Z

Toward
a Process
Pneumatology

Toward
a Process
Pneumatology

Blair Reynolds

Selinsgrove: Susquehanna University Press
London and Toronto: Associated University Presses

BT
121.2
.R48
1989

Associated University Presses
440 Forsgate Drive
Cranbury, NJ 08512

Associated University Presses
25 Sicilian Avenue
London WC1A 2QH, England

Associated University Presses
P.O. Box 488, Port Credit
Mississauga, Ontario
Canada L5G 4M2

The paper used in this publication meets the requirements of the American National Standard for Permanence of Paper for Printed Library Materials Z39.48-1984.

Library of Congress Cataloging-in-Publication Data

Reynolds, Blair.
  Toward a process pneumatology/Blair Reynolds.
    p.   cm.
  Bibliography: p.
  Includes index.
  ISBN 0-941664-97-X (alk. paper)
  1. Holy Spirit.   2. Mysticism.   3. Process theology.   I. Title.
BT121.2.R48   1990
231'.3—dc19   88-43326
                                                                    CIP

PRINTED IN THE UNITED STATES OF AMERICA

Contents

Toward
a Process
Pneumatology

Introduction

The purpose of this book is to take the first step toward the formulation of a doctrine of the Holy Spirit, God as immanent in ourselves and our universe, within the categories of process theology. This is a new, much-needed area of investigation; for while much work has been done in process Christologies, very little has been done in pneumatology.

The central theme is the relationship, specifically certain crucial parallels, between process theology and certain significant aspects of the Christian mystical tradition. This in itself is a new area of investigation in process studies. It is a most important one, because the mystical literature involves essentially accounts of direct, immediate experiences of the Spirit. Any attempt at a meaningful pneumatology must at some level address the Christian mystical tradition. Unfortunately, mysticism is often overlooked in modern theological education. This work is an attempt to remedy this oversight.

It is my contention that process theology provides a metaphysical system that enables us to clarify certain contradictory and ambiguous aspects of mysticism and therefore may serve to lead us logically and coherently into some of the deepest, most perplexing aspects of mysticism. At the same time, I am attempting to demonstrate that a process theology of mysticism has roots in certain aspects of classical pneumatology (i.e., the church fathers—Augustine, Calvin, Aquinas, and so forth). In short, process theology provides grounds for a meaningful contemporary pneumatology because it enables us to rethink and redefine certain key aspects of the doctrine historically so as to more thoroughly integrate and reconcile divine immanence with divine transcendence.

This book is divided into five interrelated topics, each of which constitutes the subject of a chapter. Briefly noting these will further illustrate the scope of this work.

Chapter 1 is largely devoted to a discussion of how Whitehead's metaphysical principles reconcile divine transcendence with divine immanence. At the same time it will emphasize significant developments and transitions in Whitehead's doctrine of God.

Chapter 2 will turn to the mystical doctrine of God, specifically as that has been represented in Dionysius, Eckhart, Suso, and Boehme. The goal of this chapter is to illustrate certain parallels between Whitehead's dipolar model of God and the conception provided by mysticism. Many scholars have understood mysticism as affirming an essentially dualistic or world-negating image of God. By that I mean that mystics have seen God as a wholly immaterial, atemporal being, totally separable from and independent of the world. My thesis is that this constitutes a onesided interpretation of mysticism, although many passages from the original mystical literature strongly support it. However, my point is that there are other passages, often ignored, in which something analogous to Whitehead's consequent conception of the nature of God emerges, that is, a sense in which God is temporal, ever-changing and growing, contingent.

Chapter 3 is an attempt to move beyond mystical metaphysics into the concrete experience of God, as evidenced in various samples from the mystical literature. The point here is that ecstasy centers upon the experience of a warm, loving reciprocal relationship between God and the world, so that again the God-world dualism is transcended. This will serve as the groundwork upon which to draw out certain parallels between ecstasy and Whitehead's concept of aesthetic experience.

In chapter 4, I turn to classical pneumatology. Classical pneumatology did not provide a concept of divine immanence that is as fully developed as might be because it yearned for a responsive but immutable God. Transcendence and immanence tended to become mutually exclusive categories. The difference in principles between process theology and classical pneumatology might be likened to a universal of the figure-ground relationship. In classical thought, God is understood as essentially static (atemporal, immutable, immaterial, wholly complete), though way in the background there is an implicit appeal to dynamic attributes (like temporality, mutability, and responsiveness). These latter attributes tend to fall into the background because of the commitment of classical metaphysics to ideals of permanence that emphasized continuity and identity. In process theology, this situation is reversed, so that the temporal, mutable, contingent side of God becomes much more obvious. A critic, then, might ponder whether or not process theology provides a coherent account of personal identity. However, that problem will not be dealt with here in any detail. Rather, it should be emphasized that the process model of God is dipolar and therefore that there is a commitment in process theology to the integration of flux or change with permanence. This is most particularly evidenced in the interrelationship of the primordial and consequent natures of God.

Chapter 5 is essentially the summary chapter. It is a further defense of process theology that will attempt to show that the advantages of a dipolar deity far outweigh the costs of a doctrine of divine mutability. This is especially evidenced in the fact that Whitehead's aesthetic provides grounds for a coherent philosophical psychology of the mystical experience of presence as applicable and relevant to ordinary experience.

In my discussions with neophytes, the suggestion was made to include in this introduction a preliminary definition of the terms feeling or prehension, creativity, and novelty. These terms are central to my analysis of Whitehead's aesthetic, are interrelated, and apparently are quite difficult for the student to readily grasp. To this end, I recommend Sherburne's work *A Key to Whitehead's Process and Reality*. This work contains a glossary and cross-references of over seventy key terms and neologisms in Whitehead. The following material is adapted from Sherburne's excerpts of Whitehead. It is intended only as prefunctory to the material in the following chapters, which will analyze and define these terms in much more detail.

Creativity

Creativity is a central but elusive concept in Whitehead that underwent a major transition, as will be emphasized in the first chapter. In many respects Whitehead's doctrine of creativity has been faulted for being "terse to the point of obscurity."[1]

My analysis of Whitehead's aesthetic will focus upon the principle of concretion: "It lies in the nature of things that many enter into complex unity,"[2] and again, "The fundamental inescapable fact is the creativity in virtue of which there can be no 'many things' which are not subordinated in a concrete unity."[3] Creativity is also the "principle of novelty." Mere order alone will not suffice for beauty. Whitehead is quite specific that the depth and breadth of experience, which is beauty, requires some "principle of refreshment."[4]

Tameness and staleness of experience must be overcome.[5] Thus the new entity that unifies the many in its constitution is different from everything else in the universe and so creates a new many that requires unification. This perpetual rhythm is the "principle of process": "There is a rhythm of process whereby creation produces natural pulsation, each pulsation forming a natural unit of historic fact."[6] The "natural units of historic fact" are actual entities, and the rhythm is the relentless alternation between one and many that repeats itself "to the crack of doom in the creative advance from creature to creature."[7]

A problematic aspect of Whitehead's thought is whether or not creativity violates the ontological principle, that is, whether actual entities are the only final realities (see next chapter). I concur with Sherburne's thesis that creativity is congruent with the ontological principle because the former emphasizes the interdependence of all actual entities. That is, the novel actual occasion or entity arises out of and is indissolubly linked to the "many," its predecessors. This point will be further explicated throughout the remainder of this work. However, the next chapter will note some difficulties incurred here, largely because Whitehead introduced creativity prior to the consequent nature of God. Thus, in Whitehead's writing prior to *Process and Reality*, creativity in many respects appeared to be an external agent with its own purposes.

Feeling or Prehension

Prehension is a technical, neutral term in Whitehead. He coined the term prehension to denote "Concrete Facts of Relatedness."[8] They constitute the actual entity and reveal its fundamental relational nature.[9]

Of particular relevance to my discussion of Whitehead's aesthetic and his mysticism is the fact that he strives to avoid any pejorative sense of the term "feeling" and thereby to overcome the reductionalism and skepticism of empiricist philosophers. Indeed, feeling has "cognitive status" in the sense that it makes truth claims. It is the most primal way in which the universe is mediated to us.[10]

The discussion of causal efficacy in chapter 1, the analysis of ecstasy in 3, and the analysis of Whitehead's aesthetic in 5 will provide further explications of the motion of feeling and its relevance to mysticism.

1
Divine Immanence in Process Theology

The purpose of this chapter is twofold. First, it will analyze how process theology makes God's immanency central; that is, it will attempt to explicate the claim that process theology is essentially, in Trinitarian terms, a doctrine of the Third Person. However, this is not to overlook the fact that the radical transcendency of God is also stressed in process thought. There is the primordial nature of God, which does not change, which is unconditioned, and which has been construed as God's moral character. Love is the most important part of that character. It is also the case that God's immanency is in an important sense God's transcendency: God is far more in things than we are ourselves, and it can even be said that the primordial nature is at least proleptically immanent through the aim toward concretion. This introductory analysis will center upon Whitehead's ontological principle, his principle of relativity, and his concept of creativity.

Secondly, it will show that a careful examination of these principles reveals them to be explicitly or implicitly making the claim that at some level our experience must include God. This will help prepare for the later discussion of parallels between Whitehead and mysticism.

The Centrality of God's Immanency in Process Thought

Though Whitehead never made explicit reference to the term "Holy Spirit," nevertheless his philosophy of organism can be shown to have made the strongest possible case for God's immanency. The following examination will show that his system does, in a fairly straightforward manner, make God's immanency a metaphysical necessity. The claim has been well established that process theology is world-affirming. Now we shall take the next step and explore how God's immanency is an inevitable consequence of this world-affirming metaphysic.

THE ONTOLOGICAL PRINCIPLE
The ontological principle is fundamental both to the principle of relativity and to Whitehead's concept of creativity. In a very abstract sense this principle is a claim that the universe, assumed to be ever-changing, is the only reality. But let us be more specific. In seeking to construct a coherent cosmology, Whitehead strives to avoid all forms of bifurcationalism. Accordingly, he

contends that there is only one level or order of reality: The space-time continuum is the one relational complex in which all objectification finds its niche. Thus, what is "real" or "actual" is that which has physically ingressed into this continuum. This continuum must not be confused with Newton's "receptive theory" of time and space. This continuum is not a fact prior to the world, something that has a being independent of the actual entities that constitute it. Rather, it is a fact derived from the general character of the world. This continuum is not a container sitting there waiting to be filled; instead it is a complex society in which all entities, including God, are obliged to conform to a social order.[1] Nothing comes from nothing; everything has to be somewhere someplace sometime. As Sherburne notes, it is here that Whitehead takes up Aristotle's protest against Plato's "otherworldliness."[2] It is Whitehead's contention that unless placed within a unified metaphysical schematization, the concept of God acquires a meaning so indefinite and indeterminate as to be unintelligible. God and the world require each other for the intelligibility of each.

This principle is of profound pneumatological significance because it eliminates the traditional ontological dualism between God and the world. Though there is a distinction between God and creatures, there is also an intimate, two-way relationship. Thus, in the following I will show that this principle yields a richer, more cogent sense of divine immanence than was possible under the dualistic metaphysical tenets of classical pneumatology (see chapter 4). This advantage is evidenced in Whitehead's ontological claims for (1) a social theory of reality in which all entities, including God, are mutually immanent; (2) the unity of mind or spirit and matter; and (3) a redefinition of nature so as to include God.

As we shall see, these claims evidence a distinct affinity with certain aspects of mystical pantheism. Boehme, for example, contended that the transcendental or eternal is not a separate order of reality but rather the inner depths and complexity of the universe. The kingdom of heaven comes from within, not from without. It is throughout the entire world, and even hell and the dead are in this world.[3] Thus, he admonishes us not to think of God as far off in an upper heaven or to suppose that when the soul departs it goes thousands of miles aloft. The next world is not some other world but just this one.[4] Indeed, God does not stand aloof or remote, but lives and dwells in the center of all things.[5] A comparable claim is to be found in *The Cloud of Unknowing* where it states that "to go to heaven ghostly," one need not "strain the spirit up or down."[6]

Although Whitehead does not explicitly acknowledge mystical sources for his thought, he does frequently refer to the experience of God's presence as depicted in the romantic poets. These latter provide a poetic rendering of Whitehead's intuition into the fundamentally aesthetic character of all reality. In Shelley, he finds the poetic expression of the flux of things. In Wordsworth, he finds the intuition of permanence. Taken together they express Whitehead's intuition of reality as an organic whole (one comprised of interrelated entities) characterized by both permanence and novelty.[7] The ontological principle is said to represent Wordsworth's intuition of "that mysterious presence surrounding things, which imposes itself on any separate element that we set up as individual for its own sake."[8] Whitehead here and also in his principle of relativity is seeking to restore the interconnectedness of reality that was destroyed by the classical doctrine of substance, especially in its Cartesian formulations.

Thus, in Whitehead there are no reservations about divine immanence. It is no accident. God is not mere construct to Whitehead but is taken to be a concretely felt reality. God is identified with the aesthetic order of the world, so that apart from God the immediacy and vividness of value is sheer illusion. Because there is no actuality without some degree of aesthetic order, there must be a transcendental valuation immanent or instanced in every occasion. Every creaturely entity points beyond itself to a permanence that transcends itself. Furthermore, what is actual is limited. In the valuing process this limitation is recognized only in regard to relevant possibilities yet to be actualized. Thus, the valuing process centers upon a dynamism that always pushes beyond all actualized values. Whitehead's claim that the universe exhibits creativity with infinite possibilities means that there must be a God as a source of value that transcends all actualization and yet is immanent in each occasion.[9]

At first glance, however, what Whitehead terms the "primordial nature of God" might seem to be an important exception to these considerations.[10] God primordially is God totally and wholly transcendent of the world. It is God as unconditioned by the world, aloof and all alone.[11]

The primordial nature of God is pure potentiality; it has no linkage to, nor yearning after, concrete matters of fact and therefore is totally void of all consciousness. "He, in his primordial nature," Whitehead writes, "is unmoved by love for this particular, or that particular."[12]

However, there are several important ways in which Whitehead's thought reconciles the primordial nature with the ontological principle. First, there is an important and elementary terminological distinction to be made. In Whitehead's system, the terms "real" or "actual" and the term "potential" are to be "taken in senses which are antithetical."[13] To speak of the primordial nature is to speak of God as the infinite realm of potentiality, that is, God as unactualized, and therefore this is not to speak of a reality or an "actual thing" above and beyond the universe. The primordial nature is said to be "deficient in actuality," far from "eminent reality," "deficiently actual," and "actually deficient."[14]

Second, the primordial nature reinforces the ontological principle. God cannot be paradigmatic in human perceptions of reality unless God is granted a mutual reciprocity with all other happenings. We must be careful not to surrender the intelligibility of God at the price of preserving the mystery of God. The primordial nature requires for its cogency integration with dynamic, relativistic elements. An exclusively static or immutable God has no efficacy for particular occasions. Taken in itself, God's eternal and immutable vision of infinite abstract possibilities does not adequately explain how God concretely functions in the world. In other words, the primordial nature is essentially aloof from all change in that the eternal objects (pure, abstract potentials) are eternal. Yet somehow the primordial nature must become involved in change; for the self-creation of every entity is the process of determining via selected eternal objects the aim of that occasion.[15]

Third, Whitehead does speak of the immanence of the primordial nature with the qualifier that this latter is not a full description of God. Whitehead must account for a concrete agency of comparison by which the primordial nature becomes relevant, and he does so by recourse to the consequent nature of God. As we shall see, the consequent nature of God is rooted in the primordial nature, so that God always functions as an organic whole. Unfortunately, however, Whitehead's separate treatments of the two natures obscures this point. In short, it is because God is assumed to be subject to the contingencies of nature and history that the eternal objects or potentialities acquire genuine relevancy. Of course, technically speaking, the primordial nature is still only proleptically immanent, because it is mediated to the world in and through the consequent nature.

Fourth, the primordial nature is in fact required by the ontological principle. This principle states that everything has to be somewhere. Accordingly, the general potentiality for the universe has to be somewhere. However, it cannot be in or part of the universe: The universe is the realm of actuality, whereas the general potentiality for the universe is the realm of pure potentiality that refers to nothing in particular. Therefore, Whitehead posits it to be in the primordial nature of God. Because of its abstract character, pure potentiality is impotent to achieve realization apart from a conceptual valuation or complete ideal harmony, which is God as an organic whole.

Furthermore, Whitehead insists that his notion of a dynamic, pluralistic universe requires potentials.[16] Leclerc emphasizes the vast importance of potentiality in Whitehead's philosophy of organism:

> There cannot be anything "novel," that is, different from what is already "actual," unless there be "entities" which are "potential...." The point is that, by the ontological principle, something "novel" cannot come into existence "out of nowhere"; it must be "given" as an "unrealized potentiality." This "unrealized potentiality" must be constituted by "entities"; the word "unrealized" simply underlines the contrast of "potentiality" with "actuality." Thus, the notion of "novelty" can have no meaning unless there be entities which are *"pure potentials."* These are the eternal objects.[17]

It should be added that actuality itself has no meaning apart from valuation, and that means potentiality. To be actual is to be finite, limited; that is, decided, and decision means choosing among relevant possibilities. Thus the primordial nature or potentiality is essential in any coherent account of either God or the world as actualities. However, later I will show that the valuation process works differently for God than it does for the world. The primordial nature means that God is an exception to the ontological principle only in the sense that God needs the world for different reasons than the world needs God.

Finally, it is important to note that the primordial nature is an affirmation of the freedom of God's sovereignty and therefore enables Whitehead to avoid overidentifying God with the world, although the two are mutually complementary. Whitehead is quite clear that God's ideals must transcend human ideals. Later I will show that this tension is the source of sin, more specifically, of the experience of alienation and nonpresence. But this does not mean that the primordial nature is thoroughly exclusive of the world. God has never been merely potential; for potentiality to some degree has been actualized or embodied somewhere in some actual occasion; therefore the primordial nature can be said to be immanent, to participate in the world. Because all entities are *causa sui* and because all self-causality presupposes an initial aim to actualize potentiality, the primordial nature is a stubborn fact that must be taken into account. No novelty would be realized unless the primordial nature is to be objectified in the world. Because genuine novelty is relevant novelty, there are grounds to assume that the primordial nature is to some degree exemplified in creatures. God's standard of value must be compatible, though not identical, with our own—otherwise God would be unknowable and of no real interest to us. Some critics (Loomer) have likened the primordial nature to love, for the primordial aim is the lure for the enjoyment of experience attained through breadth and depth of feeling. This is God as the principle of concretion. I will more fully explicate this concept in the remainder of this work.

RATIONALE
Some further explanation and defense of the ontological principle is necessary if the preceding is to be fully comprehensible. I believe that this principle can be well illustrated by appealing to the more familiar facts of life, without recourse to the recondite speculations of theoretical mathematics and physics. Indeed, that was Whitehead's intention throughout much of his writing.

To support the contention that a fully immanent God is the only viable conception of a God who is "really actual" or "fully actual," we shall examine Whitehead's line of argumentation that led up to the formulation of the ontological principle. This can be construed as also an attempt to validate the following assumption: The only knowable God is an immanent God; knowledge is impossible unless expressed in human experiential language or terms, and our most fundamental experiences are always spatio-temporal; God to be meaningful must be couched in terms of space-time. Put another way, the difficulties of divine immanence are resolvable when it is realized that there are significant analogies to the problem of human immanence.

It has been said that Whitehead did not like to argue for his position, that he tended to say, "There is their position, here is ours," and let the matter go at that. However, in point of fact this is not quite true. Various works prior to *Process and Reality* present a vigorous polemic against all forms of bifurcationism. In *The Concept of Nature*, for example, Whitehead was championing the claim that there is only one order of reality—the nature that is before us in perceptual knowledge—not two.[18]

Before proceeding into the summarization of his case, it should be noted that Whitehead in his early works did not explicitly address questions of God. The statements about God found at the beginning of each of the following sections are the implications that I see as following from Whitehead's position.

It is false to posit God as a Divine Mind dwelling in some timeless, spaceless spiritual realm independent of the universe. This follows from the fact that Whitehead rejects any sort of mind-nature bifurcation on the grounds, first, that the distinction between primary and secondary qualities is at best arbitrary. Whitehead wants to guarantee the full objective reality of time and space. So, too, do the empiricists. But Whitehead faults them precisely because their distinction between primary and secondary qualities prevents them from doing just that. What is good for the goose is good for the gander. The very same arguments that write off secondary qualities as purely subjective could also write off primary qualities (for example, time, space, solidity, inertia) as mere appearance.[19]

A second criticism Whitehead makes of this bifurcation brings God's omnipresence to the fore. God as the supreme illustration of the ontological principle is God as the supreme example of the fact that an actual entity is in potency everywhere, that every entity pervades the whole world and is in some sense present in its objective immortality in every other actual entity. This is not to overlook that God's omnipresence far transcends the capacities of any other entity. However, at this point, what is of primary interest is Whitehead's line of argumentation for this metaphysical principle in the first place.

Whitehead's second attack on this bifurcation into primary and secondary qualities is that it fostered the false conception that "an object is at one place at a definite time, and in no sense anywhere else."[20] This follows from the fact that such a bifurcation sharply divides reality into two separate realms—primary qualities, which were taken to be exclusively the property of the object; and secondary qualities, which were taken to be solely the property of the perceiver's mind. Objects were separated from the physical sensations they effected. For example, the cook is said to be in the kitchen and no place else; the sound of her voice is said to be in the perceiver's mind and no place else.

To eschew such a bifurcation, Whitehead identifies the reality of the object with the reality of its sensations. In other words, causes are assumed to be objectively in their effects. What something is, is what something does.[21]

Another way we could state the matter is as follows: While at first glance it seems easy to arrive at the simple, plain fact of where an object really is, upon careful examination, such a task proves impossible. We are unable to confine objects to any particular circumscribed place; it is impossible to draw a clear-cut distinction between the situation or position of an object and its influence.[22]

This special notion of the omnipresence of all entities has profound pneumatological significance, as we shall see. Sittler, for example, has emphasized the need for "the recovery of catholic comprehensiveness in the doctrine of grace," by which the focal point of grace is creation as the whole.[23]

Whitehead's third objection is that once reality is bifurcated into two orders, mind and nature, then the cause of knowledge is sought out in the mind of the perceiver rather than in the perceived. Nature falls out of the picture; it is the perceiver's mind and not the objects of knowledge that is of primary interest. Science, then, is unable to do its job.[24]

Fourth, Whitehead claims that the bifurcationalists were unable to explain any of the perplexities of the perceived objects by bringing in entities (for example, mind) from beyond nature. For instance, they were never able to explain why we should perceive things that are not there. "Why should we perceive secondary qualities? It seems an extremely unfortunate arrangement that we should perceive a lot of things that are not there."[25]

He attacks idealism on the grounds that such a view renders totally inexplicable the facts of which sensory experience informs us so convincingly, such as the fact that there is a world out there and that we have an instinct for action, a drive to transcend or pass beyond ourselves and to act upon something out there. We also know that a lot has happened in the past and in the remote regions of the universe, but we do not know exactly what; yet if idealism were correct, we would have detailed knowledge at our fingertips of these far-off events merely by introspection.[26]

We cannot posit God to dwell in any place else but in the spatio-temporal world. The presupposition of a timeless spaceless world outside the universe can be shown to be the unwitting consequence of a faulty definition of matter, one that Whitehead believes has the suspicious character that we are compelled to accept it upon the grounds of abstract logic rather than upon observed facts.

A second form of bifurcationalism that Whitehead attacks is that of the traditional two-term Aristotelian logic, the substance-attribute dichotomy. The proponents of this view assume that all experience is an awareness of the attributes inhering in substances. In other words, matter is the substance whose attributes we perceive.[27] The problem Whitehead sees here is this: Although they claim that time and space express relationships among substances, the fact that attributes are taken to be all we can observe means that space and time have nothing whatsoever to do with substances, but only with their attributes. Substances, then, must reside in some timeless spaceless realm.[28]

Whitehead faults this dichotomy primarily on two grounds. First, if all we can observe of matter are its attributes, then we can never really know what matter is. Physical science would be pointless; it would be totally unable ever to know or understand its subject.

Second, two-term Aristotelian logic rests on the assumption that there is a direct connection between two contrasted realities, substance and attribute. Whitehead contends that such a bifurcation is invalid because no such connection is given in experience. The bifurcationalist assumes that the attributes belong to a subject whose reality is otherwise than that ascribed to any of the attributes. But Whitehead contends that there are many clear-cut cases where the subject to which the attributes supposedly belong can be shown to be conspicuously absent. The fact that there are no reciprocal relationships between what he terms "physical objects" (substances) and "sense-objects" (attributes) is said to be "fatal" to the Aristotelian concept of matter. The bifurcation of the reality before us, the given, into substance and attribute is directly contradicted by the fact that our experience is rich in countless sense-objects with no connection whatsoever to physical objects.[29] For example, experience discloses a myriad of stray colors, tastes, smells, and so forth that adhere to no physical object. We observe the light from stars that may have ceased to exist eons ago. Since the reality of the so-called attributes proves to be exhaustive of the reality of the given, the concept of substance proves superfluous.

The only realistic conception of God is that of a spatio-temporal entity. Timeliness and spacelessness are overintellectualistic concepts. No such things are to be found; all experience is fundamentally spatio-temporal.

A third form of bifurcationalism Whitehead attacks is that found in traditional philosophic discussions of time and space, which he faults for not taking these latter with sufficient seriousness. Whitehead rejects what are termed "the absolute theories of time and space." In these theories, time and space are considered to be independent systems, separable both from one another and from events.[30]

Whitehead's first objection is that the bare time and bare space presupposed by these theories; that is, space and time as wholly independent of events, do not accord with the brute facts of experience. Time and space are inseparable from events; indeed in themselves they presuppose events, for they are abstractions from the latter. Therefore, if time and space are construed as independent of nature, we are compelled to make the most unfortunate assumption that we could not even have the smallest inkling what these data are.[31]

His second objection is to the concepts of timelessness and spacelessness, which these theories make possible by construing time and space as independent systems one from the other. Experience, too, proves them meaningless concepts: Extension, the spread of events, and time, the passage of events, together characterize our most fundamental experience of nature.[32]

Nor is timelessness a viable option. Time is something happening, the passage of events, a moving on. There is no such thing as timeless space. Experience discloses that something is happening everywhere.[33] Nor is there timeless sense-awareness or timeless thought. Sense-awareness and thought are processes; there is a passage of sense-awareness and a passage of thought.[34]

Nor can the concept of timelessness be justified by appealing to the instantaneous "Right Now" of the materialists, the notion that the past is gone, the future has not happened yet, so what we are left with is a durationless present. Whitehead rejects this position on the grounds that if we carefully analyze our experience of the "Right Now," we find that it always involves a duration, however brief this may be. Furthermore, this timeless present would make induction impossible, because nothing would then refer to the past or to the future.[35] Incidentally, this means that if we posit God as dwelling in some timeless realm, God would have no reference to history.[36]

THE PRINCIPLE OF RELATIVITY

Definition
The principle of relativity is, according to Whitehead, "another rendering of the ontological principle."[37] Therefore, it should serve to further reinforce the concept of God's immanency. To claim that "actual entities are the only reasons" is to claim that any particular actual entity, including God, arises out of a complex constitution involving all other entities. Thus all actual entities are "internally related," because the being of one determines the being of another.[38] This is the doctrine of mutual immanence. In other words, what something is depends upon what it is related to. Relationships constitute the very essence of things. From this comes the real solidarity of the universe. Nothing can exist in a vacuum; there is no such thing as total and complete self-sufficiency.[39]

Explication
We now turn to a survey of some of the main ways in which the principle of relativity makes central God's immanency. At the out it must be clearly stated that the following considerations are not intended as a "proof" for the existence of God. Whitehead himself eschewed all such dogmatic finality. Rather, the goal is to show that this principle provides certain significant advantages in speaking of the omnipresence of God.

God as the chief exemplification of the principle of relativity is God as omnipresent. God and the world are inseparably bound together, so that there is a genuine reciprocity between the two. God's transcendence does not mean God's remoteness or aloofness; neither God nor the world is self-sufficient. Without God there would be no world, and without a world there would be no God. God inherits from the world, and the world inherits from God. However, as will be explained later, God needs the world in a different sense from that in which the world needs God. My present point is to emphasize that God is objectified through the entire universe; that is, God is an item in the real, internal constitutions of all actual entities, and that, conversely, the world is objectified in God. This is Whitehead's doctrine of mutual immanence.[40] An important qualifier is necessary here. It has generally been affirmed by major theological traditions that a mutable deity renounces the divine prerogative of existing necessarily. However, in process theology, this problem is approached from a different angle. It is true that certain universes would make it impossible for a creature such as a human being to exist. However, God can exist in any possible world. God to be God requires a universe, but it does not have to be this particular one. Given different universes, God would be enriched in different ways, and therefore there would be different kinds of God. As the supreme exemplification of the principle of relativity, God has the unlimited capacity to adjust successfully to all other possible worlds.[41] Because of this capacity, God cannot fail to exist. Thus, unity with God is guaranteed; yet it is also a gift, because God has consented to be objectified in this universe as other than God could have been.

This relativistic model of God is of particular significance to pneumatology because it gives a metaphysical meaning to the central Christian affirmation that God is a God of love. This, of course, depends upon how one defines love. The process definition of love is, in brief, an empathic bond through which each significantly affects and enriches the being of the other. According to Hartshorne, love means, at a minimum, to find fulfillment only via the other and to derive part of the content of one's life from the thing loved.[42] From this perspective, it is quite problematic how the immutable God of classical pneumatology, said to be unmoved or unaffected by the world, could be the God of love. As we shall see, classical theists such as Anselm were also deeply disturbed by this problem, which they unsuccessfully attempted to resolve. This problem is not unique to process theology.

There are several other religious implications of the principle of relativity. First, absolute egotism is ontologically ruled out. No actuality can be concerned solely with itself. Because all entities arise out of a web of interrelationships, love is essential to our very existence. There is no I without a Thou. Since all entities are mutually immanent in one another, the quest for personal enjoyment is also the quest to contribute to the enjoyment of others. Second, this fact that concern for the other is an ontological factor means that it can be strengthened. This is the function of morality.[43]

Does the principle of relativity apply to the primordial nature of God? Does it call for the immanency of the primordial nature? At first glance, the principle of relativity and the primordial nature seem to be mutually exclusive categories. The principle of relativity speaks of God's deep interrelationship with the world; the primordial nature speaks of God's aloofness from the world. The principle of relativity speaks of the concrete and the particular; the primordial nature speaks of pure abstraction. In the concluding section of *Process and Reality*, this principle is spoken of only in regard to the consequent nature of God. And it is this nature, not the primordial, that is said to pass into the world.[44]

However, in Whitehead's philosophy of organism, creative purpose is seen as always being at work. In Whitehead's technical parlance, creativity is fostered through what are termed "conceptual feelings," feelings whose data are eternal objects. It is these that make for the creative advance because they envision possibilities for relevant novelty.

Phase one of concrescence, of the growing together of the many—the data—into the unity of the prehending subject, is variously termed by Whitehead the conformal phase, the responsive phase, the initial phase, the receptive phase, and the primary phase. The prehensions that constitute this phase are called pure physical feelings, responsive feelings, and conformal feelings. These feelings are said to reiterate or reproduce the datum at hand. They transform objective content into subjective feeling. They denote a receptivity to the world. Causally speaking, they represent the workings of efficient causation. However, it must be stressed that actual entities do not blindly copy or reproduce within themselves the datum at hand. Even at this phase their prehensions evidence a creative selectivity under the guidance of their subjective aims. In an important sense, then, the primordial nature is objectified in the world. All actual entities feel God's conceptual feelings (primordial nature) and so are able to liberate themselves from the tyranny of the given.

The categorical obligation evidenced here is The Category of Conceptual Valuation.[45] This obligation is also termed "the principle of intensive relevance." What is of particular importance here is the fact that Whitehead subsumes it under the principle of relativity because the former denotes the relativity of decision.[46]

In other words, actual entities do enter into each others' constitutions, but only under the limitations of the gradations of relevancy imposed upon them by the other, the prehending subject. This selectivity in responding, which is what makes for novelty in the world, is conditioned by the prehending subject's "hybrid physical feelings of the relevancies conceptually ordered in God's experience." This is God as the principle of concretion. Because the principle of relativity encompasses conceptual freedom, and because this conceptual freedom is in an important sense identifiable with the primordial nature, this principle renders God's immanency inclusive of the latter.

Much of Whitehead's pre-1925 writing on relativity seemed to be arguing indirectly or implicitly for the immanency of God, although the analogous concept is that of a very abstract geometrical order. It is a pervasive opinion that the relativists all hold that there are no absolutes. Although it is true in a sense that in Whitehead's view everything is relative, he is not the sort of relativist who rejects all absolutes. Rather, he argues that if we are to make sense of the concept of relativity, there must be within our grasp an absolute that pervades the universe. Nature is passage, change; yet there must also be an absolute or invariant geometrical framework throughout the universe, such that nature is creativity but with structure. In this sense, Whitehead's early writings might be understood as a variation of the mystical quest for the invariant.

Such a contention is not necessarily a contradiction of the ontological principle, though at first glance it may seem so. Admittedly, the suggestion that there is some reality transcendent of nature does seem confusing, since the ontological principle ultimatizes nature. However, such confusion can be mitigated if it is borne in mind that Whitehead was arguing that the space-time continuum must be uniform. He is not then arguing for some reality beyond space-time. To further clarify this point, let us examine his case against Einstein.

Specifically, Whitehead seeks to reject Einstein's concept of "causal heterogeneity" that asserts that matter generates vast distortions in the space-time continuum. Accordingly, the space-time continuum is nonuniform—in lay terms we could say "lumpy"—consisting of any number of time-space warps. Whitehead rejects such a notion on the following grounds.

Einstein overlooked the fact that uniformity is essential for knowledge and measurement. Thus, the space-time continuum must be uniform, or we must abandon all hopes of knowledge. If matter distorts space and time, what we are left with is not at all a universe, but a vast heap of monad-like natures; therefore, we would be totally at the mercy of contingency; we would then know nothing until we knew everything.[47] In other words: "The properties of time and space express the basic uniformity in nature which is essential for our knowledge of nature as a coherent system."[48] It is precisely the uniformity of the space-time continuum that provides the standard by which we can discriminate dreams from reality.[49] The notion of space-time warps would make the universe an epistemic nightmare, a madman's dream. Since dreams essentially represent distortions in time and space, there would be no way in Einstein's universe to tell if we are dreaming or perceiving reality.

Furthermore, measurement would be an utter impossibility. According to Einstein's version of relativity, we could not determine how far it is to the stars unless we knew every single object between ourselves and them. Also, valid measurement presupposes matching; that is the measurer and the measured share a common spacio-temporal order. If we hold with causal heterogeneity, measurement becomes as absurd as asking how many miles it is between New York today and Chicago next week.

Measuring also assumes that the measuring devices remain constant, that they are not subject to the mercy of local conditions. But this is an utter impossibility if the space-time continuum is warped. For example, if the space-time coordinates vary such that the yardstick shrinks and the clocks slow as they are accelerated, how can they possibly be of any use in measuring? Whitehead does not believe this problem can be surmounted by appealing to the speed of light as the absolute standard. Its velocity was determined under purely local conditions and therefore it may vary elsewhere.

It should be noted that it is precisely these epistemic considerations that led Charles Hartshorne to validate a relativistic conception of God. Knowledge demands uniformity; therefore, no matter how different we may feel inclined to make God from ourselves, still we must assume that God shares a common existence with us, if God is to be at all knowable.

In a similar vein, let us consider the possibility of an all-encompassing matrix of sensitivity pervading throughout all things. Let us call this matrix the consequent nature of God.

The problem is: How can we speak of community among ourselves, when, as true contemporaries, we cannot prehend one another? The reason why, as true contemporaries, we cannot prehend one another is that our prehensions take time; and the reason why our prehensions take time is that as contemporaries we are external to one another and therefore require time to work our way into one another.

Whitehead did not much discuss this problem. If anything, he tended to see the independence of contemporaries in a totally positive light as that by which the freedom of the universe is guaranteed.[51] Be that as it may, his system does provide the following possible solution.

The principle of relativity claims that all things are objectified in God. Of the consequent nature of God, Whitehead writes that "in it there is no loss, no obstruction. The world is felt in a unison of immediacy."[52] Therefore let us posit the universe to be the body of God. All actualization occurs within God; all things originate within a surrounding matrix of sensitivity. Since all things are internal to God, there is no time lag between the actual occasion and God's prehension thereof. God, then, can prehend all contemporaries, although the latter cannot prehend one another.

To clarify, we have at best only a very indirect contact with the external world. We know best our own bodies because we have a very intimate, that is, direct and immediate, interaction with our own physical resources. The interaction between ourselves and the rest of the world is far less intimate, coming about as it does through the indirect means of bodily actions, words, and so forth. God, as the chief exemplification of the principle of relativity, means that the relationship between God and the world is analogous to the relationship between mind and body, but with this one major exception: The human self is incarnate in an inferior fashion. Having direct interaction with little more than its own brain cells, it is grossly isolated from the external environment. In contrast, since the universe is the body of God, God's environment is wholly internal. Therefore, as Ogden emphasizes, God's interaction with every creature is "unimaginably direct and immediate."[53] God's power of empathic participation is boundless; the interaction that takes place between God and the world is not between God and only a highly select portion of the world (analogous to the fact that we have a direct relationship only with our brain cells and nervous system), but between God and the entire universe. Thus, the basis for speaking of community among contemporaries is the fact that they are together in God's prehension of themselves. In other words, there is a love and sensitivity flowing among and between contemporaries that is not of their own making and of which they may very well be unaware.

An analogous problem is: Where is the totality of the universe? The ontological principle claims that it has to be somewhere; the principle of relativity claims that this somewhere is the prehension of some actual entity; the Category of Subjective Unity claims that this prehension is the prehension of an actual entity by whom this datum is felt as one complex unity of pattern. Since no known creature is capable of such a holistic perception of the entire cosmos, the entity in question must be God. Thus, God, as chief exemplification of this principle, is God as wholly transcendent, that is, God as enjoying a unity of feeling that other creatures do not have.

The principle of relativity makes viable the concept of a Holy Spirit because it enables us to speak of a spiritual dimension intrinsic to all of nature. First, if all of reality is interrelated, then so too are the realities of fact, value and subjectivity. Indeed, the synthesis of these three elements or realities is the major theme of *Science and the Modern World*. Fact requires definiteness; definiteness requires decisiveness; decisiveness requires decision; decision requires value judgment; value judgment requires subjectivity. Therefore, since fact and value are everywhere present, so too is subjectivity. Thus, we may speak of a mental side as intrinsic to all matter.

Second, in *Process and Reality*, Whitehead is striving to avoid "the disastrous separation of body and mind, characteristic of philosophical systems which are in an important respect derived from Cartesianism."[54] Therefore, all entities are said to be dipolar, with a physical pole and a mental pole.[55]

Third, a relativistic view of reality means that nature is a vast continuum; therefore, there are no hard-and-fast dividing lines between the sentient and the nonsentient, between the living and the nonliving. To a greater or lesser degree, subjectivity is present everywhere.[56] We may say then, along with Charles Hartstorne, that even atoms have "tiny minds," being careful to note that these "minds" are the mental pole and not conscious.[57] As Teilhard de

Chardin notes, the concept of evolution means that an abnormality is an
exaggeration of what is everywhere present. The exception is never a true
exception. What is the case at the higher rungs of the evolutionary ladder is
also the case, though to a significantly lesser degree, at the lower. No matter
how much of an abnormality we may take the human psyche to be, still
something analogous to it is to some degree present everywhere.[58]

Strictly speaking, panpsychism is not a "proof" for the existence of the
Holy Spirit. Rather, it provides a better vantage point from which to speak
of the latter. Historically, the concept of spirit, both capital and small *s*, has
been totally dissociated from that of matter: Science found no need or use
for it, and the ancient spiritualists sharply divorced spirit and matter into two
separate and conflicting worlds. Panpsychism represents a first step toward
the reconciliation of the two: Properly understood, it is claiming that something
analogous to a spiritual dimension must be included in all valid descriptions
of the physical world because the latter cannot be adequately grasped without
reference to its mental or subjective side.

This point has particular relevance for Christianity. In chapters 4 and 5, I
will show that there has been an unfortunate trend in Christian throught to
view nature as merely instrumental, of no value in itself. As Reuther has noted,
one of the unfortunate consequences of classical pneumatology was that the
Spirit became antithetical to nature, which was understood as an "enemy to
be ruthlessly put under man's feet."[59] Panpsychism is an important correction
here. It emphasizes that God's love extends throughout all of the world and
is not just confined to the human sphere. The Spirit finds expression not only
in history but also in nature.

However, it should be noted that the term *panpsychism* can create some
severe problems without the necessary qualifiers. I use this term for want of
a better one and also because it is found throughout the writings of Hartshorne
and other significant process thinkers. But it is not used, not even once, by
Whitehead. It is a dangerous term because it is filled with confusion that needs
be dispelled. For one thing, it must not be confused, and it easily can be, with
animism, that is, with the belief that there is soul in everything. Hartshorne
as well as Whitehead clearly rule out such a notion. They contend that the
concept of a soul is only applicable to higher forms of life by virtue of the
fact that these possess a highly centralized structure, a nervous system. Very
low life-forms, vegetables, inanimate objects, and the like are more similar
to leaderless democracies than they are to anything else. For example, take
a carrot. Each of its constituents has a physical pole and a mental pole, so
we may speak of there being feelings in each of them. But in the carrot there
is no dominant member, like a brain, present. Thus, the carrot *qua* carrot
has no mind, soul, or personality.

Panpsychism, by attibuting a mental dimension to all entities, might be
misconstrued to mean that all entities are necessarily conscious entities. Quite

the contrary is the case in Whitehead's "reformed subjectivist principle," which will later be shown to have serious implications for our understanding of mysticism.

According to this principle, western philosophy was wrong in its pervasive and largely unquestioned assumption that all experience presupposes consciousness. Rather, Whitehead contends that consciousness presupposes experience. Fundamentally, all experience is nonconscious or unconscious feeling. Consciousness arises only "in a late derivative phase of integration."[60] Thus, the term "feeling' is itself devoid of any suggestion of consciousness. It is an all-inclusive, neutral term denoting the basic feature of all events. There is then nothing onesided about its meaning.

This principle is the centerpiece in Whitehead's attack on Hume's concept of causality. Hume's analysis of causality is cited as deficient from the very beginning because it presupposed conscious perception as the primary datum from which the apprehension of causality was derived.[61] Therefore, Hume never could elicit such an apprehension. The problem with Hume was that his overintellectualistic bias led him to begin his search for causality exclusively in terms of higher mental processes, and therefore he failed to take emotionality with sufficient seriousness. His assumption was that emotional feelings are necessarily derivative from conscious sensations. Whitehead contends that precisely the opposite is the case.[62] It is at the level of these primitive, emotional tones, only dimly grasped by consciousness, that causal efficacy is directly experienced. For example, one does not see the puff of air that makes one's eyes blink; one feels the puff make the eye blink.[63] Another example is that the behaviors of very primitive organisms with no real sensory apparatus or cognitive capacity evidence some feeling of causality.[64]

Furthermore, if Hume is correct that causality is the result of the association of familiar sensa, then the absence of familiar sensa should mark a significant decrease in causal feeling. But in point of fact the opposite is the case.[65]

CREATIVITY

Whitehead's doctrine of creativity has been a confusing and controversial issue. Nevertheless, the more obvious features of this doctrine make central God's immanency.

In *Science and the Modern World*, Whitehead's comments on God's *modus operandi* are terse and quite abstract. They center upon two principles. According to the principle of substantial activity, there is the fact of creativity, which is continuous. It is, however, wholly neutral as to form. According to the principle of limitations, it is God who structures or qualifies this ongoing creativity. Thus, God and the world are inseparably bound together because all actuality requires creativity and form (from God). It is, then, the immanency of God that guarantees order in the cosmos.

Between this book and *Process and Reality*, Whitehead significantly modified his view of God's relationship to creativity. In the former work, creativity appears exclusive of God's own nature; in the latter one, God is the supreme illustration of creativity.

To highlight this difference, God's relationship to creativity, as evidenced in *Science and the Modern World*, might be likened to a "charioteer": God is only one of several formulative elements. The horses, creativity, are the motive power of the system; and God as a kind of charioteer is the power of persuasion struggling to direct the ongoing surges of creative power that are autonomous from, but coordinate with, God. The problem with this view is that it makes creativity the one inclusive concept applying to all reality and then seems to exclude God from it as far as God's own nature is concerned. This view was later modified by Whitehead's concept of the consequent nature of God, by which the universe becomes God's actuality (or the medium of it). But in Whitehead's earlier writings, the problem still remains of positing creativity as prior to God and at the same time as essential to all actuality. In *Process and Reality* this problem is resolved by Whitehead identifying God with the reality of creativity. Thus, God might be likened to a "rickshaw driver," because God appears to have taken up the role previously assigned to creativity.

Although in the writings of the later Whitehead, creativity is in an important sense transcendent of God (that is, a categoric obligation for God), this must not be confused with the notion that creativity is allowed a reality exclusive of God. Creativity is assumed to have no reality aside from its "accidents," and God is the primordial accident.[66] In other words, creativity is both an aspect of God's own nature and at the same time that which is conditioned by God. God, then, both establishes and exemplifies creativity. This makes God's immanency a significantly more viable concept than it was traditionally, because it overcomes the severe ontological disjunction between God and the world that followed from the classical metaphysical portrayal of God as static or immutable. Whitehead's admission here of fluency, temporality and contingency in God ("creativity is always found under conditions") means that there is no need to deny the full individual reality of all creatures in God and conversely of God in all creatures.

Further light may be shed upon the relationship of God to creativity if the primordial nature is brought into view. At the end of *Process and Reality*, Whitehead writes: "The primordial nature of God is the acquirement by creativity of a primordial character."[67] The primordial nature is the grip of the creative advance. I believe that it has a vague resemblance to the Freudian *id*; that is, it represents a primordial, unconsious drive on God's part to become objectified or actualized in and through the creation of the universe. God, then, is immanent in the sense that the universe is God's material self-actualization, that is, God's body (as we shall see later).

However, a major problem with this interpretation is that, as noted earlier,

Whitehead emphatically denies that the primordial nature, as far as eternal objects *per se* go, refers to any sort of actual world. In other words, the primordial nature denotes the realm of pure abstraction or pure potentials, which by defintion are said to exclude any particular realization. Therefore, it is hard to see how there could be any impetus in the primordial nature toward any sort of actualization. That would require that this nature entertain preconceived particular realizations. Actualization requires that a potential be made relevant to a particular occasion. Therefore, if the primordial nature intended to actualize itself, it would have to be envisaging in terms of the concrete and the particular; that is, it would have to be envisaging particular exemplifications. But in the preceding passages and elsewhere Whitehead denies there are such "preconstituted particulars" there.[68]

A possible solution to this problem is to take into consideration the fact that Whitehead is not consistent in his description of the primordial nature; or perhaps it is fairer to say that he saw more to it than just the eternal objects *per se*. He also speaks of it as an "appetitive vision,"[69] an "unrest," and an "urge" for the realization of potentials.[70]

Furthermore, there are passages that make reference to some type of primordial gradation of the relevancy of eternal objects. This suggests that God primordially must have the actualization of such objects in mind. What other sense would it make for the primordial mind to valuate them? Creation or actualization denotes the realization of a potential. This requires a process whereby the potential's relevancy for particular occasions has been determined. Therefore, to posit the primordial nature as God's creative urge for self-actualization would require that it be included to determine the relevancy of the potentials it contains.[71]

If in fact there is this primordial urge in God to self-actualize, in precisely what way is the universe God's self-actualization? Whitehead calls God a "poet," which suggests that God's relationship to the universe is analogous to that of a poet to his or her poetry. However, a major problem here is that artists already manifest some degree of self-consciousness before they start their work, whereas the Whiteheadian God, described as unconscious primordially, starts with unconsciousness seeking self-consciousness. Furthermore, Whitehead's thought has suggested an alternative model. Certain process writers, like Dorothy Emmet and Charles Hartshorne, have interpreted Whitehead to mean that the universe is God's body. Such a model makes the strongest possible case for God's immanency because in an important sense it identifies God with the universe.

This model is congruent with God as instance of the ontological principle, which states that every act of becoming is the becoming of something with spatio-temporal extension.[72] It also accords well with the consequent nature of God, which is God as supreme example of the principle of relativity.[73]

The interesting question, then, is how and why is Whitehead justified in making this assumption that the universe is somehow the completion of God. The answer I propose is that the metaphor of the universe as the body of God is consistent with God as the supreme example of self-creativity. My contention is that God creates a world because God requires a body in order to attain self-consciousness. This point is implicit in Whitehead's doctrine of consciousness.[74] Thus, as noted earlier, Whitehead sees consciousness as a function of complex integrations. In order to become conscious of something, that element must stand out sharply and clearly in experience. Consciousness requires definiteness; definiteness requires contrast; contrast requires affirmation-negation. Consciousness requires the synthesis of physical feelings with conceptual ones, that is, the contract of actuality with potentiality.

Here is one crucial instance where God needs the world in a distinctly different sense from the one in which the world needs God. Whitehead describes the process of God's self-actualization in terms that have no analogy in human experience. Like all entities, God is dipolor; but unlike all other entities, God originates at the mental pole. This is God as primordial, unactualized, unconscious, but with "appetition" to become. The process of divine self-actualization begins at the level of conceptual feelings, which God already has. This process is largely an affair of God acquiring consequent, physical feelings to integrate with the conceptual ones so as to produce consciousness. There must be a phase of physical origination. God's physical pole, the world, must originate as a counterpart to the conceptual operations of the mental pole.[75] Thus, the becoming of God may be identified with the becoming of the universe. Though Whitehead does not expressly state that the universe is God's body, he tends to identify the contrast between the physical pole and the mental pole of God with the contrast between God and the world.

As a further explication of this position, I will show that process theology takes seriously and can meet various objections to this model, most specifically the objection that it seriously attenuates God's transcendency.

First, by this dynamic view of God, process theology has eliminated the major obstacle to conceiving of the universe as God's body, that is, the immutable God of classical theism.[76]

Second, Hartshorne rules out the metaphorical model of God as Father. While this metaphor is intended to guarantee the superiority of God, it does not necessarily do so. For example, children are often superior to their parents.[77]

Also, Hartshorne and others rule out the metaphor of God as cosmic monarch, although they do admit to a monarchic dimension of God. The monarch metaphor carries too many ugly connotations of God as ruthless moralist and ruling Caesar, and therefore does not square with a God of love.

Whitehead's criticism is that western theology was edited by Caesar's lawyers. "The Church," he writes, "gave unto God the attributes which belong exclusively to Caesar."[78]

In *The Seeds of Redemption*, Meland makes an analogous point:

> It is often suggested that moral will best characterizes the divine working. But moral will can be a ruthless operation, as it has been in human history. And a deity with moral will and nothing else, can be intolerable. What is it that sweetens and tempers moral will with benevolence and grace? It is a sensitive nature for whom graciousness has significance beyond sheer rectitude.[79]

God as moral will does not guarantee, indeed seems to deny, any strong sense of divine immanence. As has been the case throughout history, the intolerance and impatience of the zealous moralists and legalists all too often led them to break off relationships with and to hold themselves aloof from those they considered to be their inferiors or who would not agree with them. In chapter 4, I will show that it is precisely for this reason that Augustine denies a pantheistic option.

Third, the metaphor of God as poet is ruled out. Such a model implies that the universe is a severe power drain upon God, just as the writing of a poem exhausts the creative energies of the poet. Also, a poet does not have the intimacy with his or her own poetry that he or she may have with his or her own body. Therefore, the metaphor of the universe as God's body does greater justice to God's radical sensitivity to all things. However, certain objections might be raised against such a model.

First, one might object that such a model would posit evil to be literally within God. A viable rebuttal, however, is that empathy is the highest form of knowledge; therefore, to know suffering, God must suffer. That is, there must be suffering and pain in God, or God is not truly omniscient. Hartshorne believes that this is the very meaning of the crucifixion.[80] One is reminded of Whitehead's claim that God is "the fellow sufferer."[81] The fact that God suffers grants an eternal significance to all events; for whatever happens makes a genuine difference to God. This point has distinct relevance to the concept of *agape* or self-sacrificing love. God's self-giving in Christ is neither accidental nor an act of condescension: God finds fulfillment only through creatures, even very sinful ones. God forgives us and restores our broken relationships, and this mercy is necessary for God's own self-realization. Yet God's "sacrifice" is no less sacrificial; rather, forgiveness and mercy are intrinsic to the very being of God.[82]

The advantage of this conception is that it may provide a much more radical sense of God's mercy and as well as of evil. This point was stressed in mystical pantheism.[83] Nevertheless, one might object, the real difficulty here is how evil, in the sense of sin, can be included within God without making God sinful. In response, it might be said that God's body consists of self-deciding members that have free will. Sin is a consequence of this freedom. For example, it is true that in a sense all our outer actions and deeds are our own because they result from inner decisions by which we actualize ourselves as persons. Analogously, each creature, a constituent of God's body, is created and grounded in God's own decision and therefore is to some degree an objectification or actualization of God. Yet, it must also be recognized that the objective ground for the possibility of sin resides in the fact that some actions are more distinctively God's own actions than are others. To give a typically human example, some of our outer actions are understood to be particularly revelatory of ourselves, to give particular expression to what we are. Others are understood to be far less so, to be untypical and out of character. A strict analogy can be drawn to God. Although every creature and happening is in one sense God's own act, some are genuinely revelatory or expressive acts of God's character; others are not. Thus, the wickedness of all individuals is literally in God, but not in a way that God could be called wicked or that wickedness could be said to be the divine "character." The reality of God, as is true of the reality of all persons, is more than God's own character.[84] Thus the divine transcendence is in the context of divine immanence. God may not be fully identified with the universe any more than we are reducible to our bodies, though the latter are definitely part of ourselves.

Second, one might object that we can no longer think of God as a creator. Just as we do not create our bodies, so God had no hand in creating the universe. The rebuttal is that it is false to assume that we do not have a hand to a very significant degree in the creation of our bodies. Certainly it is the case that by diet, exercise, and the like we can and do significantly alter our bodily development.[85]

Third, one might object that such a metaphor makes God coexistent with the universe and therefore denies the eternality of God. Since the universe is slowly running down and will one day perish, so, too, God will one day die. A viable rebuttal is that this reflects a too cynical view of entropy. It is not so much the case that the universe is slowly running down as it is the case that the old is perishing to make way for the new. God, then, can be construed as eternally regenerating his body.[86] In a similar vein, Whitehead contends that the universe is in an important sense eternal.[87] Whitehead, however, is not arguing that the universe as we know it to be, as it is now, will go on forever. We are living within a vast cosmic epoch in which everything is based upon electromagnetic principles. Novelty and creativity will one day bring this epoch to an end. But that will not be the end of some sort of spatio-temporal material order; another different universe will come into existence.[88]

Fourth, one might object that the mind-body analogy is thoroughly pantheistic and therefore not amenable to Christian understandings of the Holy

Spirit. A viable rebuttal is that this metaphor is not at all pantheistic if by the term pantheism one is speaking of a blanket equation between God and the universe. There is still ample room to speak of God's transcendency; therefore, Hartshorne prefers the term "pan-en-theism." For example, God transcends the world, just as the whole transcends the sum of its parts. God transcends the world, just as the mind transcends the body. Mind is not fully reducible to body, though it is at least that. This point is important. The process conception of mind-body unity, by which the mind is said to be the size and shape of the brain and nervous system, leaves ample room to speak of the transcendency of mind over body. There are, for example, memory and imagination. By these we may transcend the spatio-temporal position of our bodies through our freedom to remember far back into the past or to imagine distant future events.

Fifth, one might object that such a model severely detracts from God's transcendency because it denies the mysteriousness of God. However, one might reply that precisely the opposite is the case. The mind-body interaction is a deeply mysterious process of which the more we study, the more we encounter new phenomena, bewildering, scarcely understood.

Sixth, one might argue that such a model violates the ontological principle. The latter seems to claim that God is just one actual entity among others, a kind of "supermember" of the universe, whereas the mind-body analogy identifies God with the universe. However, if we turn to the principle of relativity, such a contradiction may be resolved; or perhaps it is more accurate to say that all actual entities enjoy a rather paradoxical existence. On one hand, the universe consists of actual entities. On the other, the universe may be identified with any one particular entity. According to the principle of relativity, the universe is to a greater or lesser degree objectified in any given entity. This is the doctrine of mutual immanence. "Each atom," writes Whitehead, "is a system of all things."[89] Also there is Whitehead's special notion of omnipresence, which claims that any particular entity is objectified throughout the entire space-time continuum. However, God's "identification" with the cosmos must be kept distinct from that of every other actual entity. God is the supreme example of all metaphysical principles, and therefore the universe is objectified in God more completely than in any other entity. Ogden writes:

> The human self, as we noted, is incarnate in the world only in a radically inferior fashion. It directly interacts with little more than its own brain cells, and so is always a localized self, limited by an encompassing external environment. As the eminent Self, by radical contrast, God's sphere of interaction or body is the whole universe of nondivine beings, with each one of which his relation is unsurpassably immediate and direct. His only environment is wholly internal, which means that he can never be localized in any particular space and time but is omnipresent.[90]

Ogden's remarks recall my earlier argument that because God's environment is wholly internal, God is the ground of all true community. Thus, the fact that by the ontological principle God is not a wholly immaterial being means that there is a large qualitative difference between God and other entities.

Finally, it might be objected that process theology does not provide a concept of divine immanence that is congruent with Christian teaching because Whitehead's God appears more as a principle than as a person, It should be noted, however, that Whitehead's thought underwent significant modifications in this regard. In *Religion in the Making*, he rejects the notion of God as a person or divine personality as being the result of an unreflective supernaturalism.[91] Yet, in *Science and the Modern World*, he rejects Asian gods as being too impersonal. In *Process and Reality*, he speaks of the "wisdom," "patience," and "tender care" of God. Also, the unity of identity and change he attributes to God seems analogous to that found in persons.

The Centrality of God in Human Experience

As noted in the introduction, the goal now is to show that each of these principles entails the claim that, at some level, our experience includes God as a datum. Thus these principles make for what might be best termed a "secular mysticism." A fuller discussion of this notion will take place in chapters 3 and 5. However, the following preliminary considerations will prove useful.

THE ONTOLOGICAL PRINCIPLE
We shall explore four ways in which this principle can be understood as a claim that God is experientially accessible within our present mode of existence.

A most obvious way in which the ontological principle renders God experientially available is that it renders God metaphysically accessible, close at hand; God dwells within the universe, among us, not in some remote atemporal realm above and beyond the world. Since this principle eliminates the age-old ontological dualism between God and the world, because God is not the negation but the finest exemplification of metaphysical principles, it stands to reason also that God is not the negation but the finest exemplification of human experience. In other words, to seek God is not, as the traditional spiritualistic writings would have it, a purely otherworldly affair in which we must strive to put aside our humanness and to dissociate ourselves from the temporal material order. Nor is it to wait upon miraculous acts that announce that God is breaking in from without. There is only one reality—nature. The alternative view is that there are two orders of reality, nature and the supernatural (perhaps "unnature" is a better term). It is precisely this view that makes the experience of the Spirit such an embarrassment, such an alien and meaningless concept to serious modern persons, because it speaks so strongly of ghosts, disembodied souls, and the like. In sharp contrast, the ontological principle speaks of the oneness of God and nature, of God working in and through nature from within the depths of spatio-temporal reality. Conceived in this way, the experience of the Spirit loses its negative connotations; it is not some terrifying and "spooky" event in which we are grasped by some alien ghostly intruder from some bloodless beyond; rather it is to fathom the awesome and infinite depths of the universe itself. To find God we must go deeper into the world, not away from it. Sin is not flesh, it is insensitivity. Coming to sense the presence of God is a viable option for us to the extent that we actualize our potentials for maximum sensitivity to the datum before us in the empirically given situation.

The ontological principle ultimatizes the universe by claiming that it is the only real world. To some, at first glance, this claim seems to offer a too-constricting, too-limited, and uninteresting view of ultimate reality. How can the ontological principle make room for the experience of the infinite if all it puts before us is the finite?

To answer this question it is important to underscore the fact that the Whiteheadian universe is not, strictly speaking, finite; it is dynamic, openended, and therefore in an important sense infinite or unbounded. Whitehead is striving to go beyond the traditional rationalistic and scientific understandings of reality as static and simple. Traditional scientific standards such as parsimony, logic, precision, and simplicity are understood as belonging to the realm of abstraction rather than to experience. "The complexity of nature," he writes, "is inexhaustible."[92] The ultimate metaphysical truth is the infinite complexity of all things.[93] Many scientists today share this view.[94] In short, the traditional dualism between finite and infinite, or between God and the world, appears overly simplistic. Our experience of the "finite" makes for sensing the presence of God in that the awesome and inexhaustible complexity of the universe presents a myriad of intimations of the Infinite One.

In this vein, Teilhard de Chardin has made two particularly relevant points. First, the tendency toward pantheism, by which he means the tendency to perceive the universe as divine or godlike, has been historically too pervasive and tenacious not to have a germ of truth in it.[95] Like it or not, Christian theology must come to terms with pantheism.

Second, a very big problem for Christianity in the twentieth century is that the traditional, static model of God hardly seems worthy of the modern dynamics of the cosmos. Teilhard believes that there is in the making a new cosmic consciousness that is the basis for a new spirituality.[96] Many seem about to embark upon a natural religion of the universe. A "religion of the earth" seems to be fighting against a "religion of the sky." The universe is starting to play God. Many modern persons are far more captivated by the awesome wonder and beauty of the universe, with its inexhaustible profusion of structures and relationships, internal and external, than they are by the traditional Christian image of God, which to them seems too static, too transcendent, and too juridical. Teilhard believes that the only hope for a reconciliation of these two conflicting views is the process model of God, because it enables one to ascribe cosmic attributes to the Deity.[97]

He contends that a major obstacle to a mystical cosmology has been the traditional and pervasive tendency in western theology to explicate God in terms of juridical-legal concepts rather than in terms of analogies based upon the physical, natural world, which would speak of an organic relationship between God and the world.[98]

Chapter 5 will show how Whitehead's aesthetic explicates this point. At present, however, it can be said that in Whitehead God is much more than a mere judge who sits on high and hands down laws; there is a direct substantial union between God and the world.

However, there is also an important affinity between Whitehead's and the legalistic models of God. As a judge, God is essentially that agency that recalls to us our past, for which we are accountable. As the following will show, a comparable theme is found in Whitehead's contention that God mediates the past to us.

We all feel the past impinging upon us; if we did not, we would be unable to finish even the simplest sentence. We also seek to renew our acquaintance with the past, to "escape from time in its character of 'perpetual perishing.' "[99] The consequent nature of God saves the world by somehow preserving the past forever.[100] This latter point is, of course, congruent with the ontological principle: Everything has to be somewhere; the past is an objective fact with a date, so it has to be somewhere; by virtue of the fact it has perished from among us, it cannot be said to be here, so it is posited to be in the consequent nature of God. So far, all of this is quite clear in Whitehead. However, what still remains a controversial question is the exact sense in which God is the bearer of the past. To fully address this question would require an exploration of issues far beyond the range of this present work. The aspect of this question that is of particular relevance here is this: Can it be said that to feel the hand of the past upon us is also to feel the hand of God upon us? Must our prehensions of the past, that is, prehension in the mode of causal efficacy, necessarily include God? I choose to answer this question in the affirmative for the following reasons.

In his book, *An Interpretation of Whitehead's Metaphysics*, William Christian, having acknowledged that it is very problematic how the Whiteheadian God is the bearer of the past, goes on to argue that this God must be the ground for the givenness of the past. That is, it is the function of God to re-present the past to us. Thus, to prehend in the mode of causal efficacy is also to prehend God. He presents the following rationale.

Since the past has perished, it is no longer actual and therefore cannot be determinate. What no longer exists can have no impact. We cannot feel what is not there. How, then, can it be the case that we feel so strongly the impetus of the past? How do we come to finish the sentence? He contends that the only logical solution is that God re-presents the past to us.[101]

Christian, however, does not cite any specific passages in Whitehead that make such a claim. However there are some. For example, Whitehead explicitly claims that the immanency of God guarantees order.[102] Order, as defined in Whitehead, is inclusive of continuity, uniformity, and reiteration of the past.[103] Therefore, the immanency of God may be identified with the reiteration of the past.

In his discussion of the concept of nexus in Part 3 of *Process and Reality*, Whitehead seems to conclude that the consequent nature of God mediates the past to us. He posits that events in the remote past do in fact have a major impact upon us; yet it is inexplicable how we could achieve such a prehension; our memory does not go back that far. Where, then, is the complex and intricate chain of events (nexus) that interrelates us to the past? To exist is to be prehended; therefore, such a nexus must be in the prehension of some actual entity. The entity in question must be God, since this nexus is somewhere and yet is not implicated in the feelings of any actual entity of the actual world.[104]

There are numerous other passages in which it is claimed that the past in and of itself has very little impact beyond itself. God, then, must be ground for the givenness of the past; otherwise much of the past would have negligible influence, and in such a case we would be hard put to explain why the past seems so strongly deterministic. The objective immortality or "memory" of the past does not encompass its full reality; it denotes the past as present only in a very abstract and limited sense. It therefore denotes only a very weak impression of the past.[105]

Here it is important to note that even if receptivity to the past is looked at from the standpoint of selectivity and abstraction, still a prehension of God, a feeling of God's conceptual feelings, has to be in the picture. As noted earlier, what makes for novelty, what prevents the universe from being an endless series of duplications, is the fact that receptivity to the past always involves creative selectivity under the guidance of eternal objects. We do not blindly reiterate the past; in an important sense we can even be said to condition the givenness of the past insofar as we are capable of imaginatively evaluating or interpreting it; and since this interpretation (subjective form) is necessarily determined in part by our prehensions of God's conceptual feelings, our prehensions of the past necessarily involve God as a datum.[106]

The above may be further clarified in light of the following point. The ontological principle claims that there is causality: Actual entities are the only reasons. As noted earlier, prehensions in the mode of causal efficacy are essentially noncognitive, nonconceptual responses. The same is also true of aesthetic experience, and at the same time Whitehead tends to identify God's immanency with the aesthetic order of the world.[107] Aesthetic experience is in an important sense the experience of God's immanency. Because feelings of causal efficacy and aesthetic feelings are both noncognitive and nonconceptual in nature, I suspect that they may easily overlap one another. Therefore, prehensions in the mode of causal efficacy may very well include God.

According to Whitehead, the richness or fullness of feeling in the concrescing moment (aesthetic experience) is possible only by the synthesis of conceptual and physical feelings (prehensions of other actual entities). Hardly, then, is the prehension of a conceptual feeling or proposition (a lure for relevant novelty) exhaustive of the objectification of God in aesthetic experience. The immortality of the past resides in the fact that the concrescing moment includes conformal feelings of God as objectified in the satisfactions of past occasions. In other words, our enjoyment is enriched to the extent that it includes the enjoyment of our predecessors. Aesthetic experience is an affirmation of the intrinsic value of what is and has been.

Admittedly, this is an oversimplified discussion of Whitehead's aesthetic. It is intended only as preliminary to the material in the following chapters.

THE PRINCIPLE OF RELATIVITY

We shall now explore four ways in which this principle is making the claim that at some level our experience is inclusive of God. Because this principle is "another rendering" of the ontological principle, the following considerations should serve to reinforce the preceding discussion.

Since nothing can exist in isolation, nothing can be experienced in isolation.[108] It follows, then, that our experiences of the world and of God cannot be abstracted from one another. Therefore, to the extent that we experience the world, we also at some level experience God. Indeed, in Whitehead's metaphysic, every element requires every other element for its own intelligibility—elements are meaningless in isolation. The essential elements are: spacio-temporal entities, God and Creativity. Together they interpret human experience. God is assumed to be encountered within our experience; for God functions not neutrally or independently of our experience, but positively, in the service of its explication.[109] Because God had this paradigmatic role in illuminating experience, God must encompass and involve all human experience.

There is yet another way in which this principle rules out a God couched in purely abstract terms, that is, God as a mere intellectual abstraction. The principle of relativity stands in opposition to what Whitehead terms "the current view of universals and particulars," which is tied into the epistemic position of Descartes. This view contends that perception exists purely in the abstract; it is characterized only by universals. There is no such thing as the perception of a particular entity, for instance, God. Rather, we arrive at the actual entity in question by a process of intellectual inference.[110] The principle of relativity claims that such a skeptical view is mistaken: We can and do prehend particular actual entities, like God, because it is these particular actual entities that make up our real internal constitutions.

Every actual entity prehends every other actual entity. God is an actual entity; therefore, we prehend God.

The problem to be addressed here is that, taken in this way, the principle of relativity seems to be substantiating an experience of God on the basis of the premise that we experience everything that there is. Various objections may be raised against the seeming boldness of such a claim. For example, are we really all that sensitive? Does not such a claim border upon the absurd notion that we are all omniscient? If so, why is it that we do not have knowledge of everything going on in the cosmos? How is it that we are capable of perceiving the multitudinous complexity of the real world as one complex pattern, or as Whitehead says, "housing the world in one unity of complex feeling, in every way determinate"?[111]

The following considerations serve to indicate that Whitehead's position is tenable, that his philosophy of organism can deal adequately with these and similar considerations.

First, it must be emphasized that Whitehead is not dealing with perception in the ordinary sense of the term. He goes beyond traditional rational-empirical definitions of knowledge and of experience. As noted earlier, a prehension is a rather low-grade experience, one devoid of consciousness and understanding (in the intellectual sense of the term). It corresponds to the general lower way in which Leibnizian monads take each other into account.[112] In short, prehensions are vague feelings.[113] This means that on an intellectual, conscious, or sensory level, we are aware of only a very tiny and select portion of the world. On a deep and primitive visceral or "gut" level, we are feeling the entire cosmos, though vaguely so. To talk of the God experience in the most fundamental sense of the term, we must turn to that which is prior to and beneath the veneer of consciousness, and as well to that which lacks the clarity and simplicity of the sensorial.

This also means that the experience of God is a nebulous one, which is perhaps where the excitement of process theology lies. Since our experience of God is always mixed in with and part of the totality of the situation that includes an infinite number of prehensions of other entities, the experience of the divine may not emerge with sure and certain clarity. We cannot presume to know precisely what is or what is not a genuine experience of God. Whitehead is not mystical in the sense that he would hold with the dualistic affirmations of many mystics to forsake and renounce all the rest of the world in order to focus exclusively upon God. This would be an utter impossibility in Whitehead's thought. Yet, it is not inappropriate to bring in something of the mystical, that is, to assume that the more we strive consciously to fix our attention upon God through prayer and meditation, the more acutely aware of God we may become.[114]

Second, we are capable of prehending to some degree the actual world as one complex unity of feeling because the ultimate metaphysical truth is that the many seek to enter into complex unity, to become one. The actual world presents itself to each of us as ripe for integration. This point is expressed in the first of the nine categorical obligations, The Category of Subjective Unity.[115]

Third, Whitehead does not fail to acknowledge that in many ways our emotional life is limited. There are some qualifiers he places upon the principle of relativity. For example, there are "negative prehensions." These latter are defined as the "definite exclusion of that item from positive contribution to the subject's own real internal constitution."[116] On the one hand, this means that only a selected portion of the universe is felt; there is much we tune out and to which we remain insensitive. Perhaps God is tuned out, too. The principle of relativity seems compromised. Yet, on the other hand, Whitehead contends that a negative prehension is still an emotional bond to those items not felt. In a way, being insensitive is a kind of sensitivity: Those items not felt are not emotionally negligible because each negative prehension contributes to the emotional complex of the subject.[117] God, then, is never an emotionally negligible datum.

This principle claims that God is experientially available because God and the world are empathically interconnected. The Whiteheadian God is the "fellow sufferer who understands." Whitehead contends that empathy is the deepest and most primal form of experience.[118] Empathy is also central in Hartshorne's writings; he considers it to be the highest form of knowledge because it is the most informative, and therefore he posits an empathic bond between God and the world.

Essentially these considerations represent a translation of the principle of relativity into epistemic terms: To know an entity, God, is to know that entity relationally; therefore, knowledge is not impartial or detached observation from without, but participation from within.[119] On the one hand, this means that to know the world God must empathically share in it. On the other, it means that knowledge of God is a meaningless concept unless couched in terms of the self-experience of our relationship to God, and therefore God must be amenable to the terms of human experience.

CREATIVITY

Chapter 5 will present a more extensive discussion of creativity and its relationship to mystical experience or the experience of presence. The present analysis will note two basic ways in which creativity presupposes a prehension of God.

Consciousness is a consequence of the creative advance into novelty and therefore is a derivation of a more primal apprehension of God. As noted earlier, consciousness arises through the complex integration of actuality and potentiality (primordial nature), that is, the synthesis of physical feelings and conceptual feelings. The fact that we are conscious entities presupposes that we feel at some level the conceptual feelings of God, which pave the way into novelty. This means that God is somehow present in all experience and therefore cannot be restricted to the realm of paranormal events. As we shall see, this has severe implications for mysticism; in Whitehead, Spirit experiences are no esoteric realm only an elite can enter.

Whitehead contends that apart from prehensions of God there would be nothing new in the world. This is a further explication of my earlier point that God is not the negation but the fulfillment of our humanity. Whitehead's case is as follows.

All actual entities are *causa sui*. A creature is born of its subjective aim, its past, and God's initial aim. It is the status of this latter that we are concerned with here. According to Whitehead, the fact that all actual entities are *causa sui* means that the process of self-creation is initiated by the reception of an initial aim from God. The fact that we as subjects now exist presupposes that we prehended God in our process of becoming.[120]

The question now becomes, why does Whitehead make initial aims so primary in the process of self-creation? In truth, Whitehead provides no clear-cut defense of this point. Donald Sherburne, for example, has gone as far as to deny that Whitehead's system makes God indispensable to the creative process. I do not intend to undertake an elaborate defense of Whitehead on this point. However, a few preliminary considerations may prove useful to show that at least there is some degree of coherence to Whitehead's thought, even though self-creation is one of the central paradoxes of the mystical tradition (see Eckhart's doctrine of *Selbstschopfung* or autocreation).

First, self-creation is essentially a teleological process initiated by a goal to become some sort of novel entity. The past cannot fully decide what particular self or entity shall arise from the datum. The past is the many, the multitude, and therefore it is riddled with ambiguity. In other words, the multiple cannot unify itself, since it is a power of dispersion. Unity, then, requires a transcendental power. Furthermore, self-creation means that ultimately the self must decide what it is to become. But as yet the self does not exist and so cannot make such a decision. Therefore, God must make the initial decision. As the self begins to emerge, it takes into account its past, God's initial aim, and then makes its own decision.

Second, without God there is no possibility of genuine novelty. Only God can conjure up conceptual feelings that do not depend upon prior physical ones; for unlike all other entities, God originates at the mental pole. Furthermore, if we took all our cues from the world and the world alone (physical prehensions), we would see no possibility for novelty. Instead, we would assume that the future will duplicate the past. In this case, the past would fully determine the present. Novelty would be only apparent, a mere reiteration or reconfiguration of the past. Whitehead contends that genuine creativity denotes the rise of the improbable, whereas statistical probability, based upon what has been the case, assumes that the future will duplicate the present. Therefore, estimations of genuine novelty must come from an intuition of the relevancy of eternal objects in God.[121]

Whitehead contends that those, such as the British empiricists, who have attempted to account for the birth of genuinely novel ideas solely on the basis of our sensory impressions of the world, and therefore without bringing God into the picture, failed to take creativity seriously. In such a scheme, imagination is never very free, if at all, because it is thoroughly tied down to sensory impressions. Whatever it comes up with is nothing more than a highly exaggerated or distorted copy of prior sensory impressions. That is not genuine creativity; it is just the same old wine in new bottles. In this regard, Whitehead is fond of citing Hume's example of one coming up with a brand-new shade of blue that corresponded to no known shade, because it shows that even the empiricists were forced at times to admit that not all novel ideas could be accounted for by reference to prior sensory impressions.[122]

2
Process Theology and Christian Mysticism

The purpose of this chapter and the next is to provide an account of process themes found in certain mystical conceptions of God. This will be based upon a survey of various influential sources in western mysticism, for example:

Dionysius the Aeropagite, Meister Eckhart, Henry Suso, *Theologia Germanica,* Jacob Boehme, Walter Hilton, *The Cloud of Unknowing,* Teresa of Avila, John of the Cross

The choice of these particular sources was based upon the fact that they have been deemed by scholars to be among the most influential in the history of western mysticism, that they are readily available, and that they provide a substantial body of material. I do not intend to claim that they represent one particular type or several types of mysticism. Indeed, I find that there is no agreed-upon typology of mysticism among scholars. However, I have not overlooked that significant differences can be found among these sources. For example, some (Eckhart, Dionysius) stress philosophical or metaphysical components over experiential ones, while others (Teresa of Avila, John of the Cross) seem primarily oriented toward experiential rather than philosophical considerations.

At first glance, the juxtaposition of process theology and Christian mysticism may seem odd, because the two ways of thinking appear to be so antagonistic. However, this chapter will present an alternative to the pervasive assumption that mysticism represents a dualistic and world-negating concept of God. The object is to show that within certain mystical doctrines of God there are elements agreeable to process theology. Certain mystics will be shown to have placed strong emphasis upon dynamic, relativistic attributes of the deity, so that something analogous to a process model of God emerges from the literature; that is, certain mystical texts will be shown to reveal numerous instances in which the *via negativa* or "negative theology," with its allegedly dualistic metaphysic, issues forth into an "affirmative theology" that centers upon the oneness and mutual interdependence of an evolving God and universe.

Dionysius the Aeropagite

The writings of Dionysius the Aeropagite are one of the earliest sources of the western mystical tradition. The author or authors, date, and exact place of these writings are unknown, but historical studies suggest Syria between the fourth and fifth centuries, A.D. This author enjoyed enormous popularity during the Middle Ages and had great influence upon famous scholars, such as Peter Lombard, Albertus Magnus, Thomas Aquinas, and many others. His writings should have particular relevance for process theology because they have had considerable aesthetic appeal. For example, the fifteenth chapter of his *Celestial Hierarchy* constituted the canon of symbolic angelic lore both for literature and for architecture throughout the Middle Ages.

This chapter will attempt to illustrate the process themes in Dionysius, according to a discussion centering upon the following points:

1. that the Dionysian God is neither remote nor static. The "negative theology" is counterbalanced by an "affirmative theology";
2. that this point can be highlighted by his concepts of sin and salvation, which transcend all such dualisms.

At first glance, the *via negativa* would seem to present an inordinately dry, static, inanimate conception of God. Dionysius iterates and reiterates that God does not change, grow, move, indeed has no "being," is not a "life."[1] This conception, of course, renders him totally at odds with process theology.

But the *via negativa* proves to be more complex than it first appears. We can glimpse here an inner tension that ultimately eliminates any thoroughly static image of God. It is as if Dionysius were claiming that his system is openended as regards the question of whether or not God is dynamic, because ultimately no real answer can be given, save in the terms of very paradoxical formulations. Dionysius expressly states that the meaning of the *via negativa* is that we may elevate ourselves to God only by "paradox" and "absurdity."[2] This means that nothing logically consistent can be said regarding a dynamic side of God. A dynamic God cannot be ruled out across the board; that would be too rational. Rather the *via negativa* strives to speak paradoxically of a dynamic God, so that He is said to be the one who "neither remains immobile nor moves,"[3] who "moves only in an immobile fashion."[4]

It is also important to bear in mind that the *via negativa* makes a much broader claim than merely that we cannot know what God is, that nothing affirmative can be said of Him; it also expressly claims that God transcends all negations. We can neither affirm nor deny anything of God, because all affirmation and all negation stand on this, our side of God's transcendence.[5] In other words, the *via negativa* ultimately negates the negations. As such, there are three ways in which it can be construed as granting a dynamic God. First, claiming that God is the negation of all negations is the mystic's way of ascribing to God the fullness of all being, and therefore absolutely everything must be predicated in Him. Second, it means that we can bring in through the back door a dynamic conception of God insofar as we are compelled to negate those negations by which He is rendered static. Third, at the very least, it means that if we cannot know what God is, neither can we know with any real surety what God is not. Spoken of either positively or negatively, the subject of God is one of pure idle speculation; no dogmatic statements can be made one way or the other. A dynamic or mutable God is therefore just as viable as a static or immutable one.

Dionysius at least anticipates process theology in his realization that the nature of God is by no means simple, that a complete account of God will contain potentially conflicting elements. The advantage of process theology is that its concept of a dipolar deity provides a reconciliation of these elements, for which Dionysius failed to provide a satisfying account.

There is one very intriguing passage in Dionysius (*Les Noms Divins*, 9, 19) where he strongly implies that whether or not it is viable to speak of God as dynamic depends upon whether one wants a thoroughly pious account of God or one that is metaphysically satisfying. To render God as static is to pay God compliments, but such a static God does not complement metaphysical endeavors. He begins by raising this question: "What do the theologians mean when they say that God descends into all things and that the immobile moves?" He goes on to say that piety forbids us from ascribing any movement whatsoever to God, movement in a straight line, circular motion, mixed motion, movement by transmutation, alteration. But, he continues, we are compelled to say that it is God who is omnipresent and everywhere exercises his providence, for He envelops all things.[6] At this point, as if to say that one cannot absolutize the pious or static conception of God when it comes to God's *modus operandi* with the world, he goes on to speak of the "movements of the immobile God," for example, movement in a straight line, which signifies the immutability of the divine process; and circular motion, which signifies that God envelops all intermediaries and extremes, and returns to Himself all that has departed from Him.[7] The spectacle of life on earth is an immense aesthetic content streaming back into God.[8]

In this respect it is important to note that Meister Eckhart acknowledges this dynamic side of the Dionysian God; he quotes Dionysius as having spoken of souls catching the tide and flowing back into God as God flows back into Himself.[9]

To further emphasize that the *via negativa* in no way implies a rejection of matter, the body, and creation, we turn to the centrality of eros in Dionysius' mysticism.

At the outset, it is important to note the conspicuous absence of pessimistic, world-negating statements in this author. Rather, Dionysius claims that the *via negativa*, by virtue of its erotic dynamism, surpasses or transcends all such distinctions made by means of spirit-matter dualism. There is no reference to an introverted retreat from creation. Ecstasy means standing outside oneself, not retreating into one's spiritual center. The movement to God is an ecstatic movement of the whole cosmos; therefore, neither matter, nor body, nor desire for created goods can impede this motion. The necessity of this extroverted movement is clearly emphasized at the very beginning of *La Théologie Mystique*, chapter 1. The all-inclusiveness of God is the central theme of this work (see 4, 14; 7, 3 and 5). God is eros, the uniting power that permeates throughout the whole of creation from the highest beings to the lowest. This dynamic power safeguards the harmony and synthesis of the elements, guarantees the indissoluble stability of the universe, assures the unity of soul and body, and accords deification. The omnipresence of God, the Holy Spirit, is not the negation, but the affirmation and guarantee of the material world, not the destroyer, but the perfecter of nature.

The mystical theology of Dionysius is not a purely abstract philosophical construct showing little or no interest in personal experience. Although it is true that Dionysius provides no real description of mystical experience, autobiographical or otherwise; nevertheless, the central theme of his mystical theology is how to reach the most direct possible experience of God. Because such a direct experience would be rendered impossible if our thoughts should come to stand between ourselves and God, he admonishes the reader to abandon absolutely all mental operations. His mystical theology is no abstract intellectual system; rather, it is a striving to demolish any sort of intellectual or philosophical conception of God, to grossly accentuate the ascendancy of the experiential over the realm of intellectual abstraction. Indeed, this basic theme is reiterated continually throughout all his writings. For example, in *Les Noms Divins*, 7, 3, we read that since God surpasses all reason and intellect, the manner most worthy of knowing Him is to know Him by unknowing in a union that transcends all intellect.

To gain further insight into the dynamic side of the Dionysian God, we turn to his "affirmative theology." Already it has been shown that his concept of eros makes central God's omnipresence. However, there are some further important considerations that need be noted here. Many commentators speak only of the *via negativa* in Dionysius. This of course easily translates into a thoroughly aloof, otherworldly God; according to the *via negativa*, absolutely nothing of the creaturely, not even being or existence itself, can be predicated of God. Thus, God appears to be the total and complete negation of the world, which excludes any real sense of His immanency. However, a most important point to be made here is that Dionysius also speaks of what he terms an "affirmative" theology.[10] In chapter 3 of *La Théologie Mystique*, he states that whether or not theological discourse follows either the "negative" (*via negativa*) or the "affirmative" way depends upon the reference point of the discourse. If the discourse moves from the inferior to the superior, from the world to God, this is the "negative theology," and to the extent that we reach the summit, the volume of our thoughts diminishes to the extent that finally we can say absolutely nothing. On the other hand, if the starting point is God Himself, so that the discourse moves from God to the world, this is the "affirmative theology," by which we can say what God is.[11] He has placed God in a relativistic context; this renders his conception analogous to process thought.

The world-affirming character of this "affirmative theology" is well evidenced by the fact that it liberally ascribes highly anthropomorphic, cosmic attributes to God. Indeed, it tends to identify God with the universe. God is termed the "Lord of Lords," "King of Kings," "Ancient of Days," "Saint of Saints," "Sun," "Star," "Fire," "Water," "Rock," "Cloud," "in a word all that which is and nothing of that which is."[12] In this context, Dionysius, citing First Corinthians 15:28, states that "God is striving to be all in all."[13] Certainly he does seem to be claiming that the universe is God's body.

There are, however, at least two other ways in which this "affirmative theology" can be construed as claiming that the stuff of the world is the stuff of God. First, in his Christological formulations, Dionysius states that through the Incarnation the Eternal received temporal extension.[14] Consequently, he rules out any sort of docetic dualism; for he contends the mystery of the Incarnation is that, in Christ, God Himself took up the very essence of mankind.[15] Thus, something analogous to Whitehead's ontological principle seems to be involved here. This principle speaks of the ontological unity of God and the world, and in Dionysius this fact constitutes the true meaning of the incarnation. There are not two separate realities, the natural and the supernatural, but only one: By the incarnation, God, supremely united His divine nature with our lowly nature, that we might come to the perfect and divine life. Holy Communion, then, is said to represent our "deification," that is, the fact that our baseness becomes bound to His infinitely divine stability, so that we become members of the divine body of Christ.[16]

Second, in his briefly explicated creation myth, God is depicted as dynamic, as continually expanding and contracting. Everything in some way preexists in God, so that creation is said to be an outward diffusion or differentiation of God analogous to rays emanating out from a center point.[17] This concept seems analogous to the consequent nature of God by which God's nature is said to pass into the world.[18] Also, another process theme implied here is that God in some important sense needs the universe. Dionysius thinks of God as a supraabundance that spills forth into all things, as if to alleviate a tremendous internal pressure created by an excess or surplus of libidinal energy that must be discharged.

On the other hand, there is also the matter of God contracting in on Himself, that is, salvation. As was noted above, Dionysius sees salvation as a matter of everything flowing back into God. He writes that "according to the Holy word, 'All things come from Him and all things return to Him.'"[19] This seems analogous to Whitehead's claim that "every actuality in the temporal world has its reception in God's nature."[20] It is also analogous to Whitehead's contention that the concept of "static completion" is inapplicable to God.[21] Consequently, Dionysius speaks of the "circle of eros," by which he means that God's desire, like a circle, is without end.[22]

Insofar as Dionysius contends that in God all exist in a "synthetic union,"[23] he seems to be congruent with Whitehead's claim that in God the many become one. Nevertheless, the meanings of the two conceptions diverge; for Dionysius this synthetic union means total and complete homogeneity; Whitehead considers true unity to be a complex pattern of contrasts.[24] But there is not total and complete disagreement here either: In Dionysius, complexity is applicable to God insofar as it may be said that, in pouring forth from Himself, God moves from total and complete homogeneity to the complexity of the multitudinous differentiation of all life. Relatedly, Dionysius seems to share Whitehead's conviction that all of reality is interconnected insofar as he contends that eros is the suressential force, the "power of unification and connection,"[25] pervading all being, and that therefore all entities mutually attract one another.

Dionysius' view of the biblical images of God is quite interesting in this context. He seems to parallel the central epistemic tenet of process thought that the only viable God is an anthropomorphic God. After having spoken of God strictly in terms of the *via negativa*, by which He is said to be totally void of all that belongs to the sensible or creaturely,[26] Dionysius takes up the matter of the highly anthropomorphic, physical images of God found in the Bible. What he now claims in effect is that the *via negativa* ultimately proves impractical; it is simply too much for us;[27] there is no way we can come to make sense out of this thoroughly intangible God.[28] Thus, the physical metaphors of scripture are a necessary accommodation to our natures; as physical beings, there is no other way we could come to grasp the mystery of God.[29]

It is obvious, then, that Dionysius' rationale for anthropomorphizing God is quite different from that found in process theology. He takes these biblical images and symbols as merely a kind of accommodation. His acceptance of them is not in strict accord with process claims for an anthropomorphic deity. From the perspective of process theology, the problem here in Dionysius is what possible meanings these biblical images would have if they do not in some way correspond to the actual nature of God. (See chapters 4 and 5.)

In sum, distinct parallels exist between the negative and the affirmative theology and Whitehead's concept of the primordial and the consequent nature of God. The *via negativa* or negative theology seems analogous to the primordial nature insofar as the former speaks so strongly of turning away from the world, from the concrete and the particular, of groping after God as He is totally and completely alone in Himself. Analogous to Whitehead's contention that the primordial nature of God is God as in some important sense unreal or nonexistent, the *via negativa* expressly denies God "being."[30] In sharp contrast, the affirmative theology, by speaking of the outgoingness of God, of God pouring forth from Himself in "an unlessened stream into all things that are,"[31] of a God who is "all that which is," seems to speak of a God who is objectified in, hence consequent to, the world. In other words, just as Whitehead's distinction between the primordial and the consequent natures of God makes for an ambignous model of the deity, so too does Dionysius' distinction between the affirmative and the negative theology, by which God can be said to be transcendent and yet radically immanent, accessible and yet remote, this-worldly and yet otherworldly. At the very beginning of *La Théologie Mystique*, this ambiguity comes through strongly in Dionysius likening God to a "darkness brilliantly shining forth from bleakest obscurity."[32] However, this discussion is subject to a most important qualifier. There is in point of fact a major discrepancy between the *via negativa* and the radical transcendency of God in process thought. Hartshorne, in contrast to Whitehead, contends that the absolute nature of God can be known absolutely. The baffling mystery that eludes all human comprehension is the relational nature or the radical immanency of God. This is because only most imperfectly do we enjoy any degree of real intimacy with things and therefore we are total strangers to sensitivity on the magnitude an scale of the radical immanency of God. We will remain stupefied at the extent and intimacy of God's relationship to the universe, a point also echoed in Teilhard de Chardin.

The preceding considerations may be reinforced by a discussion of Dionysius' concepts of sin and of salvation. First, his concept of evil seems analogous to the general trend in process literature to view sin as a failure to actualize potentials. Dionysius, like process thought, stresses the innate goodness of creation. Earlier we noted his claim that absolutely no evil comes from the fact of having a body. He strengthens this implicit claim for the innate goodness of the material order by stating that nothing, not even a demon, is evil by nature.[33] Evil is the failure to attain the perfections appropriate to one's nature.[34]

Analogous to Whitehead's famous contention that it is the *telos* of the universe to be beautiful, Dionysius contends that all creatures, even the most despicable, seek beauty. In short, evil *qua* evil, evil is a lesser or inferior form of beauty; it is "nonbeing" or "being without," a "privation."[35] In other words, evil is the failure to attain to those perfections proper to one's own nature. We are said to be evil by virtue of what we are not rather than by virtue of what we are.[36]

It follows that sin does not denote the reality of some huge, unbridgeable ontological gulf between God and human beings, which has been an unfortunate consequence of much classical theism. It is true that the latter understood the gap that sin creates between God and us to be accidental. Yet, as we shall see in chapters 4 and 5, this radical doctrine of sin has in fact functioned as an ontological gap. Dionysius, however, avoids this pitfall. Not only does he teach that human nature is innately good but also that all beings continually participate in God, who abandons no one.[37] This point seems analogous to Whitehead's claim that all entities continually receive initial aims from God, whether or not they actualize them.

Attaining mystical unity with God has nothing whatsoever to do with any form of self-annihilation whereby we are purged of our humanity. Dionysius' view of nature is too optimistic for that. Indeed, humans *qua* humans are said to be essentially angelic or divine in nature. Dionysius speaks of eros as enabling us to be transformed in our entirety (body and soul together and united) to immortality and the perfect life. Mystical unity denotes the wholeness of the self. That our self-identity is retained in mystical unity is well evidenced by his statements in section 1 of chapter 3 of *La Hierarchie Ecclesiastique*. There he likens "perfect divine conformity" or the "imitation of God" to an artist modeling or reproducing something by keeping his attention riveted upon it. In other words, we become one with God, become His true self-manifestation, and yet we still remain ourselves, just as the artist totally absorbed in the model still remains the artist.

Finally, one might be tempted to think that Dionysius has a thoroughly predestinarian understanding of divine providence, since he speaks of all things as having "preexisted" in God. If so, this would place him at odds with process theology. However, numerous passages reveal that Dionysius, as congruent with the central tenets of process thought, sees the realities of sin and of salvation, of good and of evil, as consequences of human freedom: *Les Noms Divins,* 11, 2, 3, 4, 5; *La Hierarchie Celeste*, 3, 3; *La Hierarchie Ecclesiastique*, 2, sec, 1, 3; sec, 3, 4–8; 3, sec, 3, 1, 7.

On one hand, these passages define evil as essentially chaos, so that purification denotes the soul having been brought from disjunction to conjunction, from discordancy to inner harmony, that is, the unification of our multitudinous thoughts, feelings and desires.[38] Eros is "the power of unification";[39] thus, he writes that "deification," that is, assimilation to God, renders us insensible to the domain of oppositions; and that thanks to our yearning after the One, all that was disordered in us is now ordered, and all that was shapeless is now given form.[40] Understood this way, the thought of Dionysius seems congruent with Whitehead's contention that the ultimate metaphysical truth is that the "many" seek to become "one."

On the other hand, Dionysius expressly claims that the soul is free to decide its own course of action, so that this process of unification excludes any sudden or miraculous and coercive transformation of the will by God. Certainly his likening of the process of divine conformity to the work of an artist suggests that what we receive of God is something analogous to initial aims, something which it is up to us to actualize. Furthermore, it is a gradual process by which the beauty of our superiors attracts us to attain higher and higher degrees of perfection. Consequently, there is no room here for any form of rugged individualism. In contrast to interpreters like R. Jones, who understand the Dionysian path to perfection as a solitary one that the soul travels alone, Dionysius makes it quite clear, especially in his writings on the ecclesiastical hierarchy, that one does not become awakened to God in a vacuum; the spiritual depth one might attain has everything to do with the spiritual depths attained by others. To participate in God is first of all to participate in the beauty of the other. Mystical union is the culmination of a social process by which divine perfection, as reflected in the beauty of one's contemporaries, gradually awakens the soul's desire for unity with God. He writes that the desire for the ecstatic experience of mystical union with God is gradually awakened in us by those more advanced.[41] Since it seems to be the case, then, that we are more pulled along by what is out front rather than pushed from behind, it seems safe to say that Dionysius approximates Whitehead's concept of God luring us on.

It should be emphasized that this luring on to perfection denotes a continual ongoing process of spiritual growth. The mysticism of Dionysius does not consist of a unique or ultimate state, eternal and static. On the contrary, he states clearly that there is no level of mystical unity that cannot be further deepened. There is always room for a further perfectioning.[42]

Meister Eckhart

Down through the ages, the writings of the famous German mystic Meister Eckhart (1260–circa 1328) have been inspirational but nonetheless quite confusing and controversial. He has been claimed as a loyal Catholic, a heretic, a pantheist, a proto-Nazi, and the father of German idealism, to name but a few labels.[43] Also, he was a most unsystematic writer; his phraseology and expressions were too recondite for his contemporaries and would also appear to be so for modern persons, and only partial English translations are available of his writings. This makes his teachings a very difficult subject to study.

Despite these difficulties, it is possible to show that distinct process themes consistently emerge from his writings. For organizational purposes, the following analysis has been divided into two major sections, each of which deals with a major issue in Eckhartian scholarship.

First, I shall attempt to define Eckhart's concept of manifest reality. This will deal with questions such as: Is the temporal material order real in Eckhart? Does he transcend the mind-body or spirit-matter dualism? To what extent does he evidence a relational or relativistic understanding of reality? Is it fair to say that his mysticism is world-renouncing?

Second, I shall turn to an explication of those items in Eckhart's doctrine of God that appear analogous to the main tenets of process theology. Relevant

questions here are: In what ways does Eckhart evidence a bipolar conception
of the deity, so that something analogous to Whitehead's distinction between
the primordial and the consequent nature of God emerges from his writings?
Put more specifically, is Eckhart's deity dynamic and in some important sense
consequent to, hence contingent upon, the universe? Might the universe be
said to be God's body? In what ways does his doctrine of the Trinity absolutize
a relativistic model of God?

Process theology is a world-affirming doctrine of God because it centers
upon the ontological unity of God and the universe. In contrast one pervasive
interpretation of Eckhart is that he writes off manifest reality, spacio-temporal
reality or the sensory world, as a mere illusion and hindrance that must be
pushed aside if we are to attain God. However, I intend to show that this
is a most superficial interpretation of Eckhart, that in point of fact his basic
theme is that reality is a living whole, that what is paramount in his thought
is the unity of time and eternity, of spirit and matter, of soul and body and
of the human and the divine.

ARE TIME AND SPACE REAL IN MEISTER ECKHART?

Rufus Jones, the noted authority on mysticism, has written that one of the
most baffling problems in Eckhart is the meaning of time and space.[44] Are
they facts of reality or mere appearance? Are they real or are they merely
illusionary? He draws attention to passages in Eckhart that strongly suggest
that the only reality is time-free and space-free, that time and space are mere
illusions because they have no place in eternity.[45] These are the so-called
"hard" or "dark sayings," which center upon Eckhart's claim the "God is
truth, but things in time are not truth."[46] The temporal world seems unreal,
a mere shadow of the real seen through the lenses of time and space.[47] For
example, we read that at its apex the soul has nothing whatsoever to do with
time,[48] that heaven touches neither time nor place,[49] that nothing hinders the
soul's quest for God as much as time and space, and that the most blessed
are those set above time.[50]

But does Eckhart really mean business with this static concept of Eternity?
Is it really so disjunct and separate from spacio-temporal reality in his system?
I contend that Eckhart places some very severe qualifiers upon these "dark
sayings." Whitehead speaks of the temporal passing into the nature of God.
Likewise, Eckhart's concept of the Eternal Now (*Ewige Nu*) claims that time
and eternity are inseparable realities that interpenetrate one another.[51]

The Eternal Now is one of the most unique concepts in Eckhart's thought.
It is said to be grasped or touched by the apex or the highest and purest part
of the soul. Eckhart misleads the reader by his claim that at this level the soul
has nothing to do with time; there is no room in his thought for an ahistorical
centerpoint or apex of the soul; it is there that the whole of history centers
itself, for it is there that God is said to have created all of the past, all of

the present, and all of the future.[52] Relatedly, Eckhart seems to equate the soul with a binding together of time and Eternity: His favorite theme is that the soul stands between these two, and there is at least one passage that speaks of the necessity of a meeting or mediator between the things of time and the things of Eternity.[53] Such a binding together of time and Eternity is said to require a likeness between these two realities. This notion further reinforces our contention that time and Eternity represent one reality, not two, in Eckhart.

Consequently, the soul, caught up in the eternal now, is rendered the highest possible degree of time consciousness. To transcend the temporal is to grasp the fullness of time. Eternity or the Eternal Now is not the negation but the fullest affirmation, indeed, the very meaning of time; the eternal now is the ultimate culmination of all time: *"in dem nu ist al diu zit beslozzen."*[54] As the ultimate culmination or effect of time, it is said to be a fusion of all of the past, all of the present, and all of the future into one ever-present now. To step into eternity is to step into all time, all history, all at one.[55] This means that eternity can be said to transcend time, if by time we mean the materialistic sense of the term—time as a series of disjunct, separate episodes of past, present and future by which all that is immediate is a durationless present exclusive of the realities of the past and the future. When Eckhart writes that in Eternity there is no "before," or "after," no "yesterday" or "tomorrow,"[56] he means that there is no sense in which we can speak of a past that has perished and a future that is yet to be; rather, what is immediate in the Eternal Now seems to be the mystical equivalent of Whitehead's concept of the Right Now as a duration, an unbroken synthesis of past, present and future. Thus, in God there is neither yesterday nor tomorrow, for in God all time is here now.[57]

There is yet one other important way in which Eckhart's thought fuses together time and Eternity. Accepting Whitehead's definition of time as passage or change, one may conclude that Eckhart's Eternity is essentially temporal reality because it is described in terms of process. Eternity is not static; it is dynamic, an "eternal becoming." Eckhart writes that temporal becoming is a work of eternal nature and therefore has neither beginning nor end, and that the Holy Spirit is the author of "becoming" in Eternity.[58]

IS ECKHART A RELATIVIST?

To further reinforce the preceding point, it should be noted that Eckhart evidences a relational or relativistic concept of reality. He provides two metaphors to illustrate this point. One is that reality is said to be analogous to the human body, of which all the parts are united, such that for example the eye is part of the face and the face part of the eye. Thus, "all things are one, all in all united." The other is that, in the Kingdom of Heaven, there is no such thing as separateness or exclusiveness. Roughly speaking, each appears to be part of the reality of the other because each possesses in himself what the other has.[59]

Consequently, he seems to evidence an evolutionary conception of reality. All creatures appear to have a common heritage, so that the nature of any one creature is said to leave its imprint on all the others, including even the angels themselves.[60] Life, then, is likened to a tree, and creatures are said to come to be in a manner analogous to a tree sprouting forth roots.[61] Here it is important to note Benz's point that the term "evolution" was first introduced not by the nineteenth-century Darwinists but by the eighteenth-century German mystics, many of whom were much imbued with Eckhart.

WHAT IS THE RELATIONSHIP OF SOUL TO BODY?

As explicated in chapter 1, it is the bifurcation into two separate realities, mind and nature or relatedly mind and body, which renders manifest reality unreal, a mere illusionary appearance. Consequently, the reality of the manifest is guaranteed to the extent that mind and body are seen as one reality, as a unity. Congruent with his relational view of reality, Eckhart's thought can be shown to fall within this second category. The oneness or unity of mind and body constitutes a major theme throughout his writings.[62] We find Eckhart speaking expressly of the oneness of mind and body as an ontological unity or fusion of essences, said to be analogous to the reality of food being converted into one's body.[63]

Eckhart, it would seem, totally eschews anything resembling what centuries later would become known as Cartesianism—the dualistic concept of the soul as an extensionless point that has no direct or intimate contact with the body, save at the pineal gland. Rather he understands the soul to have a far more intimate and extensive relationship with the body; he renders it synonymous with the inner depths or reality of the body itself; he claims that the soul pervades or extends throughout the entire body and therefore there is no bodily part that does not have an inner spiritual dimension to it. At one point he takes issue with a scholar who would confine the seat of the soul to the heart; to Eckhart the entire body is the home of the soul.[64]

Consequently, he chastises those who would speak of themselves in dualistic terms by saying my body does such-and-such or my soul does such-and-such, as if these two denoted separate spheres of operation. Eckhart claims that soul and body taken together constitute the individual. Furthermore, he argues that absolutely no part of the body, not even the smallest member, can be abstracted from the soul, because the source of all life is the "great oneness" of soul and body.[65]

What is also stressed in Eckhart is the complexity of the soul. This further strengthens the case that the soul is some form of physical reality. He likens it to a house, which implies that it is three-dimensional and partitioned. It is not the static simple monad of the Neo-Platonic tradition. Eckhart, like later mystics such as St. Teresa and Boehme, conceives of the soul as a rich, complex structure; therefore, the frequent dualistic interpretation of Eckhart's mystical concept of the soul as a flat, unidimensional entity is not correct. Eckhart has an essentially dipolar conception of the soul as consisting of a male and female component.[66] The male component denotes the soul's traffic in God, that by which it transcends the world; the female component denotes the soul's traffic in corporeal things.[67] These two components are taken to be inseparably united, the male permeating the female.[68] This means that sensitivity to God and to the world are bound together. The female component is particularly relevant to the issue at hand; it shows that Eckhart has transcended any sort of spirit-matter or spirit-sense dualism by which the sensorial is relegated to the status of an antagonistic and inferior world that must be banished if we are to attain to God. Rather, by its very nature the soul is sensual. Indeed, the senses can be thought of as its outward projection. Thus, according to Eckhart, if the soul is thought of as a house, then the senses may be thought of as its front porch.[69] The sensory world is a very real part of our spiritual life and therefore must be taken seriously. The soul itself seems to have a physiological substratum. Also, we see something here of Whitehead's concepts of physical and conceptual prehensions. The male component seems analogous to conceptual prehensions insofar as it denotes that power by which the soul transcends the given. The female component appears equivalent to physical prehensions because she denotes a receptiveness to the datum at hand. The fact that Eckhart takes the fusion of these two elements to be indispensable seems analogous to Whitehead's contention that one's self-consciousness or self-identity is rooted in the intertwining of physical and conceptual prehensions.

Later this theme is emphasized in the writings of Boehme. Soul or spirit and body are mutually interrelated, each being a kind of food and home for the other. A disembodied soul would be quite crude, having no real knowledge of itself.[70] A soul without a body could hardly be said to exist, because it would have no character or identity.[71] The soul is manifested throughout the entire body and the relationship of the members of the body to the soul is likened to that of the branches to the tree.[72] Thus, the soul is not merely some strange organ affixed to the brain; it seems to denote the totality of our being. Boehme, perhaps more so than Eckhart, rejects the bifurcation of reality into the separate worlds of mind and nature or matter. There is no passive, inert matter, for all matter is alive and has a subjective or spiritual side. According to Boehme, there is nothing that close not have its soul and body.[73] This point is very analogous to the doctrine of panpsychism elaborated in chapter 1.

Another important parallel between process theology and these mystics is that the former speaks of reality not only as dynamic but also as intermittent. Likewise, becoming not being dominates Eckhart's concept of the soul. He is fond of likening the soul to fire or to a flame, which implies that it is ever-changing as well as flickering or intermittent. In contrast to classical Christian thought, he contends that the soul is by nature perishable and so would die were it not for the presence of God.[74]

IS HIS MYSTICISM WORLD-FLIGHT?

Still, it would be easy to write of Eckhart's mystical way as a thoroughly world-negating enterprise whose aim is self-annihilation. In his writings there are numerous sayings to support such a contention. For example, he writes that even as a cask cannot hold two liquors, all creatures must be poured out if they are to have divine joy.[75] Similarly he writes that even as a vessel totally empty of everything, including air, rises up to heaven, the soul empty of all creatures rises up to God.[76] Of fleshy or carnal desire, he writes that there is none without spiritual harm, because the desires of the flesh and of the spirit are contrary to one another. Therefore, he continues, the less one pays attention to creaturely things, the more the Creator pursues him.[77]

However, I want to argue that such statements taken out of context totally misrepresent Eckhart's thought. There is also a positive side to Eckhart's mystical way that needs be stressed and generally is not. When that side is seen, his mystical quest appears to be an essentially world-affirming one that centers upon the oneness of the Divine and the human.[78]

This touches upon a crucial difference between Eckhart and process theology. His claim to be identical with God is pantheism not pan-en-theism. Process theology does not identify the human soul with the essence of God, because we are accidents of God.[79]

However, Eckhart's concept of mystical unity is not self-annihilation; rather, it involves a two-step process: One must renounce the self and the world in order to rediscover them in God. God, then, is not the negation but the fulfillment of our humanity, for only in God do we come to know our humanity and all things in the highest.[80] To speak of mystical unity is to speak of self-affirmation in the highest degree. Indeed, the self or ego now appears infinite. Jones writes: "Personality is *real* from all eternity, and even at the highest point of the soul's 'union' with God, personality remains unlost—the soul still finds itself."[81] In other words, to identify God and the human spirit, as does Eckhart, is also to speak of a retained personal dualism in the sense that the ego or self or the human subject is still distinguishable from God. According to Eckhart, his "discovery" is that God and I, this earthly person before you, are One, that I am the unmoved mover, who moves all things.[82]

But how can Eckhart, on the one hand, speak of something tantamount to self-annihilation or self-dissolution, and yet, on the other hand, speak of finding in God the reality of the self? Here Eckhart's thought appears paradoxical only if it is viewed in terms of the traditional canons of western metaphysics, where the self is seen as a permanent or indestructible subject undergoing adventures of change. If, however, process categories are employed, what he says makes sense: Process thought contends that the self in point of fact is intermittent, a series or society of perishing selves. Therefore, to speak of the self is also to include or make reference to the reality of self-loss. But let us be more specific.

Earlier it was said that becoming, not being, dominates Eckhart's concept of the self. What was meant is that his mystical quest centers upon the reality of self-transformation. When he seemingly speaks of self-annihilation, it is not annihilation in the strict sense of the word that is meant; rather, it is the fact that the old self or selves perish to make way for the new. His concept of atonement is essentially indebted to the East rather than the West.[83] He parallels Athanasius in contending that God became a man that we might become God.[84] Thus, when he raises the question of the fruits of Christ's humanity, the answer he provides is that it denotes the perfecting of our humanity through the fusion or ontological unity of human nature and divinity.[85] The suffering humanity of Christ is the affirmation of our humanness, "the praise of all creatureliness."[86] Consequently, we should gladly accept our physical lot, no matter how painful it may be.[87] In sum, Eckhart here seems to approximate the process conception of God as fellow-sufferer insofar as he seems to take the reality of God's suffering as that by which life is rendered meaningful and bearable.

Relevant here is Eckhart's concept of *Abegescheidenheit*, freely translated as "detachment" or "disinterest." It has been said that no concept is more pervasive throughout his writings.[88] But what does this concept really mean? Does it mean that we are to maintain an introverted aloofness from the world? At first glance, it may seem so, but upon careful examination it appears that Eckhart does everything possible to avoid the stereotype of the mystic as the aloof introvert or lazy contemplative all alone on the mountaintop. According to Blakney:

> The evidence of Eckhart's life and teaching are against translating this word in the usual sense of "solitude, seclusion, or detachment." He did not recommend monkish solitude, nor the detachment which suggests a lack of interest.[89]

In his famous work, *Die Rede der Underscheidunge* (The Talks of Instruction), Eckhart devotes section 6 is exclusively to the topic of *Abegescheidenheit*. There Eckhart expressly claims that one attains to God not by introverted world-flight but by learning to sense the presence of God in absolutely everything. In other words, we attain God by our recognition of the ontological unity of God and the world. He writes that the more everything is regarded as divine, the more God is pleased with us.[90] Those who feel they must withdraw from the world and cloister themselves up in the church are those who are not yet fully conscious of God's omnipresence and therefore are easily distracted from Him. In contrast, the man to whom God is everything because he is fully conscious of God in all things does well everywhere.[91]

In this same work, Eckhart takes up the question of the relationship of the inner to the outer life, the relation between the life of introspective contemplation and the life of action. The point he stresses is that the soul is a unity; therefore, one must be careful to avoid neglecting either the inner or the outer realm, that all activities and actions might manifest the soul's unity, that all activities might lead one back to inner unity. When the two sides work together, that is best of all, and one is then working together with God.[92] Eckhart contends that one should note carefully whether or not in a state of introspective withdrawal from the world one feels any urge to get back to work. If one does not, if one finds oneself bordering on a state of total and complete apathy, one must do everything possible to break free and return to work; for such a state, in which one does not work, is harmful and destructive to one's nature.[93]

Consequently, we find Eckhart stressing that these alluring ecstasies are secondary to a life of loving ministry to the needs of others. Furthermore, such ecstatic experiences are not all due to God; and even if they are, they are merely the preliminary stage in our spiritual development. By these experiences God lures us on to love, so that as we grow in love such experiences will come less readily. Therefore, even if one were to enter into the introverted ecstatic state that St. Paul once did, and if one knew at the same time of a sick person needing soup, it would be better for the ecstatic person to break free and feed the sick one. St. Paul himself tells us we must be willing to give up these rapturous reveries for the sake of the other when he writes (Rom. 9:3): "I could wish to be severed from Christ for the love of my brother."[94]

Among the *Sprüche (Fragments)* we find a similar claim. Eckhart states that no one in this life can exempt himself or herself from outer work. Even those devoted to the life of contemplation cannot refrain from the active life. To have virtues is to apply them according to time and place. Those who have devoted themselves exclusively to the life of contemplation and have eschewed all work have seriously deceived themselves.[95]

His work *Von Abegescheindenheit* (On Disinterest) is intended to provide a synopsis of this concept. Unfortunately it is brief, terse and vexing. The most apparent theme is that *Abegescheindenheit* does in fact denote an apathetic withdrawal from the world. Despite the fact that the masters as well as St. Paul ultimatize love, disinterest is ranked superior to either love or humility.[96] The disinterested one is said to have no regard or desire for anything, neither to love nor to hate; he or she is said to be dead to the world and to have no experience of physical reality, for he has no appetite for anything earthly.[97] Eckhart raises the question; What is so noble about disinterest? He answered that the disinterested mind is unmoved by any sort of affection, sorrow, slander or vice, analogous to a mountain remaining unmoved by a small breeze.[98]

However, this text may exhibit a much more positive meaning. Disinterest does not mean uninterest in the world, but rather patience and endurance amidst the struggles of life. It should be borne in mind that in perhaps one of his most famous sayings Eckhart writes: "That a man has a restful or peaceful life in God is Good; that a man endures a painful life is better; but that a man has his rest in a painful life is the best of all."[99]

If, on one hand, Eckhart can state that the disinterested one is "dead to the world" and has "no experience of physical reality," on the other he seems to be claiming that the disinterested one evidences the healthiest possible openness and receptivity to the temporal world. There is only an apparent contradiction here; what Eckhart is striving for is a well-balanced spiritual life, a harmonious blending of action and contemplation. Although disinterest is extolled above love, honored above humility and more than mercy, these qualities are included in the notion of disinterest, which is their root and without which they would quickly degenerate into absurd caricatures of themselves. For example, there is said to be no disinterest without humility, and disinterest is ranked higher than humility because without the former the latter would quickly become self-abasement and therefore self-destructive.[100]

By disinterest it would seem that the person becomes a whole, a living unity. Eckhart claims that each person is really two people—the inner or spiritual man and the outer or carnal-sensual man. (Note that earlier these were termed the male and the female respectively.) These two must be unified; thus, he contends that the soul must not squander its strength of the outer man, so that one lives like an animal without intelligence; nor must the soul squander all its strength upon the inner, so that one becomes a senseless, aloof, and dispassioned intellect; the soul must have access to the senses as needs be and to the extent that it can guide and lead them; and furthermore, though one may see fit to withdraw into himself and become senseless and rapt, still it must not be forgotten that "God demands of every spiritual person that he love with all the powers of the soul." This means that manifest reality must be taken seriously. To deny or suppress the outer man is to destroy the soul. Indeed, the senseless one, who "robs" the outer man of all powers of the soul is put on the same level as the "animal people," who rob the inner man of all power.[101] Thus, Eckhart surmises that "disinterest is best of all because it unifies the soul, purifies knowledge, kindles the heart, quickens the desires, and enhances all virtues."[102]

ECKHART'S DOCTRINE OF GOD

Eckhart's doctrine of God consists of a myriad of obscure, tangled and scattered passages. As one toils through these, it world be easy to conclude that he evidences a thoroughly world-negating concept of God; everywhere the *via negativa* predominates. Nevertheless, I want to contend that a careful reading will show that Eckhart's deity is far more complex and dynamic than the static simple monad of the classic *via negativa*.

Is Eckhart's deity dipolar? The answer is affirmative insofar as Eckhart seems to evidence a complexity or ambivalency within his concept of the Deity; his central theme is the differentiation of the Deity into God and the Godhead (*Got und Gotheit*). According to Eckhart, these "are as different as heaven and earth."[103] Might then this distinction correspond to the distinction Whitehead makes between the primordial and the consequent nature of God? Let us first examine how the Godhead appears analogous to the primordial nature.

The Primordial Nature and the Godhead

Analogous to the primordial nature, the Godhead denotes God as the unconditioned unconscious "all-possibility," that is, God as an empty, indeterminant abstraction. To be more specific, first the Godhead is said to be God in "the all-possibility of His unmanifest isness."[104] Like the primordial nature, it is God's wealth of potentiality. This means that, like the consequent nature, God manifests Himself through the realization of certain potentials.

We find Eckhart speaking indirectly of the Godhead as the potential for the universe; that is, in the passages in question he does not speak of the Godhead *per se*, but he does at least speak of God in terms analogous to Whitehead's concept of initial aims. Eckhart claims that everything in the ✓ universe corresponds in some degree to a preceding image or model of that thing in God.[105] This must not be confused with predestination, with God ordaining whatsoever comes to pass. Rather, analogous to initial aims, it is God as holding forth a highly idealized model of the thing that way or may not be the case in reality. To clarify, it is important to note that Eckhart claims a Dionysian understanding of evil as a negative fact, a "robbing" of the creature's *wesen*, that is, its nature or being, like blindness robbing the eyes of sight.[106] In contrast, what God has in mind is the *wesen* of the thing, hence the thing in all its perfection. Eckhart may have drawn this notion of *Bild* from the Platonic concept of "idea." The latter is also Whitehead's source for the notion of eternal objects. This marks an important affinity between Whitehead and Eckhart.

Second, analogous to the primordial nature, the Godhead is the realm of total and complete abstaction in which there is no room for the concrete, the particular, or the individual. The Godhead is God all alone with himself, totally apart from the world and therefore "free of everything."[107] Therefore, the soul sunk and lost in this "desert" is said to have its individual identity destroyed, to become a nothing.[108] In the Godhead there is absolutely nothing for us to seize. "In the barren Godhead," Eckhart writes, "there is neither form nor idea," for it is "the empty formless nature of divine unity," a "supra-nothingness."[109] Thus we should come to love God strictly in impersonal or abstract terms as a "not-God, a not-person, a not-spirit, formless, for He is a pure light dissociated from all duplicity, in Whom we eternally sink from nothingness to nothingness."[110] But could we ever come to love this abstract God, this God of indifference and bloodless perfection? Can it ever be real to us? It would seem that Eckhart has made the Godhead meaningless to us by rendering it a bare "nothing" for human thought. In this respect, Eckhart himself writes that nothing can be said of the Godhead "except that it is nothing."[111] One comes to suspect that Eckhart understands the Godhead as God in some important sense as unreal or nonexistent. There are, however, two other relevant points that need to be made here.

One is that he claims in effect that the Godhead denotes God as deficient in actuality, by denying God (the Godhead) *wesen* ("*got is weder wesen* . . . ").[112] Blakney seems to attenuate the text by translating, "God is neither a being. . . . "[113] But the article is omited in the German, so the passage is more correctly translated as "God has neither being. . . . " Thus, void of all being, the Godhead certainly would denote God as nonexistent, as a nonentity.

The other consideration that needs to be kept in mind is that Eckhart seems well aware that the Godhead, insofar as it denotes God lost in pure abstraction, does not provide a satisfying or exhaustive account of the deity. This is analogous to Whitehead's contention that the primordial nature, insofar as it denotes God totally abstracted from commerce with particulars or concrete matters of fact, does not provide a full description of God. According to Eckhart, in and of itself the Godhead does absolutely nothing. "God works, but not the Godhead"—that is the central theme.[114] We may speak of God but not of the Godhead. There is nothing to talk about: It is said to have nothing to do, to have nothing going on in it, and not to be on the lookout for something to do. Obviously then, for all practical purposes, the Godhead is meaningless. Consequently, Eckhart tells us that we cannot call this do-nothing Godhead "Father." All that we receive we receive from the Persons of the Trinity.[115] In other words, it is not the Godhead but the personal God that we must reckon with. The Godhead is an abstraction and so a fiction, no more real than, say, human nature minus individual persons. Analogous to the fact that in and of itself human nature does nothing, individual persons do, in and of itself the Godhead does nothing, God as person does.[116]

Third, like the primordial nature, the Godhead seems to denote God as void of all consciousness. The Godhead is said to be void of intelligence and therefore to know neither this nor that.[117] Analogous to Whitehead's claim that God as primordial neither loves nor hates,[118] Eckhart writes that "God is non-loving, above all love and affection."[119] Elsewhere this unconscious side of God comes to the fore in Eckhart's concept of "pure disinterest."

Accordingly, this state of pure disinterest is defined as "empty nothingness," for it attends to no objects.[120] From the very beginning, God (the Godhead) has evidenced pure or "unmovable disinterest"; indeed it gives Him His status as God. Therefore, the creation of heaven and earth is said to have affected Him as little as if He had not made a single creature, the martyrdom of the Son is said to affect Him as little as if the Son had not become human, and He is even said to pay no attention to prayers and good works.[121] In sum, the Godhead, like the primordial nature, seems to denote God as void of all physical feeling, all feeling for the world, "untrammelled by reference to any particular course of things," as Whitehead would say.[122]

So far, the Godhead has been spoken of solely in static and aloof terms. What is stressed is the immeasurable gulf between it and all creation; it is God as wholly other than the world. In chapter 1, however, it was shown that no matter how remote and static the primordial nature may be construed to be, still there is an impetus within it toward the creaturely. Indeed, it was said to be God as the unconscious seeking consciousness. Can such a dynamism be attributed to the Godhead?

Perhaps Eckhart, like Whitehead, was struggling to reconcile change and permanence metaphysically. There are passages in which he strives to counterbalance the severity of his otherwise static Godhead by counteremphasizing its dynamic, immanent aspects to the extent that it has been said that he drives "fearlessly on to the conclusion that everything in the universe is a differentiation of the Godhead."[123] If he gives great weight to the ontological gulf between the Godhead and all creatures, he also gives equal weight to their ontological unity. Eckhart does not hold strictly with his contention that the Godhead is unmanifest; rather, it is said to be manifested in everything. For example, all creatures are identified with the Godhead.[124] Likewise, he contends that when God made man, the whole content of the Godhead was united to or oned with man.[125] Christ is said to be a revelation of the entire Godhead.[126] Eckhart is fond of describing the Godhead as a "onefold stillness" that none can fathom; but one must note carefully that he defines stillness or rest in an unusual sense of the term as the "freedom of all movement" rather than in the ordinary or static sense of the term as immobility or the absence of motion.[127] Consequently, God's nature is described as a flowing-forth nature.[128] The Godhead is frequently characterized as flowing in things. One passage is particularly potent in this respect, as it has the Godhead flowing everywhere every place, that is, in the Father, in the Son, and in the Holy Ghost, as well as within time, eternity, and all creatures.[129] In sum, the Godhead denotes a mighty current impeded by none and manifested by all. It is no wonder then that the Holy Spirit is likened to "wind."[130]

The question now becomes, What accounts for this powerful impetus, for this going forth of God?

Eckhart's God and Consequent Nature

In chapter 1, I contended that the primordial nature is God's primal urge for self-consciousness that is fulfilled only through the reality of creation. Analogously, in Eckhart the universe is no capricious overflow or whim on God's part; it is the self-actualization of the Godhead—God as emerging forth from the abyss of His nothingness to become an object of consciousness to Himself. We see in Eckhart something of the central claim of the ontological principle that physical reality is the only reality: God to know Himself must become tangible to Himself: Therefore, Eckhart says in the same breath the God is "inseparable from all self-manifestation," and that He "is more in things than they are in themselves." Eckhart likens this process of God going forth from himself into Himself to a mirror reflecting back sunlight. Analogous to the fact that a mirror sends back sunlight, the soul sends back a divine reflection to God. Just as sun and the reflection are the same thing, the expression or Word of God becomes God.[131] The eternal "birth" of God through the Son is the central theme in Eckhart. This birth is said to be accomplished by God speaking forth all things through Him. The "birth of God" is equated with all things "pouring forth" or coming to be. [132] "Why did God create the world?" he asks. "Only this, that He might be born in the soul," he answers.[133] In short, God becomes as physical phenomena express Him. This means that there is a continual interchange between God and the universe, a continual action and reaction of God upon the world and the world upon God. God is the supreme effect as well as the supreme cause and therefore is said to be the end as well as the beginning and middle of all things.[134] Consequently, Eckhart speaks of God as deriving His divinity from the world. It is God's nature to give, but He cannot give unless in our humility we are prepared to receive His gifts. If then God is to be God, if He is to "exercise" or manifest His divinity, he needs our humility. Therefore, our humility "gives God His divinity."[135] Certainly a God consequent to the world is a God vulnerable to the world. Thus, Eckhart contends that if we refuse God's gifts we do Him great harm.[136]

We are now in a better position to understand Eckhart's concept of God's "immutability." First, the central theme in Eckhart is that there is no self unless there is self-consciousness, unless the self has brought itself into intuition and become an object unto itself. "If I were king," he writes, "yet unaware of this fact, I would not be king."[137] Analogously, God to be God must go forth from Himself to bring Himself into intuition. His eternal joy consists of encountering Himself in the other, as we shall see in the following discussion of the Trinity. It is because of this double or circular movement of coming and return, of going forth from the self to enter into the self, that God is said to be immobile. In this vein, Eckhart writes that the joy that liberates all things is that they may go forth only to return to themselves and therefore remain immobile in themselves.[138]

Second, Eckhart's frequent claim that God is immobile or unchanging is best interpreted to mean not that God is excluded from becoming, but that the becoming of God is eternal. As noted earlier, Eternity, which Eckhart does in fact identify with God,[139] is said to be an eternal becoming. Since this eternal becoming of God is said to have neither beginning, middle, nor end, He is also said to be a "becomingless becoming."[140] In other words, claims for the immutability of God are in essence claims that the divine process is immutable. God is incessant change and therefore is undisturbed by change. Nothing can impede the becoming of God, for whatever happens contibutes in one way or another to His eternal process of self-actualization.

The Universe as God's Body

Is, then, the universe God's body? Though Eckhart does not explicitly address this question one way or the other, I contend that an affirmative answer is the logical consequence of the preceding analysis. To further strengthen the case, however, the following considerations might be presented.

First, the ontological principle claims that God is not the negation of all metaphysical principles but their finest exemplification. Eckhart states something approximating this point in his appeal to the fullness and complexity of God. Accordingly, he takes issue with those who would deny all categories of being to God; rather, he contends that "God lacks none of these and yet none of them include Him."[141] Consequently he takes the *via negativa* of Dionysius to mean that the difference between God and the world is one of degree, not kind. God is described as a supra-everything, a supra-life, a supra-light, a supra-being.[142] He raises the question, "What is God?" He answers it by saying, "All that is better substance than not substance and better to be than not to be."[143] Therefore Eckhart's claim that the creature is a "nothing" compared to God must be understood in a positive rather than a negative light. It is not to speak dualistically of God as the negation or exclusion of the world; rather, it is a claim for the all-inclusiveness of a God who contains all being within Himself.[144] In other words, God's fullness is the fact that He includes the infinite plenitude of all reality within Himself. The universe is God's wealth. God abstracted from the universe is nothing, for the richness of God is His richness "in all things," is the fact that He has poured Himself forth into all things.[145] Consequently, God is defined as the "negation of negations." This means that absolutely nothing may be denied, excluded, or separated from Him, It is therefore analogous to Whitehead's claim that in God there is no loss, no obstruction. Eckhart writes that every creature contains within itself a negation: It posits itself as this and not that. For example, an angel is an angel, not some other creature. But God is the negation of all negations and therefore posits Himself as all others, for nothing is external to Him.[146] The universe, then, may be thought of as God's body because it must be included within the reality of God. Consequently,

Eckhart claims that "all creatures are in God" and therefore may be identified with the Deity. Elsewhere a similar idea is expressed in Eckhart's claim that none can grasp God, not because He is exclusive of all things, but because "God Himself is in all things and is all things in all things everywhere all things everything."[147] In this respect it is important to note that on two separate occasions Eckhart uses the soul's relationship to the body as his metaphor to explicate how God is the innermost being of all things. God's relationship to ourselves is said to be analogous to the soul-body interaction. As the soul is the life force flowing through the entire body, so God is the life force flowing in the soul.[148] As the soul is the core of the eye, so God is the core of the creature.[149]

Second, a particularly strong affirmation of the universe as the body of God comes from Eckhart's contention that God made the world out of Himself. God in Himself is said to be matter and form, so that creation is described as God extracting Himself forth into differentiation. In other words, creation is God's self-creation by which He enters into the complexity of His being.[150] He moves from a totally homogeneous mass into the multitudinous diversity of all life.[151]

Third, like Whitehead, Eckhart assumes that the universe is co-eternal with God. Whitehead writes that God was not before the world but with the world. "As soon as God was," writes Eckhart, "He created the world." Nothing, then, separates God's existence from the birth of things. By the same act in which He posits Himself, He posits the world.

Fourth, one of the major themes in Eckhart's *Daz Bouch der Gotlichen Troestunge* (The Book of Divine Joy) is the oneness of God with our bodily feelings, especially those of pain and suffering. Whitehead speaks of God as a "fellow-sufferer." Analogously, Eckhart finds comfort and joy in the compassion and sympathy of a God who "feels my pain before I do."[152]

If Eckhart takes the universe to be God's body, then one would expect to find him claiming that we are part of a larger life, are in fact a life in God. In fact, he claims that the higher grades or levels of the contemplative life consist of an experiential recognition of this point. He writes that all creation is a life in God, and that what is God is God. The soul's recognition of itself as a life in God provides unspeakable joy.[153]

The Trinity in Eckhart

Eckhart does not provide a systematic doctrine of the Trinity. However, his sparse and scattered comments on the subject will serve to further clarify and explicate certain process themes in his thought.

Whitehead ultimatizes complexity; classical theism ultimatized simplicity and therefore defined God as a static simple monad. Eckhart's concept of the Trinity guarantees the complexity of God, because it denotes God as the eternal differentiation into persons in the literal sense of the term, that is, as centers of self-consciousness. Eckhart echoes Whitehead's principle of relativity in his contention that God must be understood relationally; this is, God is said to consist of two things—nature and relationship or a "seeing again."[154] This *widersehen* or *relatio* is the key to why there is a Trinity in the first place. Analogous to Whitehead's contention that the grasp of complexity or contrast is the source of all consciousness, Eckhart contends that God would have no self-consciousness, no personality, unless there is a differentiation into self and other. Eckhart writes that God without the Son would be deprived of all self-intuition, for He would then appear to Himself not as a self but as an empty void. Therefore, God eternally wills to differentiate Himself into self and other, into Father and Son, in order to bring Himself into self-consciousness by intuiting Himself in "an other person."[155] Later I will emphasize that a comparable theme is found in Boehme.

Henry Suso

The writings of Henry Suso or Heinrich Seuss (circa 1300–circa 1366) represent a footnote to the teachings of Eckhart. He never wrote nor apparently ever attempted to write a systematic textbook on speculative mysticism;[156] rather he strove to present an alternative version of Eckhart's teachings in a form elementary enough to be understood by untrained minds.[157]

THE LITTLE BOOK OF TRUTH
The process themes in this work may be summarized according to the following four points:

Eternity and Time
In Eckhart we found that Eternity is not the negation but the culmination of all time as synthesized into an ever-present Now. Suso makes this same point in the following succinct way:

> Question: A word that was said previously still puzzles me: that a man can in this world attain the state in which he understands himself to be one with that which has ever been. How is that possible?
> Answer: A master [i.e., Eckhart] says that eternity is a life which is above time, and includes all time within itself without any "before" or "after," and whoever is carried up into the eternal Nothing possesses all in all, and therein he has neither "before" nor "after." Indeed a man rapt up today would not have been there for a shorter time, speaking in terms of eternity, than he who was taken up a thousand years ago.[158]

God and the Godhead
As does Eckhart, Suso distinguishes between God and the Godhead. Whether

or not the Godhead, as opposed to the personal God, has a real existence was a point much debated by the Scholastics.[159] Suso's view seems to be that this "Nothing" or "silent hovering darkness," this God lost in pure abstraction is a false God, a deficient God. It appears real to us only as a consequence of faulty human reason. In and of itself, it has no real existence, for it is but one aspect of the living, personal God.[160] In Suso, the Godhead denotes God as the undifferentiated, God as a simple monad. As such, it can hardly denote the full reality of God, because God is diversity in the highest unity. In other words, the Godhead seems to denote God-as-yet-to-be, that is, the starting point from which God moves forth into self-actualization through His self-complexity.[161]

In the fiftieth chapter of his book, *Life*, Suso takes up the question: What is God? There we get a clear sense of God's movement or pouring forth from simplicity to complexity.[162] As to why there is a Trinity in the first place, Suso's answer in part is that this self-complexification is the source of God's self-consciousness: To become conscious of Himself, God must diversify Himself into self and other. But this other must also be God; otherwise, the object of His consciousness would not be Himself.[163]

Suso does claim that God is totally self-sufficing, not dependent upon anything. But as he continues in his exposé of the Trinity, there is a very important sense in which it can be said that God needs the world, that God totally alone with Himself is not enjoyable to Himself. In Dionysius, God seemed analogous to a supra-abundant productive power or energy that by virtue of its restlessness could not remain bottled up in itself. At first glance, Suso seems to be making much the same point. But if his argeement is examined more closely, he seems to have accentuated the moral component more heavily. Hartshorne has claimed that, in God, altruism and egotism are one and the same or at least not incompatible but complementary.[164] In the same vein, Suso seems to be claiming that God, to enjoy Himself, must be true to Himself; and to be true to Himself is for God to be ture to His morality; and to be true to his altruistic moral fiber God must create a world, because that is what moves Him to share Himself with others. Put another way, the ontological principle claims that what is real is what is actual. Analogously, Suso seems to be claiming that for God to have virtues is for God to apply them. In other words, God would not be real to Himself unless He applies Himself to creation.[165] The universe then is the pouring forth of God Himself and therefore may be identified with Him. The Holy Spirit, God's omnipresence, signifies that He is the supreme effect as well as the supreme cause of it all, the end as well as the beginning of all things.[166]

The Oneness of Mind and Body

For many years Suso practiced the most austere and gruesome forms of asceticism. Knowing this, one might easily suspect that his thought centers upon a very sharp spirit-matter dichotomy. However, quite the contrary is the case in this particular work. At the outset he makes it clear that unity with God transcends all such dichotomies. To war against the flesh is futile; it destroys the wholeness of the self. He confesses that the ascetic route is a perversion of the truth.[167] What does it mean to be inner or self-abandoned, to be "totally resigned" to God? According to Suso, it means the oneness of soul and body; that is, to be at peace with oneself because the inner and the outer man have become a harmonious whole. He chastises those who have gone to extremes and have adopted exclusively either the intellectual life of contemplation or the physically demanding life of action.[168] The point here seems to be that God and only God is the source of self-unity; without God in their lives, human beings tend to absolutize one aspect of themselves to the exclusion of all others, so that for some, life is all mind, all intellect, and no body, and for others, it is all body and no mind. The Holy Spirit signifies the unity of all life, that by which any such spirit-matter or mind-body dualism is abolished and flesh and soul made one.

Mystical Unity as Self-Affirmation?
In process thought, the equivalent of the mystical concept of oneness with God or the birth of God in the soul is the actualization of initial aims, by which God is said to be objectified in the world. As these initial aims are provided by God in order that we may enrich or further perfect our humanity, the omnipresence of God stands for the affirmation of our fullest possible humanness.

However, quite the opposite appears to be the case in Suso. At first glance his concept of mystical union seems to denote the negation or privation of our humanness. In this work there are a number of "dark sayings" that speak of the total annihilation of the self in God.[169] Furthermore, those in unity with God are said to be "deprived of their being," "dehumanized."[170] Indeed, the Nothing is said to be that" in which all things are annihilated internally as to their own selfhood."[171]

But these dark sayings are not the whole story in Suso. They are sharply contradicted elsewhere.[172] What, then, are we to make of this confusion in Suso? There is an ontological unity with God, and therefore our humanity is annihilated; there is not a genuine ontological unity, and therefore our humanity is preserved; there is an ontological unity with God, and therefore our humanity is strengthened. I contend that there is a great unresolved tension in the work of Suso between orthodoxy and a kind of pantheism. One must bear in mind that Suso was a student of Eckhart, and that at the time Eckhart was being condemned twice-over as a heretic, largely due to the pantheistic themes in his works. From his pantheistic side, Suso strives to speak of the ontological unity of God and the universe, of the fact that we ourselves as ourselves are in an ontological sense identifiable with God. But at the same time he must be careful not to overstep the bounds of classical theism. The latter contends that the human and the divine, God and the world, do not mix, that they are in fact two separate realities. Therefore, he vacillates between claiming either that there is an ontological unity and as such the human factor has to be collapsed out or denying the reality of such a unity in anything but a figurative sense so as to maintain a strict dichotomy between the human and the divine. In another work, however, he gives much freer reign to his pantheistic tendencies, and so we are there able to grasp more clearly some significant process themes.

THE LITTLE BOOK OF ETERNAL WISDOM

God as the Tender, the Sentimental, and the Poetic
Process theology views with disdain the static, abstract God of classical theism, alternatively termed the Ruthless Moralist, the Unmoved Mover, the Ruling Caesar, or the philosopher's God. In its place, stands the Whiteheadian God as tender poet. Suso's thought moves in this direction, and this in two ways.

First, there is the question of style. He is essentially a poet with a great disdain for abstract philosophical concepts. He prefers a loosely constructed rhapsodic exposé as opposed to tightly organized intellectual or philosophical argumentation. The dialect of this work, his native Swabian, is practical, vivid, full of popular lore, and unfettered by either grammatical or logical conventions.[173] As heir of the great German *Minnesinger*, his writing is full of parallelism, alliteration, and sentences interspersed with rhyme.[174] He prefers to express in concrete, often highly imaginative images what a more intellectual mind would have expressed in the abstract. Thus, for example, he speaks of the wounds and blood of Christ rather than of the atonement. He evidenced a great disdain for the intellectual life of his time and for the ensuing concepts of God.[175]

Second, the essentially Christocentric nature of this work shows that the impersonal abstract Godhead or Nothing has been pushed aside for the personal God in Christ. The central theme is that God is to be thought of as a tender lover, and so those who fear Him as a strict judge know Him not. Thus, something of the consequent nature of God, of God as receptive and yielding, breaks through, in two main ways.

On the one hand, he evidences a highly accentuated preference for a God in the feminine form over a God in the masculine form. On the other hand, there is something very physical, almost erotic, about his concept of God. This comes from the fact that in Suso's unrestrained application of medieval love-lore to Christ, He ends up being described in highly sensual and feminine terms as "sweeter than honey," "so lovely to embrace," and so on.[176]

The Oneness of God and the World

Suso is not a metaphysician by any stretch of the imagination. However, there is at least an implied metaphysic in this work: the ontological oneness of God and the world, of the spirit and nature. This follows from the fact that the central theme of this work might be best described as follows: There is absolutely no way to Divinity save through humanity. Process theology has argued on epistemic grounds that the only viable God is an anthropomorphic God. Analogously, Suso contends that "the beginning of the school of Wisdom . . . is to be read in the open and wounded book of My crucified body,"[177] for the only way God could render Himself meaningful to us is through His own genuine humanness.[178]

God as Sufferer

This work has often been severely criticized because its chief emphasis has been placed upon the extreme physical suffering of Christ.[179] Indeed, to Suso, God's sufferings did not cease at Golgotha but are eternal. However, to one familiar with the tenets of process theology Suso appears in a much more positive light. It is not so much the case that Suso was guilty of a morbid sadomasochistic preoccupation with pain and suffering, though he may have overstated his point here and there, as it is that he was affirming the realization of an empathic bond between God and man. This of course represents one of the most fundamental tenets of process theology: that God is a matrix of sensitivity, a fellow-sufferer who empathically participates in all human suffering.

Theologica Germanica

While there are numerous passages in this work (Anon., 1497) that would support a dualistic interpretation of mysticism, nevertheless, a careful reading suggests a world-affirming view point more evident than some critics would allow.

REALITY AS RELATIONAL

Mystical consciousness, as represented in this work, seeks oneness or unity with the cosmos more deeply than the mere poetic use of the term would imply. It seeks to break down all the fictive barriers that exist between human beings, God and the cosmos. There are not two orders of reality, but only one holistic system. Heaven, for example, is not some separate order of reality above and beyond the world, but the rich inner depth and complexity of the spacio-temporal world. Thus, the temporal world of the senses is described as "a Paradise and outer court of heaven."[180] Paradise is described as "all things that are."[181] The fundamental mystical intuition is the interdependency of all reality, the fact that All is One: "God is the One, and must be the One, and God is All and must be All. . . . Now he who would hold to God loves all things in the One which is One and All."[182] Because reality is in essence communal, all valid knowing is in terms of sharing, participation and empathy. Mystical consciousness is more than mere cognition; indeed, cognition and the intellect are eclipsed by the fact that reality is a synthesis. Thus, intellect, the world of analysis, is in an important sense a fiction. Spirit, represents more than a mere testimony to historical truth or to the authenticity of Scripture; it refers to the depth and complexity in the present structure of experience. It is not "knowledge or belief" to say that one knows such-and-such because it was read in Scripture. Many things are said to be known by this kind of awareness, yet not loved.[183]

Suffering is central in this work, but it is not the suffering that comes from a morbid guilt complex or a sadomasochistic disposition. Rather, it is the kind of suffering that comes from an appreciatory awareness of reality. To love God is to empathically share in God and therefore to suffer; For God is not immutable deity but a personal sensitive God who is deeply moved and troubled by the sins of the world. Indeed, God is said to be so grievously affected by sins that He would willingly suffer agony and mortal death to wipe out sin.[184] God's salvific activity is essentially the realization of an empathic bond between God and ourselves. To save us, God took human nature upon himself, took to himself "all that is in me, inward and outward."[185] Because God suffers, the "godlike and deified" person should mourn over sin.[186] Sin, then, would appear to be essentially insensitivity, the breach of relationships. Thus, "the more the Me, the Mine, the I abate in the self, the more God Himself increases in him."[187] The Dark Night of that Soul or period of alienation is the result of a false dichotomy between self and other that must be overcome. Therefore, it is said to be by the "false light" of sin that one seeks out a God exclusive of all relationships with creatures, beyond all suffering, unmoved by the world. This sinful soul "arrogates to itself what belongs to God; and not that which is God insofar as He is man and dwells in a deified man."[188]

However, mystical unity is not the annihilation or abolition of the self or self-consciousness. The "Voice from Heaven" says, "Man, know thyself."[189] Unity with God is pointless unless there is a retained personal duality, because it is in God that we find our true selves. God and all the things that God has done are said not to make one blessed, "lest I feel, taste, and know them in me."[190]

VIA NEGATIVA AS AFFIRMATIVE

This work does not understand God to be wholly separated from or other than the world but contains more than one telling claim for the ontological unity of God and the world.[191] This means that the *via negativa* is in fact testimony to the fullness and all-inclusiveness of God, from whose own being nothing, not even finite reality, can be excluded. This richness, this complexity of God eludes all cognitive apprehension. Therefore, God is termed the "nothing," not because God is in fact a void, but because creatures cannot apprehend the complexity of God's all-inclusiveness.[192] To seek God we must put aside clarity and exactness. Purgation is night, obscurity, though ultimately it becomes day, illumination, insofar as we come to appreciate the radiant fullness of God. The claim that to know God we must "rid ourselves of things" is essentially an appeal to put aside clarity in favor of depth and complexity. To be a thing is to be simple clear, distinct, this and not that. But to think of God as something, a this or a that, would violate the all-inclusiveness of God. If God were a thing, a this and not a that, God would not be All in All.[193]

THE GODHEAD AND GOD

This work makes a distinction between the Godhead and God that is somewhat analogous to the distinctions Whitehead makes between the primordial and consequent natures respectively. I emphasize the word distinctions, because in this work, as in Whitehead, there is little effort to fit God back together again once He has been bifurcated, although Whitehead is the more cogent in this regard. The Godhead seems to be God as an indeterminate abstraction, untrammeled by the world. It suggests God as potentiality yet to be actualized. It is God "as a state, and not as a working, so long as it is without any creature."[194] The Godhead is said to be without conscience, action, pain, suffering, or trouble.[195] Neither will, knowledge, manifestation, nor anything named or pictured is said to be ascribable to the Godhead.[196] The Godhead then is not in all respects comparable to the primordial nature. In chapter 1, I stressed that the primordial nature is God's moral fiber, whereas the Godhead is void of conscience. Also the primordial nature was depicted as a drive for self-actualization and that implies need and pain, which are excluded from the Godhead. It is therefore difficult to see what purpose the Godhead serves, unless it is a ploy to set up a false antithesis between God and the world that is later resolved.

God as God appears to be God as a concrete personal entity. The implication is that God becomes actualized by virtue of the divine experience of the world. From the "revealing of Himself to Himself" there "arises distinction and personality."[197] This work seems to understand the perfections of God as potentialities that require a world of order to become actualized. Though God possesses every excellence, "none of them can be worked and practiced without the creature, for in God without a creature, there is only a being and a flowing, but not a working."[198] God's being is not complete without a world, so the world is of no mere external consequence to God. God does nothing in vain, so creation is not an arbitrary decree or motiveless act on God's part.[199]

This analysis is only suggestive. The following is intended to show that Jacob Boehme provides a much clearer explication of these themes.

Jacob Boehme

Jacob Boehme (1575–1624) was one of the founding fathers of the Protestant mystical tradition. His thought was influential in the work of such thinkers as Fox, Law, Blake, Hegel, Saint-Martin, and Tillich. His influence, however, was in many respects attenuated by his esoteric symbolism and awkward, unsystematic prose. His writings have been termed a "melange of chaos," "dreary wastes of words that elude comprehension."[200] Yet, it should not be overlooked that his extensive use of the esoteric and magical symbolism of alchemy and astrology in itself points to a distinct affinity between his thought and process theology. His language might be understood as an appeal to an essentially aesthetic-affective orientation to reality in which appreciatory awareness eclipses cognition and in which reality is grasped in a more dramatic, poetic fashion than is possible in more precise, neutral formulations. One is reminded of Whitehead's famous dictum that "exactness is a fake" and of Maslow's argument that mystical experiences are best worked out in terms of the poetical, the metaphorical, and the inexact rather than the framework of a cold, precise scientific approach.[201] Indeed, it was Boehme's contention that the organized religion of his day had desacralized much of life, that it had become "stone houses" that ignored the importance of the first-hand experience of God's immanency.[202] However, it would be a mistake to assume that Boehme overlooked the need for systematization. In his *Sendbriefen*, for example, he admits that his work *Aurora* is confusing. He claimed that it was only a childish beginning that required clarification.[203]

Hartshorne and Reese, though they omit a specific critique of Boehme, make strong claims for a distinct affinity between Whitehead and Boehme.[204] They observe that Boehme was one of the first to see that the Unmoved Mover is in God but is not God in his concreteness, that God is "a living, sensitive, free personality, preserving all actual events with impartial care and forever adding new events to his experience."[205]

The following is intended to show that these claims are justifiable in reference to specific aspects of Boehme's thought.

THE *UNGRUND* AND THE PRIMORDIAL NATURE

Whitehead claims that the ultimate metaphysical principle is creativity. As was noted in chapter 1, the primacy or priority of creativity over God does not mean that first there was creativity and then there was God. The interrelationship of God and Creativity is from all eternity. Whitehead claims that reality has two forms, the actual and the merely potential. God has never been merely potential, because the primordial nature has been actualized to some degree in some actual occasion somewhere. But any particular phase of this actuality was once merely potential.[206]

Berdyaev and Whitehead had no direct communication with one another, but there are remarkable parallels between the two thinkers. Perhaps this is because they both shared a common ancestor, Schelling, who was an adept of Boehme. Berdyaev in his appropriation of Boehme, or more specifically of the *Ungrund* or *Gotheit*, speaks of "freedom," "creativeness," "spontaneous activity," although he avoids terms such as "potential" and "possible."[207] He sees in Boehme's concept of the *Ungrund*, or Divine Nothing, the creation of the world by God as a secondary act. Freedom is not created by God but is rooted in the Nothing or *Ungrund* from all eternity, out of which the holy Trinity, God the Creator and Redeemer, is born.[208]

Boehme does not speak in the terms of Whitehead or Berdyaev, but there are distinct similarities. He seems to contrast two forms of reality: the nonbeing or *Nichts*, by which he asserts the priority of freedom or creativity over God, and determinate actuality. The *Ungrund* is described as a stillness, a void in which there is nothing to be seen. Analogous to the Godhead mentioned earlier, it is without character, pattern, life; it is unrevealed, unknowable.[209] It is said to be unactualized will (*unessentialischer Wille*),[210] which suggests that it is an unfathomable depth of creativity ready to be revealed, realized, embodied, and represented in material and visible forms. In the last chapter, I spoke of the primodial nature as an appetition to become. Comparably, Boehme speaks of a primodial will (*Urwille*), which is God struggling to project himself into actuality. Thus, the *Ungrund* is said to be a search after something (*Wille ze Etwas*).[211] The "first principle" is the "hunger for substance." The *Nichts* is seeking to become an *Ich* so that the *Ungrund* becomes known as a life.[212] The *Ungrund* ultimately has a positive meaning. It seeks to actualize itself through the full, rich plenitude of empirical reality. It is said to be all in all and therefore comparable to nothing.[213] All things are "from it, in it, by it."[214]

GOD AS CONSEQUENT, INTERDEPENDENT

It is interesting to consider the possibility that Boehme may have evidenced a stronger sense of God's contingency that Whitehead ever did. While Whitehead did not introduce that consequent nature until quite late in his writings, the majority of Boehme's texts are in one way or another an explication of his concept of creation as God's own self-discovery and self-actualization.

Boehme seeks to preserve the mystery of God, or God's radical transcendence, but within the context of divine immanence, so that each magnifies the other and so as to avoid the pitfalls of a spirit-matter dualism. He is quite explicit that the mystery of God is mystical pantheism. That is, the great mystery (*Mysterium Magnum*) is the unfathomable intimacy of God with all things—how God is so near to all things and fills all.[215] Although creation is said to be incomprehensible mystery,[216] Boehme claims that he knows how it took place, that the world is an emanation of God.[217] The world is seen as a pouring forth of the imagination of the Eternal, a mirror of Eternity, a revelation of the Eternal.[218] This rather Platonic claim that the things of the world arise through participation in the eternal is also central in Whitehead.

However, his concept of *creatio ex deo* is not fully amenable to process; for in process, initial aims have to be actualized through the free self-decisions of creatures in order to become effective in creation. Also, Boehme's fundamental appeal is to extrarational authority. Boehme understands his doctrine of creation as the actualization of God, to be grounded in and congruent with scripture (Romans 2:36, John 9:15). Boehme's claim is that an ontological unity or mutual reciprocity between God and the world underpins the whole doctrine of revelation. If God had made the world out of nothing or out of some material external to his own nature, then there could be no revelation because the world would have nothing of God in it. God would be off, beyond and outside the world, and so would not be known in the world.[219] The nondualistic affirmation marks an important affinity with process; it approaches the central claim of Whitehead's metaphysic, namely, that the universe is not a second pinciple that stands against God.

According to Boehme, it is God Himself who has a body, and this corporality, *Leiblichkeit*, is not foreign to the being of God but is an element proper to the perfecting of God's own being.[220] This notion has distinct affinities with the secret teachings of the cabala, though it is hard to prove a cabalistic source for Boehme.[221] A similar notion is found in the writings of Schelling and Oetinger, both of whom were students of Boehme. According to Oetinger, "corporality is the end of the ways of God," and by this same formula Schelling expresses the essence of his philosophy of nature.[222] The Kingdom of God, as understood by Boehme, is an attempt to absorb creation into the Kingdom of Light, into a heavenly corporality identical with the luminous body of God.[223] Thus, the self-manifestation of God implies a process as much preservative and soteriological as creative. The evolution of the universe forms a kind of prolongation or continuation of creative evolution into the Kingdom of God. The ultimate goal appears to be the total manifestation of the forms and powers hidden in the depths of the *Ungrund*, that is, the full self-realization of God.[224]

In Boehme, God is not merely active but also passive. Boehme is quite specific that the eternal process of creation is God's movement toward personality and character. As Stroudt has observed,[225] the process of creation is that by which Boehme's God, natureless, passionless, but with a will to become, strives to introduce Himself into actuality so that He can feel, find, and behold Himself. Boehme understands God as a relational being, in strict analogy with the human soul. Just as the latter must go forth from itself to have knowledge, so God must go forth from Himself in order to bring Himself into intuition.[226]

This evolution of divine consciousness is not possible in Whitehead. God does not become conscious but always was, because there has always been some kind of world.

However, this process of self-consciousness has some affinity with certain aspects of Whitehead's aesthetic (see chapter 5) in the sense that Boehme emphasizes the apprehension of complexity as the key to the depth and breadth of experience by which the universe is apprehended as meaningful. Thus, a positive contribution of Whitehead's aesthetic is that it may provide a more formal, technical rationale of certain points of Boehme's doctrine of the divine consciousness for which he failed to provide a coherent account. According to Whitehead's theory of prehensions, "consciousness is how we feel the affirmation-negation contrast."[227] Boehme at least seems to be making an analogous point. God as a totally simple, homogeneous entity is void of self-consciousness and so must self-differentiate into contraries to attain self-awareness.[228] Thus, it would appear that in Boehme an aesthetic orientation toward unity in diversity is the ultimate metaphysical principle. God as absolute is God as the One. The universe as other than God is merely the many as many, the multitude. God as in an important sense relative or contingent is the integration or synthesis of the many into one in the unified active-passive content of God's experience.[229] This emphasis upon multiplicity as a perfection, not a privation, of God, places Boehme outside classical theism. His emphasis upon the freedom of God places him outside pantheism, which admitted of no accidents in God. Thus, pan-en-theism may be a more adequate metaphysical schema for what he was seeking through an analysis of his mystical experiences.[230] But what kind of experiences are we talking about here? The problem is that Boehme, like other mystics discussed in this chapter, seems to have been more inclined toward metaphysics than toward providing an in-depth account of his personal experiences of God. Thus, the interesting question remains: What sorts of Spirit experiences mystics have had that lead them to speak of a mutual reciprocity between God and the world. This is the subject of the next chapter.

3
Mystical Ecstasy

From the largely metaphysical portrayal of divine immanence, let us take the logical next step and attempt an experiential one. Many Christians have spoken of the experience of having the Spirit. How might process theology contribute toward to fuller understanding of this experience? In partial answer to this question, the present chapter is intended to demonstrate that the Christian mystical tradition may provide process theology with highly useful and advantageous insights toward this end. Historically, mysticism has yielded the most detailed accounts of the experience of having the Spirit. My claim is that there is a distinct affinity between mystical ecstasy and aesthetic experience in the Whiteheadian sense of the term. In chapter 5, I will more clearly delineate Whitehead's concept of aesthetic experience. However, this chapter will examine in detail the nature of ecstasy. This will serve as the groundwork for my concluding remarks in chapter 5. My contention is that mystical ecstasy centers upon a mutual reciprocity between God and the world and that in turn God's presence is objectified or manifested in and through fullness of feeling. The ecstatic, as one twelfth-century mystic wrote, desires that God ". . . might pervade her (the soul) wholly in the deepest affections and to the very ground of the heart."[1] I am attempting to present an alternative to the pervasive interpretation of ecstasy as world-flight or as world-negating state of mind characterized by emotional withdrawal and deadening. According to *The Cloud of Unknowing*, even in the fourteenth century, the golden age of mysticism, ecstatics were faulted for being "lazy contemplatives" who turned their backs on the world. Modern scholars such as Poulain contend that ecstasy is a purely intellectual act, devoid of all emotion.[2] Others such as Delacroix and Leuba, who rarely cite first-hand sources, contend that ecstasy marks a continuous simplification, impoverishment, and stagnation of the ecstatic's psychic activity and inner spiritual life.[3]

It would be rash to deny some degree of truth to these and similar claims. The mystical literature often depicts the Spirit and emotionality in dualistic terms as highly antagonistc foes. The mystical literature yields numerous arid, ascetic passages that speak of the purgation of the aesthetic-affective side of life. Witness, for example, the following passages from St. John of the Cross:

> The radical remedy lies in the mortification of the four great natural passions, joy, hope, fear, and grief. You must seek to deprive these of every satisfaction and leave them as it were in darkness and void.[4]

However, it is my contention that these passages represent only one side of the mystical quest for God. In many respects a mystic appears to be one who sets up false dualisms or dichotomies only to overcome them. In point of fact, the Christian mystics understood the ecstatic experience of unity with God to be an experience of an essentially emotional nature and origin. This is especially true of John of the Cross, who is often depicted as one of the most ascetic of all mystics. The subsequent excerpts will demonstrate that in ecstasy one is seized by an "emotive flood" of such intensity and incomprehensibility that it can be understood only by those who have experienced it. Thus "fire," "heat," "warmth," "conflagration," "glowing" (as an iron in fire) are expressions met with constantly in the mystics' descriptions of the consummated ecstatic union and its intense emotional content.[5]

The Question of Technique

The mystics evidenced a great disdain for ascetic practices and techniques because these tend to interfere with the spontaneous flow of experience and life. The dynamic side of the mystical conception of God is particularly evidenced in the fact that ecstasy is fluid, not static or fixed, and therefore it cannot be circumscribed by certain procedures. In chapter 5, I will show that this mystical emphasis upon ecstasy as a sudden, illuminating flash of insight is congruent with Whitehead's aesthetic. At present, I am emphasizing that mystics for the most part promote freedom and creativity over order. In general, the first-hand mystical literature tends to eschew all systems and categories, looking for truth in the immediacy of personal experience.

For example, *The Cloud of Unknowing* denounced those who had identified contemplation with all sorts of unique physical postures, on the grounds that the proper contemplative attitude is oriented toward the whole person rather than to precious, encapsulated practices.[6] Recently, Krishnamurti has attacked the special cross-legged meditation practices for this same reason.[7] Walter Hilton decried rigorous ascetic practices and techniques on the grounds that they destroyed the unity of the soul and body. He claimed that suffering or mortification of the flesh was a hindrance to the fervor of love in contemplation, because this can be felt only in the greatest repose of soul and body.[8] Furthermore, "no certain rule can be laid down" for contemplation.[9] Over a century later, St. John of the Cross had some harsh words for those who had gone to excesses with various ascetic practices as if to completely divorce themselves from their bodies. He took this to be a form of prideful insensitivity, one that destroys the wholeness of self by absolutizing one aspect of our existence over all the others.[10]

Furthermore, ecstasy cannot be circumscribed by any set procedures. Strict ascetic discipline and mystical experience do not necessarily go together.[11]

John's appeal to spontaneity and creativity is especially evidenced in *Dark Night*, 1,8,3. Apparently his purpose there is to further instruct those who have used meditative techniques for some time, but who have become arrested upon a spiritual plateau. His antitechnique or antiroutine is to help such persons further advance by letting go of all techniques.[12] In other words, the final goal is beyond any technique, so that one has to go a route that leaves behind all technique in the end. As we read in *Ascent*, "In order to come to that which you do not know, you have to go via a way you do not know."[13]

St. Teresa is skeptical about ascetic practices. A "sweet disorder" is said to dominate her works, providing an outlet for her natural spontaneity.[14] In itself this provides an interesting parallel to the nonlinear web-like quality of Whitehead's exposition. According to Teresa, introspection, the journey inward to God, is not a rigid, narrow path but calls for freedom and flexibility. The "mansions," or dimensions of the unconscious, are not "arranged in a row one behind the other" but "some above, others below, others at each side."[15] Once inside itself, the soul must be allowed to roam freely through these mansions.[16] The mystical path is an openended, come-and-see approach. Personal experience worked out in highly imaginative terms takes precedence over tradition, institutionalized religion, and especially over rigid dogmatic formulations. Boehme, for example, levied many bitter criticisms against the churches of his day for having allowed faith to collapse into mere intellectual ascent to doctrine, for having lost all sense of loving spirituality through an obsessive preoccupation with doctrinal purity.[17] Even though various mystics seem to have prepared for their extraordinary experiences through the study of a tradition, they were not reassured by that study. For example, Teresa studied the contemplative manual of Francisco de Osuna, but she doubted the validity of the states they described. The same is also true of Madame Guyon and Francios de Sales.[18]

However, the following material provides some necessary qualifiers to these considerations. Despite this emphasis upon freedom and spontaneity, certain mystical sources recognize a necessary interrelationship between form (pattern, structure) and transformation or ecstatic experience, which is often misunderstood to be structureless, contentless, timeless. To the mystic, however, God is no apophatic void, but a concrete personal presence. Ecstasy, then, is no blank state of mind, but one rich in affective content.

God's Touch Gently Exercised

Process theology makes central the sensitive, tender elements of God.[19]

I shall note four ways in which these elements characterize certain first-hand accounts of ecstasy. This is also to claim that emphatic sensitivity, not stoical resignation, characterizes the mystical quest.

First, the mystics tended to allegorize God as an artist. Already we have noted that Dionysius likened the process of deification to an artist modeling something. This trend can be traced back to an even earlier source of Christian mysticism, the third-century Alexandrian, Plotinus. Aesthetic passion seems to be the vehicle of unity with a God who allures rather than coerces. He writes:

> We are like a choir who stand round the conductor, but do not always sing in tune, because their attention is diverted by looking at external things. So we always move round the One—if we did not, we should dissolve and cease to exist—but we do not always look towards the One . . . but when we do behold Him, we attain the end to our existence . . . . Then we no longer sing out of tune, but form a truly divine chorus about Him; in the which chorus dance the soul beholds the Fountain of life, the Fountain of intellect, the Principle of Being, the cause of good, the root of soul.[20]

It is interesting to compare this dynamic side of ecstasy, this rhythmic dance around a divine Corypheus, with certain passages in the apocryphal "Hymn of Jesus," where the Logos or Christ says to the disciples: "I am the Word who did play and dance all things. Now answer to my dancing, understand by dancing what I do . . . . Who danceth not knoweth not what is being done. I would pipe and dance ye all!"[21]

In the work of the Flemish mystic and Benedictine Abbot Blosius (1506 – 1565) creation is assumed to be continuous and so God is likened to a skillful artist "who delights in touching up his picture here and there, adding or changing a color."[22] Thus, his "hard sayings," the so-called Dark Night of the Soul, have a positive dimension if they are looked at in terms of his overall aesthetic framework. Suffering is not damnation; it is not punishment at the hands of an angry God. Rather, suffering is central to the process of spiritual growth. Thus suffering is best thought of as a growing pain. The soul, writes Blosius, is prepared by afflictions, as fire prepares the wax to take on the form desired by the artist.[23]

Second, feelings of sweetness, gentleness, and tenderness frequently characterize the mystical apprehension of the Spirit. Bishop Ambrosius (circa 340–387) writes of ecstasy:

> if it [i.e., the soul] abandons itself entirely to the Word, it seems to it that it hears His voice without its seeing Him, that it perceives the fragrance of his divinity. . . . Suddenly the smelling of the soul is filled with a spiritual grace, it feels a gentle breath in which it perceives the presence of Him Whom it seeks.[24]

Cassianus (circa 360–435) speaks in the same metaphorical terms:

It often happens that during the divine visits that we are filled with fragrances, with a sweetness that it is not in our human power of capacity to attain, so that the soul, languishing with pleasure and delight, is transported in the ravishment.[25]

This same mode of expression is also found in Suso:

His mental powers were filled with a sweet heavenly fragrance, as when one pours a good balsam from a jar and the jar afterwards still retains the good fragrance. He perceived this heavenly fragrance for a long time afterwards and it imbued him with a heavenly longing for God.[26]

St. Angela of Foligno (1248–1309) writes:

Unto the soul (not drawn forth out of darkness) is then vouchsafed the utmost knowledge of God which I do think could be granted. And it is given with so much clearness, sweetness, and certainty, and hath such depth that the human heart cannot attain to it.[27]

Elsewhere she again emphasizes God's boundless tenderness toward the soul.[28] Comparably, Lucie Christine (1844–1908) writes of the "Divine Charm" emanating from God:

And again, O my divine spouse, what is that *language without words* by which Thou makest the soul feel Thine infinite tenderness! The soul understands that mysterious voice, and yet she cannot put into words any of those things which she has heard.[29]

This likening of God to an affectionate, gentle suprapersonal spouse is quite common throughout the mystical literature, as for instance in St Teresa, St. John, St. Bernard, Blosius, Surin, Hugh of St. Victor, St. Gertrude, to name but a few. It seems to parallel the fundamental contention of process theology that God is a loving and unlimited companion. Thus, of the ecstatic union with God, Catherine of Siena writes: "Secrets are revealed to a friend who has become *one thing* with his friend and not to a servant."[30]

Francois de Sales (1567–1622) stresses the gentleness of God's touch almost to the point of rendering ecstasy a state of static repose:

The soul, then, being thus inwardly recollected in God or before God, now and then becomes so sweetly attentive to the goodness of her well-beloved, that her attention seems not to be attention, so purely and delicately is it exercised; as it happens to certain rivers, which glide so calmly and smoothly that beholders and such as float upon them seem neither to see nor feel any motion, because the waters are not seen to ripple or flow at all.[31]

Though often faulted for his arid asceticism, St. John of the Cross makes frequent references to the Holy Spirit as a noncoercive personal power, as a "touch most delicate."[32] In *Ascent*, he tells us how it is that all things gentle and soothing may lead us to God.[33]

Third, the mystical literature tends to allegorize God in the feminine form. This calls to attention the empathic, receptive, preservative aspects of God, as these traits have been traditionally identified with femininity. Aside from Henry Suso, two other pronounced examples of this tendency are Dame Julian of Norwich (1342–1415) and John of the Cross. In the writings of Julian we find a chapter entitled "Jesus Our Mother," in which she writes:

> Our Kind Mother, our Gracious Mother [i.e., our Mother by nature, our Mother in grace], for that He would all wholly become our Mother in all things. . . . The Mother's service is nearest, readiest, and surest: (nearest, for it is most of nature; readiest, for it is most of love; and surest, for it is most of truth). This office none might, nor could, nor even should do to the full, but He alone. We wit that all our mother's bearing is us to pain and to dying: and what is this but that our Very Mother, Jesus, He—All Love—bearest us to joy and to endless living, blessed may He be![34]

It is to be noted that the Sophia or feminine aspect of the Word is central to John's bridegroom mysticism. At the beginning of *Ascent* (1,2,4), he states that the goal is unity with the divine wisdom, who is the divine bride of the soul. Although his initial nuptial symbolism pictured the soul as the Bride and God in the masculine as the bridegroom (*The Spiritual Canticle*), his system underwent a complete turnaround. Thus, the soul becomes the Bridegroom and experiences God as a woman who gives him her breasts.[35] The soul then exclaims upon experiencing God: "Beauteous art thou in thy footsteps and thy shoes, oh prince's daughter."[36]

A corresponding theme is to be found in the mysticism of the Eastern Orthodox. For centuries, the Sophia has represented God's wisdom. She is pictorially represented as a young woman, not a mother; she is the erotic side of God.[37]

This tendency to picture God in the feminine can be understood as serving the aesthetic purpose of assuring a "warm" spirituality, of guarding against a too-abstract, colorless, and emotionally sterile approach to prayer life. As Mallory notes, it is therefore possible that contrary to what feministic theologians may say the overmasculinization of God, so characteristic of western thought, has been more detrimental to men than to women. Women may reap great benefits from a thoroughly masculine God, because they can use this image as a libidinal springboard to an emotionally rich prayer life. It is the men who reject the warm side of spirituality, who have great difficulty working up their affective motivation. In the past, perhaps Mary and the female saints pictured as young women helped men attain an emotional access to God. In recent years, with the downplaying of devotion to female figures, there has been an increasing emotional sterility evidenced in the prayer life of men. P. van Ginneken, for example, compared the spirituality of a large number of Benedictine nuns and monks. He concluded that a great difference exists: The nuns tended to emphasize the emotional aspects of religious experience; the monks tended to reject such experiences.[38] Mallory's own extensive psychological study of Carmelites yielded similar results.

Fourth, various mystics speak of a curious spiritual phenomenon, God enfolding the whole of a person's being in an affectionate "hug," "embrace," or "clasp." This of course concurs with the spouse metaphor. It is found in the writings of St. Bernard, Gerson, Blosius, St. Teresa, Antoine due Saint-Esprit, Ribet, Denis le Chartreux, Marie d'Incarnation, Marguerite-Marie Alacoque, St. Gertrude, St. John of the Cross, According to Angela, on one occasion when she begs God to give her physical proof of the revelation she has of Him, God answers: "I shall give thee a better sign, that thou shalt constantly feel in thy soul. . . . Thou shalt be embraced by divine love and be inwardly illuminated by the knowledge of God."[39]

In the confessions of St. Augustine the word "embracement" (*amplexux*) is used no fewer than three times as a description of mystical union with God.[40] St. Gertrude(1256–1303) writes:

"Very often I felt that the friendly gaze rested upon me and that in a vivid clasp [*dans une vive entreinte*] Thou embraced my soul. But however admirable these signs of favor have been, they have never been of a power comparable with the wonderful gaze of which I have just spoken."[41]

According to Marina of Escobar (1554–1633):

When I was overcome with sickness and troubles I saw the divine Majesty, Who said to me mildly: "Thou art weary, wilt thou come with Me?" "Surely," I cried, "I should be enraptured if I might follow your Majesty." The Lord accepted my assent and pressed me to Him in a very intimate union [*me serra sur lui, dans une union tres entroite*].[42]

P. Lyonnard speaks of the "omnipotence with which it takes possession of the whole of one's being, the infinitely strong and sweet hug (*entreinte*) with which God unites the soul with Himself."[43] In her work on Purgatory, one of the most famous on the subject, Catherine of Genoa (1447–1510) contended that even souls in Purgatory were subject to this divine embrace.[44]

In process terms, one might interpret these experiences as representing a direct apprehension of oneself preserved or woven within the consequent nature of God, which is a "tender care that nothing be lost," and which accepts us as we are and not as we might be; that is, it includes or "prehends every actuality for what it can be in such a perfected system—its sufferings, its sorrows, its failures, its triumphs, its immediacies of joy—woven by rightness of feeling into the harmony of the universal feeling.[45] In Teresa this theme works itself into the unique, concrete metaphor of God as being like the finest woven cambric cloth.[46]

This emphasis upon God as an affectionate lover helps establish the following theory of mystical redemption.

Mysticism as Affective Redemption

The pervasive, dualistic interpretation of mysticism emphasizes the "cold," empty, somewhat depressed attitude of ascetic distance from emotionality. I shall present evidence for an alternative viewpoint: All that really interests the mystic is the affective side of life, and it is passion in its most extreme form that constitutes mystical union with God. The mystical view is that our hunger for emotional satisfaction and stimulation, when given meaning and an aim, leads to what might be termed "affective redemption." In his discursive writings, Thomas of Aquinas reduced the concept of *desiderium Dei* to an intellectual desire or curiosity, but then he had a mystical experience and quit writing. The mystic, however, establishes a much broader context for such a theme.[47] As was implied in the previous discussion, to know God is primarily to experience God in a warm, loving relationship. Attraction, desire and union as fulfillment of desire, that is the mystical way. This is, of course, congruent with the previous contention that the mystical God, like the Whiteheadian one, works in a gentle, noncoercive, alluring manner. According to Recejac, "Mysticism claims to be able to know the Unknowable without any help from dialectics; and believes that, by the way of love . . . it reaches a point to which thought alone is unable to attain."[48]

"This monk can give lessons to lovers!" exclaimed Arthur Symons upon reading John of the Cross.[49] Comparably, Underhill writes: "The mystic's outlook, indeed, is the lover's outlook. It has the same quality of selfless and quixotic devotion, the same combination of rapture and humility.[50]

Numerous extracts can be easily compiled from the mystical writings to illustrate this principle of affective redemption. "For example, some critics have contended that the ecstasy of Plotinus was purely an affair of the head entirely disconnected from the heart. But however dispassioned and arid Plotinus the metaphysician and philosopher with his immutable, passionless deity, Plotinus the ecstatic is sure that it is a union of hearts, purely an affair of the passions. Ecstasy is only for the desirous, for the one who has that "loving passion'" that "causes the lover to rest in the object of his love." Only "by love He may be gotten and holden, but by thought never." Elsewhere he writes:

> Some there are that for all their effort have not attained the Vision; the soul in them has come to no sense of the splendour there. It is not taken warmly; it has not felt burning within itself the flame of love for what there is to know.[51]

The erotic similie of marriage is used by this hard-headed philosopher to depict ecstasy.[52]

In Eckhart it is the passions (*Zorn*), this power always fighting its way back to its origins (*Kriegende Kraft*), that unite us with the Holy Spirit.[53]

Richard Rolle speaks of ecstatic unity in erotic terms, adding to it his passion for music:

> . . . speaks the loved to the heart of the lover; as it were a bashful lover, that his sweetheart before men entreats not, friendly-wise but commonly and as a stranger he kisses. . . . anon comes heavenly joy, and it marvellously making merry melody, to her springs; whose token she takes. . . . This ghostly music, that is unknown to all. . . . No man there is that his had known, but he that has studied to God only to take heed.[54]

The Spirit as manifested through a nondiscursive, purely affective intuition is the central theme of both *The Cloud* and another old English work *An Epistle of Discretion*. In the latter we read:

> For silence is not God, nor speaking is not God; fasting is not God nor eating is not God; loneliness is not God nor company is not God; nor yet any of the other two such qualities. He is hid between them, and may not be found by any work of thy soul, but all only by love of thine heart. He may not be known by reason. He may not be gotten by thought, nor concluded by understanding; but He may be loved and chosen with the true lovely will of thine heart. . . . Such a blind shot with the sharp dart of longing love may never fail of the prick, the which is God.[55]

In the words of the sixteenth-century French mystic Surin:

> True devotion does not consist in reasoning and speculation and a lot of brain-work, but in submission and humility of the heart which, being joined with love, not only unites the heart with God, but brings as well a great enlightenment, for Divine love is a clear fire from which men receive great abundance of exhalted thoughts: so much so that it is a bad mistake to cumber the mind with one's efforts to reach it too much. Love is an easy-flowing river which carries of understanding and knowledge gently to the soul.[56]

Surin's point seems to accord particularly well with the thesis that the *via negativa* is an affirmation of the fullness, the richness of God.

Two particularly apt illustrations of the fundamentally personal and romantic nature of mysticism are, first, *Confessions Aminatis* (A Lover's Confession), by the Benedictine nun Gertrude More (1606–1633):

> Never was there or can there be imagined such a Love, as is between a humble soul and thee. Who can express what passes between such a soul and thee? . . . O Love, Love, even by naming thee, my soul loseth itself in thee. . . . Nothing can Satiate a reasonable soul, but only thou. . . . Nothing can bring us to this sight but love. But what love must it be? . . . It must be an ardent love, a pure love, a courageous love . . . to give all for love is a most sweet bargain. . . . O let me love or not live![57]

Second, in *Das Fliessende Licht der Gottheit,* Mechtild of Magdeburg writes:

> The soul spake thus to her Desire, "Fare forth and see where my Love is.
> Say to him that I desire to love." So Desire sped forth, for she is quick
> of her nature, and came to the Empyrean and cried, "Great Lord, open
> and let me in!" Then said the Householder of that place: "What means
> this fiery eagerness?" Desire replied, "Lord I would have thee know that
> my lady can no longer bear to live. If Thou wouldst flow forth to her, then
> might she swim: but the fish cannot long exist that is left stranded on the
> shore." "Go back," said the Lord, "I will not let thee in unless thou bring
> to me that hungry soul, for it is in this alone that I take delight."[58]

This provides further evidence that, to the mystic, God is the object of very
intense erotic desire. This fact opens up whole new vistas for interrelating
eroticism with spirituality. For example, instead of considering mystical union
as a sublimation of unfulfilled sexual desire, it is possible that precisely the
opposite occurs; that is, we project our unsatisfied desire for God, an erotic
desire, onto other objects of desire, such as the man-woman relationship.[59]
This may point the way for a future approach to spirituality congruent with
a society becoming more and more aware of the centrality of eroticism for
giving meaning to life.

However, it must be emphasized that a broader view and definition of
eroticism is presupposed here than is ordinarily the case. For example, Van
Ussel emphasizes the personal intimacy of eroticism rather than the aspect
of sexuality (mere genital stimulation), which can be most impersonal and
nonintimate. He, along with Ledergerber, assigns eros a significant role in
healing or wholeness:

> Eroticism is something like God's breath over his creation. Things which
> appear to be separate are experienced as being connected with each other.
> Man is small, powerless, temporal, mortal and cannot answer the question
> about the meaning of his existence. But if he opens himself up, then he
> receives eyes that see "more"; he feels and knows more. He becomes big,
> great, and important because he participates in transcendence, a meta-
> physical, cosmical, mystical or religious experience. The view of life and
> the world becomes a whole, everything is connected with everything else.[60]

John of the Cross is a particularly interesting example of this kind of
understanding. Many interpret him to be one of the most arid and dualistic
of all mystics. However, we have already had occasion to note that the
interpretations of John's mysticism as a strictly ascetic, celibate lifestyle in
which all the emotions must be strictly bridled is too literal and onesided. Let
us go into more detail. A. Vergote, in developing a psychological approach
to the study of ecstasy, remarks:

> Certainly tradition bases the so-called supernatural order on the natural

desire for God. But this desire became conceived of as a metaphysical, intellectualized entity. Its orientation was conceived of intellectually, which was indeed unavoidable within a philosophy which thinks of man according to the order of the theoria. . . . Let us not forget that the thinking self is secondary; the first self is the bodily self, that is, the libidinal self.[61]

These remarks invoke something of the reformed sujectivist principle. We submit that a comparable theme can be found in John of the Cross. A careful reading shows that the deepest center of the self, the locus of mystical unity, is the passions. Like Whitehead, John contends that human beings are primarily feelers, and only secondarily thinkers and sensors. It is the "will with its four passions" that governs the soul.[62] Thus, neither intellect nor sense can serve as "proximate means of union with God."[63]

His fundamental commitment to an aesthetic-affective pneumatology may be further illustrated by reference to a statistical survey of his theological terms as compiled by Mallory. The picture that emerges is that he had scant interest in the usual areas of abstract, intellectual theological speculation, and he evidences a richly developed vocabulary of human affect. The *Concordance* to his works shows only a few sentences on baptism, the eucharist, the sacraments, the Fall, paradise, sinners, sins, salvation, predestination, evil, justification, redemption, mortal and venial sins. He wrote only one page on the Trinity, two pages on the eternal Father, four on the Son of God, four on Jesus, five on the Holy Spirit. Obviously fine-point Trinitarian distinctions do not occupy his mind. Nor do psychological distinctions interest him. For one supposedly committed to a rigorous spirit-matter or soul-body dualism, he spends little if any time on the topic. Even though from time to time he uses terms that accord with a dualistic framework, he gives little attention to the incorporeality of the soul's center. Throughout his writings he only three times uses the term "incorporeal" and then only in regard to incorporeal visions.[64] At no point does he specifically state that the soul is something immaterial. There are only two-and-one-half pages on the flesh, only one paragraph on incorporeality and one-and-one-half pages on corporeality.[65]

His exclusive preoccupation with emotionality is further evidence by: (1) a fine precision of terms for describing various degrees and kinds of desire; (2) the exactness of terms for describing the object of desire, God or otherwise. This is evidenced by the amount of attention he gives to the will (eleven pages), appetites (ten pages), pleasures (eight pages), affections (eight pages), sensual desires (eleven pages). He has a rich vocabulary for describing degrees of desire: movements of the will (*movimientos de la voluntad*), inclinations (*inclinaciones*), leanings (*asimientos*), likings (*aficiones*), fondnesses (*afectos*), affections (*afecciones*), attachment (*arrimo*), yearnings (*ansias*), tastes (*sabores*), appetites (*apetitos*), desires (*deseos*), delights (*gozos*), pleasures (*gustos*), passions (*passiones*), covetousness (*codicia*), avarice (*avaricia*), concupiscence (*concupiscencia*), vice (*vico*); to love (*amar*) to like (*querer*), to desire (*desear*), to crave (*apetiecer*), to love vehemently (*adamar*), to please (*agradar*), to be pleasing (*gustar*), to satisfy (*contentar*), to enrapture (*embriagar*).[66]

To illustrate his exactness in using terms for describing the objects of desire, let us note that he had fourteen pages on the love of God and seventeen pages on the love from God, *amor de Dios* as distinguished from *amor*. He uses a certain set of terms, *ansias* or yearnings and the symbol of the flame to refer to the erotic desire for God. *Ansias* is found five times in *Ascent*, his earliest work, sixteen times in *Dark Night*, and fifteen times in *Canticle*. In *Flame*, his last work, this term appears only once, having been replaced by the symbol of the flame, used over forty times. He never refers to the desire for God as concupiscence, and the act of desiring creatures, *apetecer* (to crave), is never used in regard to desiring God; rather, he uses the verb *desear* (to desire), which is almost exclusively reserved for that purpose.

The dynamic aspect of God, which corresponds to the eros in Dionysius, is represented by John's special term "force of love" (*fuerza de amor*). Here, too, fine distinctions are made. There are about eight references to God's force of love for man, about thirty-one references to man's force of love for God, and about twelve references to man's force of love for creatures. It is important to note that he identifies this dynamic side of God with the Holy Spirit.[67] In addition to this term, he provides a whole family of symbols to express desire and its effects: a spark, a burning flame, a wound, a flaming sword, inflammation of the heart.[68]

John does attempt to formulate ascetic teachings whereby the mystic becomes purified of all emotional gratification through an affective asceticism. However, the problem arises that one can find pleasure in the experience of God's sensitive love. John spends the last part of *Ascent* and almost all of *Dark Night* trying to work out a formulation whereby one can enjoy highly pleasurable experiences in and through unitive prayer without becoming egotistical. His solution seems to be that God's love has the paradoxical effect of producing deep-seated pleasure while at the same time purging one of all self-love.[69] As Fortmann has said, in affective prayer the libido is "self-cleaning," because it is less fixated on the self.[70]

Unfortunately, John reflects all too briefly on the psychological and theological basis of this paradox. Thus, the problem regarding the reconciliation of emotional gratification and altruism has yet to be resolved.

Certain aspects of process thought are applicable here; indeed, they may very well hold the key to this solution. For example, Hartshorne has devoted much attention to the reconciliation of altruism and egotism. Certainly it seems congruent with the principle of relativity to state that concern for the self is also concern for the other, because that other is ontologically part of the self. Or, one might consider a point much emphasized in Hartshorne: Since each of us is ever changing, each of us is in point of fact a nexus, a society of ever-perishing selves. Therefore, the seeking of self-pleasure is altruistic;

it is in fact the seeking of pleasure for someone else, for that new and distinct self in the future.[71]

The following subsection will show that a comparable emphasis upon the ontological unity of self and other is a central feature, if not the *sine qua non*, of ecstasy.

Ecstasy as Emotive Flux

According to Whitehead's reformed sujectivist principle, our most primal level of experience is an unconscious affective flux. Among certain texts of the Christian mystical literature such an experience is given a deeply spiritual meaning. Christian mystics tend to describe the unitive ecstatic feeling in its more intense manifestations as a vehemently irrupting divine emotive flood ("*on est envahi par un flot divin*," to quote Poulain), which breaks forth from the depths of the soul's substance. When the ecstatics experience the Spirit present and active in their souls, they feel great surprise and awe; for they find themselves seized, penetrated by a new expansiveness and fullness of feeling that they do not properly apprehend. But they abandon themselves to that affective stream—"*ils se laissent aller à ce courant*"—because they have constated from the first that it is a devout occupation.[72]

It was this kind of experience that Bernard of Clairvaux had in mind when he wrote:

> The Word utters no sound, but penetrates; it is not full of words, but full of power; it strikes not on the ears, but caresses the heart; the form of its face is not defined, and It does not touch the eyes of the body, but It makes glad the heart, not with charm of colour, but with the love It bestows.[73]

There is, however, one problem with this description: The Spirit seems characterized as an impersonal It. Elsewhere we can find numerous descriptions that more thoroughly emphasize the personal side of God.

Madeleine has provided a graphic description of ecstasy as eruptively gushing forth in floods of feeling. She speaks of being "flooded by waves of tenderness"—"*les flots de tenderess qui m'inondent*"—by the deepest and sweetest feelings.[74] She describes herself as being sunk in an intoxicating ocean of unknown voluptuousness.[75] She feels as if an invisible fire penetrates the whole of her being, and she feels her heart more and more kindled and moved to the extent that she could beat such feelings.[76]

According to Lucie Christine, the soul in ecstasy "looses herself in the ineffableness of the Divine Ocean, and has no longer any consciousness of herself except by the exquisite sentiment which this vision, this knowledge which inflames her with love, procures her."[77] Ruysbroeck speaks of God as a "Sea that ebbs and flows."[78]

This allegorizing of the Spirit in dynamic, fluid terms as a sea, ocean, river, flowing light, living fountain, and so forth, is common throughout the mystical literature. Such metaphors are found in Eckhart and Dionysius, as noted earlier, and also in Mechtild of Magdeburg, Tauler, David of Augsburg, Blosius, Mother Elizabeth Daurelle and many others.

The fact that such metaphors are borrowed from the realm of the impersonal should not obscure the point that this "ocean" of Spirit is experienced as an all-encompassing matrix of sensitivity and affection that repersonalizes rather than depersonalizes. The hard edge or border of personalities seem transcended so that they flow together, mutually enriching one another. Whitehead's metaphysical basis for this experience is the doctrine of mutual immanence or the principle of relativity. In chapter 5, I will attempt to demonstrate a significant parallel here with Whitehead's concept of concrescence or aesthetic experience (the many becoming one). At present, however, the goal is to further clarify the mystical concept of unity.

Ruysbroeck also speaks of the Spirit as a "storm of love," in which the two lovers, God and the soul, "melt into each other."[79] Comparably, P. Lyonnard (1829–1897) speaks of feeling wrapt up in an all-consuming heat, the "furnace of divine love."[80]

This concept of Spirit as an affective flux that is a gentle but powerful emotional invigorator (the lure for feeling in Whiteheadian terms) is apparently what Teresa has in mind when she likens the various degrees of contemplative prayer to various ways of watering a garden.[81] Elsewhere, speaking of one of her ecstasies in which she beheld the Persons of the Trinity, she writes: "It seemed to me that the soul was drenched with the Deity in the same way as a sponge dipped in water is drenched with this."[82]

Teresa is not alone in using this image. Marie d' Incarnation also compares the soul in mystical union to a sponge soaked with water.[83] A similar idea is expressed in Blosius's statement that in union the essence (*essentia*) of the soul is so completely drenched with God's own essence (*essentia Dei perfus*) that it becomes God-colored (*tota Deicolor*).[84]

These remarks illustrate the incomprehensible intimacy experienced between the self and God, which is everywhere stressed in the mystical literature. Note, for example, the previous quotation from Ruysbroek. Likewise, St. Bernard writes that the soul and God are "mingled with each other."[85] Elsewhere Teresa writes: "As when two things, which have previously been separate, have become one, the soul has become entirely at one with God."[86]

The exact nature of the oneness or unity of God has been a controversial topic in the commentaries. On one hand, what the mystic seems to express is an empathic sharing or participation in God rather than a dissolution of the self. But the language of mystics is often ambiguous, so that on the other hand they seem to express a confusion of essences, hence a loss of self-identity, which is non-Whiteheadian. For example, Eckhart makes numerous references to an empathic sharing in God. Not only does he speak of the great joy of experiencing oneself to be a life in the interior of God, which means to find oneself participating in the internal life of God, but also of the fact that "the eye by which I see God is that same eye as that with which God sees me."[87] He also states: "If I am to know God directly, I must become completely He and He I so that this He and this I are one I."[88] Eckhart is a prime illustration of the ambiguity of mystical language. On one hand, Eckhart's own *Ich* appears retained, in fact it becomes projected to infinity. On the other hand, his language is suggestive of a confusion of the essence of soul with the very essence of God. This is faulty empathy and non-Whiteheadian, because it does not allow for a retained personal duality between God and the soul. Similar problems can be illustrated by the following examples.

Ellina von Crevelsheim seems to speak of an empathic participation in God when she writes that she "saw the interior of the Father's heart," and was therefore "bound with chains of love, enveloped in lights, and filled with peace and joy."[89] But, as we shall see, it is not all peace, joy, and bliss that the mystic seeks.

According to Janet, the noted French psychiatrist and expert on mysticism: "If one sympathizes strongly with a person, if one in a high degree shares in his feelings and actions and lives the same life as he, one will finally end up resembling him. . . . When one is united with a person, one may not only share his joy, one must also know how to suffer with him and share his sufferings."[90] Thus, it was the case with many Christian mystics that their highest desire was to share empathically in God's own suffering, for instance, Suso (as we saw in chapter 2), Boehme, Catherine of Ricci, Magdalene of Pazzi, Therse Neumann, Mary of Moerl. This desire to participate in one's own person in the sufferings of Christ attains its highest fulfillment when, in the contemplation of His passion, this de-votional exercise is transformed into a directly experienced reality, as happens in many cases.[91] For example, numerous ecstasies have been reported as lasting as long as twenty-four hours, during which time the ecstatic is a "deeply engaged participant" in the scenes of Christ's passion from Gethsemane to Golgotha. By "deeply engaged" is meant not a passive observation but an empathic reliving of these events physically as well as mentally. Gemma reports having felt the pain of the crown of thorns on her own head, and describes her experience of the stigmata (8 June 1889) as follows: "I saw Jesus: His wounds were uncovered, but in place of blood they flowed flames. In the flash of an eye these flames touched my palms, my feet, and my breast. I felt as though I were dying."[92]

Again and again the mystics assure us that ecstatic unity means empathic participation rather than the dissolution of the self. A favorite metaphor used by the mystics to illustrate this point is that of a piece of iron thrown into a fire; this image can be found in the writings of John of the Cross, David of Augsburg, St. Bernard, St. Bonaventure, Eckhart, Tersteegen, and Blosius. For example, writes Boehme:

I give you an earthly example of this. Behold a bright flaming piece of iron, which of itself is dark and black, and the fire so penetrateth and shineth through the iron, that it giveth light. Now, the iron does not cease *to be*; it is the iron still.[93]

In other words, as the coldness and rigidity of a hunk of iron is melted away in a fire, so the icy, stony heart is melted away in God's love. Ecstatic unity is a supreme instance of self-affirmation achieved through the gentle perfecting and fulfillment of our latent potentials for sensitive, appreciatory awareness. Five hundred years before Boehme, Richard of St. Victor, a mystic it is unlikely he read, wrote: "As the difference between iron that is cold and iron that is hot, so is the difference between soul and soul: between the tepid soul and the soul made incandescent by divine love."[94]

But the question still remains whether mystics such as Madeleine evidence a retained personal identity or whether they have become so completely identified with God that there is self-loss, hence faulty empathy. The iron metaphor above is particularly ambiguous in this regard. Is it not the case that if we place iron in fire, it can become so altered from its previous state or in fact can melt away, so that we can no longer say that iron is present? In chapter 5, I will suggest ways in which Whitehead's aesthetic provides a precise terminology to overcome this ambiguity. The following discussion will further highlight this ambiguity in mysticism. Though a dissolution of the self is implied in many passages, others seem to claim that ecstasy is a continuous process of personal growth and development.

Ecstasy as Process, Not Static Repose

The affective theory of redemption allows one to refute the quietistic interpretation of ecstasy as a condition of static repose. Rather, ecstasy is understood as a continual process of self-growth throughout one's entire lifetime.

It is true that mystics frequently describe ecstasy as a state in which they are seemingly "conscious of nothing," "absorbed in nothing at all."[95] St. Teresa once described ecstasy as a "sleep of the powers of the soul."[96] Augustine Baker once likened the soul in ecstasy to an eagle who is "with great stillness, quietness and ease, without any waving of the wings at all."[97] Miguel de Molinos (1640–1697), whose quietistic teachings were condemned by the Catholic Church, gave the distinct impression that there was great virtue in doing nothing at all, that all spiritual and mental activities were bad and also unnecessary. In one of his condemned propositions he wrote: *velle operari active est Deum offendere* (all activity is offensive to God).[98] Much of the modern, "pop" mystical or transcendental cults are crudely quietistic in this sense. One is taught by simple exercises to attain a state of mentally vacant placidity in which one simply rests.

It is no surprise, then, that the charge of "holy indifference," of fostering a meaningless state of blank consciousness, has been hurled frequently against the mystical tradition. Doubtlessly some have perverted the teachings of the mystics to justify coming to a mental plane of utter stillness. The following material, however, provides a more accurate alternative to this somnolent interpretation of ecstasy.

Two of the giants among the mystical scholars, Underhill and Baron von Hügel, emphasize that the concept of "rest" or static repose is applicable to ecstasy in mere appearance only. They offer an interpretation of ecstasy that renders it amenable to concrescence, where aesthetics belongs in Whitehead. Something of the reformed sujectivist principle is central in the following account of ecstasy by Underhill:

> Psychologically, it [ecstasy] will mean the necessary depletion of the surface-consciousness, the stilling of the mechanism of thought, in the interests of another center of consciousness. Since this new center makes enormous demands on the self's stock of vitality its establishment must involve, for the time that it is active, the withdrawal of energy from other centers. Thus the "night of thought" becomes the strictly logical corollary of the "light of perception."[99]

Baron von Hugel terms the mystical way the "ascetic-aesthetic" path to God. He therefore carefully differentiates between quietism and mysticism:

> Quietism, the doctrine of the One Act; passivity in a literal sense, as the absence of imperfection of the power or use of initiative on the soul's part, in any and every state; these doctrines were finally condemned, and most rightly and necessarily condemned; the Prayer of Quiet and the various states and degrees of an ever-increasing pre-dominance of Action over Activity— an action which is all the more the soul's very own, because the more occasioned, directed, and informed by God's action and stimulation—these and the other chief lines of ancient experience and practice remain as true, correct, and necessary as ever.[100]

The doctrine of the One Act taught that the merging of the will with God was the one act never to be repeated. Once done, then, the self had nothing more to do than to rest in the divine life. This corresponds to Tillich's concept of the final trance, which he mistakenly attributes to mysticism. The following survey of first-hand sources is intended to show that such a static interpretation is false.

Ruysbroeck (1293–1381), one of the great masters of introversion, sternly denounced quietism: "Such quietude is nought else but idleness, into which a man has fallen and in which he forgets himself and God and all things in all that has to do with activity. This repose is wholly contrary to the supernatural repose one possesses in God."[101]

Madame Guyon (1648–1717), a contemporary of Molinos and usually taken to be a typical Quietist, also stresses the dynamic, activistic side of ecstasy.[102]

We have already seen that Teresa sees a vast emotional impetus in ecstasy. This is important because Teresa's writings, like the writings of all introspective mystics, evidence such a strong connotation of an introverted withdrawal from experience, as if like a turtle she curls up in her shell and goes to sleep. Though she frequently describes ecstasy in rather somnolent terms (the soul is "fast asleep in God," "the body is as dead"),[103] her primary contention is that the deeper the ecstasy, the more affectively aroused and "awake" the soul is to God. Thus, Teresa is not describing a state of consciousness comparable to the normal waking state, but neither is she describing a perceptual blank; rather, she seems to be describing a nonreflective state of dream-like consciousness totally absorbed in almost violently dynamic experiences. At one point she likens the impetus of ecstasy to that of a bullet leaving a gun.[104] Therefore, she sees fit to differentiate ecstasy from the state of sleep or from a lapse into an unconscious stupor.[105] At many points she seemingly stresses that ecstasy is a vast impetus for extroverted activity.[106] This "flight of the soul," this expansiveness of feeling, is a description of ecstasy common throughout the mystical literature, as in Suso, Maljovanny, Amiel and Bernado de Laredo.

However, the way in which many mystics and others have interpreted such experiences may represent a severe problem from the standpoint of our developing process pneumatology. It should be obvious by now that process thought stresses, in fact centers upon, the unity of mind and body. Indeed, the body is seen as the locus of all experience. Frequently, however, ecstasy is claimed as an out-of-the-body experience, or at least as one in which the ecstatic completely dissociates from the body. For example, G. A. Coe in *The Psychology of Religion* writes that the "basal fact" in ecstasy is "a shifting or retraction of attention with respect to the mass of organic and other sensations upon which our habitual sense of the body rests."[107] Teresa and many other mystics have tended to describe ecstasy as a form of disembodiment. Elsewhere her rationale for such an assumption seems to be the complete and total absence of sensory functioning in that state. This is also Coe's point. However, from the standpoint of Whitehead, the mere absence of sensory functioning is not at all grounds upon which to argue for disembodiment. If anything, consciousness dominated by nonsensory modes of experience might very well provide the framework in which one could enjoy a more intimate feeling of identification with one's own body than is available through sensory channels. That is because the derivation of one's experience from one's own body is essentially a non-sensory process, as will be explicated in chapter 5.

Therefore, it is interesting that elsewhere Teresa is much more guarded and hedges considerably over whether or not these "flights" denote a genuine separation from the body.[108] St. Catherine of Siena states that ecstasy is characterized by the complete and total absence of all sensory functioning, but she denies that this implies that the soul is separated from the body. She claims that the voice of God told her that in ecstasy all the bodily powers are "united and gathered together and immersed and inflamed in Me."[109] Dionysius and also Walter Hilton strongly emphasize that unity with God involves the whole person, body and soul together. In short, everything takes place as if the soul draws the body after it. Thus, Teresa significantly qualifies her dualistic theme by writing: "My body became so light that it no longer had any weight, so that in fact sometimes I could not feel my feet touch the ground."[110] In modern times, Pratt reports a comparable experience from one of his respondents during prayer:

> It is a singular feeling . . . which comes to me when I pray, that while I pray I feel my body is lifted up from the floor and I feel light and floating, so to speak, in the air. . . . I feel no weight of body and my body becomes as light as a feather.[111]

Such "levitation" experiences are so commonly reported among the mystics that Ribet has remarked that "there are but few ecstatics who have not been seen, at one time or another, during their ravishment elevated in air without support."[112]

The unity of mind and body is a central tenet in Whitehead's philosophy of organism. This suggests grounds for an alternative interpretation of these above experiences. Rather than the mystics' claims for disembodiment or separation from the body, such movement sensations imply a psychophysiological mechanism whereby brain cells governing motor behavior become quite active during ecstasy. This claim, however, will not be further explicated; it is intended only to suggest that ecstasy might well entail highly complex physiological events.

What the mystic actually experiences is not disembodiment or levitation in the literal sense of these terms, but rather a powerful emotional uplift. These ecstasies involve a radical and positive change in body image by which the body is no longer felt to be a heavy, disturbing, or distracting influence. The ecstatic undergoes a heightened experience of mind-body unity or harmony, characterized by overwhelming feelings of physical well-being and new-found emotional invigoration. A more solid feeling of oneself results. This is clear in the graphically described ecstatic reveries of Madeleine and also in the case of Miss Beauchamp. The former writes:

It is like an electricity in me, a kind of compressed stream that seems about to explode. . . . Is it not absurd that I, at the same time as I cannot even speak, feel how cries of joy, hymns of glory and love (*des chants de gloire et d'amour*) gush within me?[113]

Likewise, Morton Prince described the "levitation" experiences of Miss Beauchamp by feelings of "lightness of body, of physical restfulness and well-being, besides those of exaltation, joyousness and peace."[114]

But what of the introspective ecstatic experiences?

Mallory's research provides an illustration of the aesthetic character of these experiences; that is, they entail very rich inner experience. She finds that the introspective, unitive prayer as practiced by the modern Carmalites evidences a very pleasurable bodily component, though this is more obvious among the nuns than the friars. This prayer experience involves an affectionate intimacy with God that borders almost upon sexual relationship.[115] This experience corresponds to John's own experience of the deeply pleasurable bodily aspects of unitive prayer. Despite his strong dualistic and ascetic tendencies, his emphasis is placed upon the wholeness of persons. Physically as well as spiritually, body and soul together, we participate in God.[116]

Furthermore, introspective mysticism, at least as represented by Teresa, denotes a complex process of personal growth in the sense of an ever-deepening self-awareness. The main theme of her *Interior Castle* is the introspective journey through the so-called "interior mansions" or subconscious depths of experience, until God is encountered at the center of the soul. Thus, unity with God is the process of the irradiation into consciousness of the complex inner world of experience beneath the veneer of sensory awareness. Teresa, then, faults those who live solely by the senses for living on "the outer walls of the soul" and claims that they will be turned to pillars of salt for not turning inward.[117] In chapter 5, I will emphasize that a comparable emphasis upon precognitive, subconscious experience is central to Whitehead's aesthetic.

So far I have attempted to refute or repudiate the quietistic interpretation of mystical ecstacy on the basis of a rephrasing of the earlier affective-flux theme. However, there are several ways to show that in the life of the mystic it is not immobility that reigns, but becoming.

The mystical way does not consist of a unique state; it is above all a development, a progression of interrelated states, a lifelong process of spiritual growth. For example, in Blosius the mystical quest for unity appears to be an organic process of transformation. There is, he contends, no union with God that may not at any moment become more sublime. "However far the servant of God may have advanced," he writes, "he must never lay aside the desire of future progress."[118] Clearly, then, mystical perfection is not a static, once-and-for-all affair. According to Madame Guyon, the interior life is a rich, complex life; it consists of an endless series of interrelated stages, so that "what makes for the perfection of one stages makes for the beginning and the imperfection of the stage which follows."[119] Centuries earlier, Walter Hilton spoke of at least three stages of spiritual growth, all of which are good but which get progressively better.[120] Teresa is especially careful to warn of the great dangers of self-complacency, of forgetting that there is no state of unity that cannot be further deepended, of overlooking the fact that unity with God is not something permanent, static, or guaranteed.[121]

Where the mystics might have been mistaken as having acclaimed a blank or emotionally void state of mind is in fact not that at all, but rather a period, sometimes many years long, of painful emotional lethargy and overall depression, commonly termed "the dark night of the soul." It has also been termed a "dark" or "negative ecstasy." Teresa provides graphic descriptions of such states.[122] If unpacked, this dark night serves to further reinforce the aesthetic dimensions of mystical experience. It is in fact a powerful impetus toward emotional growth. To be more specific, here and in chapter 5, I will suggest ways in which this alienation experience is a function of a budding awareness of frustration relative to God's lure for feeling.

The mystical route is not "cheap grace"; it is not an escape from the serious business of judgment and chastisement, though its fundamentally aesthetic emphasis is often interpreted that way, as for instance by critics like Nygren. The ecstatic raptures by which the mystic is awakened to the ineffable beauty and splendor of God lead to a painful awareness of his or her own imperfections and unworthiness, and with this goes a deep-seated feeling of alienation. The Dark Night is in part the mystics' claim in effect that nothing can be more humbling than the experience of great beauty, which awakens us to ways higher than our own and therefore in an important sense provides an acute sense of chastisement. This is somewhat analogous to Meland's point that our problem is that we have been too much humbled before great tyrants and not enough before beauty.[123] Being humbled before great beauty does offer a kind of chastisement and judgment, but it does not oppress or generate resentment; it does not destroy, but moves us beyond ourselves, lures us out of our self-centered complacency.[124]

This arid period of alienation is testimony to a lack of wholeness in our emotional lives. The soul is struggling against a God who is luring it on to greater depth and breadth of feeling. This is a prime example of the broad cosmological aim of eroticism: the redemption from emotional disintegration and stagnation. John addresses this theme in his last writings.[125]

This theme is quite pronounced in the writings of Suso, perhaps even more so than in John or Teresa. Suso's *Leben* devotes chapter after chapter to a very graphic, dramatic portrayal of a ten-year struggle against a God who seems to be luring him toward a greater degree of emotional maturation and fulfillment than he is prepared to accept. His Dark Night set in after twenty years of blissful monastic isolation.[126] Later, having undergone many illnesses and trials, including the accusation of having fathered a child, he complains to God and is answered: "Well, what has become of that noble chivalry? Who is this knight of straw, this rag-made man? It is not by making rash promises and drawing back when suffering comes that men win the Ring of Eternity which you desire."[127]

No doubt this overly masculine and stern portrayal of God is too suggestive of the insensitive Ruling Caesar to be fully compatible with process thought. Nevertheless, in certain respects Suso's prolonged "negative ecstasy" is suggestive of God as the lure for feeling. Suso was by nature an introvert, and he sought out a very secluded and sheltered life; he was an artist and a recluse, with all the dreamer's dread of the real world.[128] Thus, for him, this dark night represented a period of sensitization, of emotional stimulation and maturation, pushing him out of the peaceful confines of his monastic isolation into the rough-and-tumble of the real world, from isolation and illusion to emotional participation in life, however painful that may have been. He then becomes a whole person, for he begins to actualize certain "masculine" potentials of his personality left dormant and suppressed by his cloistered monastic life. This implies that mysticism is in a certain sense world-affirming, which is the subject of the next subsection.

Ecstasy as World-Affirming

Serious objections have been raised against mysticism on the grounds that it denotes a split between God and the apparent world, a split that process theology strives to overcome. The Christian mystic has been characterized as tending to feel that real growth has less to do with how he or she deals with the world, with moment-to-moment living, than with special and apart procedures. The secluded monk isolated from the world is the person believed to be grappling with what is most real.[129] Thinkers such as Bonhoeffer, Teilhard de Chardin, and process theologians have been deeply concerned with this split.

These objections, however, are in many respects onesided. Mysticism appears to be an attempt to overcome all false dichotomies between the self and the world. Arbman, for example, contends that an aesthetic-like intuition of things in their full concreteness characterizes all the higher forms of mystical absorption, to which Buddhism, yoga and all the higher forms of Christian mysticism aspire.[130] For example, when a yogi has attained perfection in *samadhi*, he is said to be in a position to make everything between heaven and earth, from the coarsest to the finest and most abstract thing, the object of ecstatic fixation. His mind (*citta*), freed from all obscuring elements, reflects all things in their true nature and in a direct, unclouded clarity.[131] Also, one of the classical Indian texts (Vedic), the Brhadaranyaka Upanishad (2, 3:6) says that in the identity of the soul (*atman*) with the Brahman, one is enabled to grasp the innermost and true essence of the reality of everything.[132]

The first-hand literature is replete with accounts of ecstasies centering upon an exalted appreciation of Nature and Process that leaves the ecstatic with an overpowering certainty of having attained identity with as well as important insights into the structure of the universe. Such insights are assumed to be of a more fundamental form of reality than those available through the ordinary workings of the senses. Although the mystics often speak of a noetic quality, such ecstatic experiences of external reality are more like nondiscursive states of pure aesthetic feeling than they are like states of intellectual comprehension.[133] Commonly reported are feelings of awe and reverence at the ineffable depth and complexity of all things and as well a profound intuition of unity accompanied by the insight that "All is One." Life is experienced to have deep, profound meaning. The universe is felt to be alive, to be a divine, friendly, and loving presence—indeed the body of God. In short, this cosmological side of mysticism represents a concrete apprehension of the Spirit as a subjectivity and sensitivity within all things, variously described as a life, consciousness, or a living presence.[134] One would expect such experiences to be characterized by increases in feelings of joy, tenderness, and love, in short, by an ever-growing sensitivity to life.

This experience of expanded depth is one major characteristic of Whitehead's aesthetic (see chapter 5). It agrees with the observation that most mystical experiences occur outdoors. The pervasive trend in the mystical literature (as in Eckhart) to identify God with the wilderness, desert, or mountains may not represent world-flight but rather the seeking of a vantage point from which enriched experience or heightened perception is possible. These out-of-the-way places make possible experiences of expanded depth. This, in turn, implies enhanced self-expressiveness, for the self is able to more fully identify with the surrounding world. There is an implicit appeal here to Whitehead's concept of concrescence: By gaining these transcendental vantage points, one is better able to contain and integrate experiences that otherwise might have overwhelmed the self.

Another implicit parallel to Whitehead's aesthetic is that the latter centers upon the fusion of sense and affect (see chapter 5). In comparison, reality grasped through deeply impassioned perception, through the eyes of love, so to speak, is a major theme in mystics such as William Blake.[135] In other words, rather than a secret closet or hiding place separate and apart from the world, the internal or subjective self becomes a multidimensional space fused to the external world and adding meaning to it. Fact, value, and subjectivity are one. This is also the essence of Whitehead's thought (see chapter 1). Also, this is cosmological mysticism in the best sense of the term: "The doors of perception are cleansed" so that "everything appears to man as it is, infinite."[136] This is also Boehme's highest aspiration: that the eye of time be fused with the eye of eternity.[137] It is also the fundamental contention of the

Theologia Germanica. Many themes of introversion are evidenced in this work. Again and again it emphasizes that "peace and rest lie not in outward things."[138] Yet, carefully read, a strong extroverted mood of cosmic adoration comes to light. The deified one is said to love everything because everything is God: "Now he who will hold to God loves all things in the One which is One and All."[139]

Teresa, often depicted as a purely introspective mystic, knows of such an exalted extroverted vision, although she fails to provide much detail.[140] So, too, does the blind Lucie Christine, who makes obvious the mystical notion of the world as an outpouring of God's own dynamic becoming.[141]

Blosius, like Teresa and Lucie Christine, is generally described as an introverted mystic. He writes that, to see God, one must "introvert himself" — turn himself into his own soul, for there he will find God.[142] Yet there is also an extroverted side to Blosius. Like Eckhart before him, his theme is that we must learn to see God in everything. For truly spiritual people, all things that they see and hear give them an immediate impulse toward God.[143] Indeed, all of creation is said to be a self-expression of God: "Whatever was made was made like Him."[144] Elsewhere there are numerous implicit references to visions of God's omnipresence: He is said to be wholly in every created thing. "Everywhere He is present with all His being": God is in the earth, sea, and air. He refers us to Jer. 23:24: "I fill the heaven and earth."[145]

Jacob Boehme was especially prone to the ecstasies of cosmological mysticism. In his life there were at least three distinct onsets of illumination, all of the "pantheistic and external type," during which "he looked into the deepest foundations of things."[146]

Several other noteworthy instances of cosmological mysticism are to be found in the writings of Geoge Fox. As in Boehme's case, there is here an insistence upon having received an ineffable revelation of the profound depths and unity of objective reality.[147]

Comparable ecstatic experiences of the ineffable richness and complexity of external reality were claimed to be had by both Ignatius Loyola and his coworker, Frans Xavier. Loyola relates that on the way to the church some distance from Manresa, he sat down to rest for a moment by the roadside. Suddenly and unexpectedly the eyes of his soul were opened and drowned in light. He emphasizes that this experience contained no ordinary sensory elements: Rather, he conceived in an ineffable way a wondrous number of truths. They were so many and the light was so clear that he felt himself entering into a new world. So rich was the knowledge communicated to him and so sublime its nature that everything he had learned in his sixty-two years of life, either by studies or supernatural channels, could not be compared with what he received on this one single occasion.[148]

Similar experiences have been reported by the great mystical reformer of the occidental monkish orders, and by Benedictus of Nursia (as later described in Gregory the Great), and by Swedenborg, J. B. van Helmont,[149] Tauler and John of the Cross (see especially BK. 2, xxvi, *Ascent*), to name but a few.

In a few cases where such ecstasies are not explicitly described, there is at least implicit acknowledgment of their validity. One example is Blosius; another is Hilton. At more than one point the latter severely qualifies his otherwise world-negating outlook, as if to say that we come to God by going into the depths of the world, not above and beyond it. He claims that love of the world is not necessarily worthless or vain but depends upon whether or not it fosters spiritual growth.[150] The highest form of spiritual experience is said to be love springing from a direct apprehension of the divinity of Christ united to His humanity.[151] This implies an ecstatic intuition of God and the world as one. Elsewhere he tells us that "it is good to see God in the material world, with the inward eye,"[152] and also that the highest gift of the Holy Spirit is a wisdom enabling us to see all things in relation to God.[153]

Cosmological ecstasies such as these also predominate in the literature on spontaneous conversion experiences. God as a lure for depth and breadth of feeling is implied in James's finding that one of the most common features of conversion is feelings of a beautiful newness both within and without. A Whiteheadian theme is strongly implied in loss of fear: Nature is no longer felt to be threatening because it is felt to be the manifestation of a gentle, sensitive matrix or nature within nature.[154]

This experience of the universe as a living, sensitive presence rather than ultimately indifferent is neither unique to twentieth-century writers, such as Bucke, nor to Christian mystics, but is found in India as early as 1000 B.C. in the identification of Brahman with the universe. In Egypt it is found quite early in the identification of Ra, Isis, and Osiris with everything that exists. This squares with Whitehead's contention that empathy is the most primal of all responses.

A final point concerning the world-affirming character of ecstasy is that all cases seem to evidence a heightened sense of social obligation. The empathic experience of God's great love and sensitivity actualized in and through all things leads the ecstatic to an all-embracing love for the world and consequently to a great impetus to do good. In Whitehead's *Adventures of Ideas*, a major theme was the reconciliation of passive contemplation with action and adventure. A comparable theme is to be found in many mystical circles. In praise of the active life, Hilton tells his fellow contemplatives: "You should love and honour particularly those that lead an active life in the world. . . . Put yourself beneath their feet."[155] In *The Cloud*, the two manners of lives in the church, the active (bodily works of mercy and charity) and the contemplative, are said to be so coupled together that neither can be had without the other. Thus, "man cannot be fully active lest he be contemplative" and vice versa.[156] There are, for example, numeorus passages in the writings of Teresa that make it clear that the apparent world is the arena for spiritual growth.[157] This same theme is emphasized in Tauler and also in Eckhart and John of the Cross.

In summary, the mystical literature provides a concrete illustration of an aesthetic-affective pneumatology that is of meaning and value, given our typical experience as secular persons, and given that life is taken to be of ultimate significance as the basis of all religious thought. The fundamental mystical intuition of God as diffuse in the cosmos provides the basis for a spirituality in which purity is not found in a separation from the temporal-material world but is formal in a deeper penetration of the universe. Because the mystical tradition evidences themes analogous to Whitehead's philosophy of organism, a process theology of mysticism seems to be viable. The question now is what are the costs and advantages of a process theology of mysticism, relative to the tenets of classical Christian pneumatology. This is the subject of the next two chapters.

4
Process Theology and Classical Theism

Introduction

In this chapter, I will compare and contrast some of the central tenets of classical Christian pneumatology with those of process theology. I want to provide a selective focus those aspects of pneumatology that must be taken into account in a process critique, so that when an improved doctrine of the Spirit is provided, that doctrine comes to fit not simply within philosophy but also within the framework of the church. I will also emphasize that process theology has roots in certain key historical aspects of the doctrine of the Spirit. However, my focal claim is that a process theology of mysticism points the way to solving problems of pneumatology that Christian theology has failed to solve, relying as it has done on Neo-Platonic or Aristotelian metaphysics. Thus I am committed to showing (1) the failure in representative nonprocess accounts and (2) evidence for success in process accounts. The core issue at state in this conflict is God as responsive and therefore in an important sense mutable. The Christian affirmation of God as love includes the notion of a mutual reciprocity between God and the world. This reciprocity is a central tenet in the metaphysics of process theology. Traditional theology, however, denies that this reciprocity is true unless it is carefully qualified (and by traditional theology or classical theism I mean the theology of Augustine, Anselm, Aquinas, and Calvin, for example).

The God of classical pneumatology is the biblical God, the loving Father, revealed in Christ, who guides the world toward its fulfillment with tender care. Indeed, one must not overlook the centrality of biblical authority in classical theism. Many texts and statements of classical theists were not intended to answer philosophical or metaphysical questions, but rather to be exegeses of scripture. My critique of classical theism is not a quarrel with its faith in the authority of Scripture. Following Scripture, classical theists speak of God in a way later to be emphasized in process theology as an eminent Thou whose relationship to other creatures is anything but purely nominal or external. God is an eminently personal and social deity who creates and judges all things and so acts through tenderness and mercy to bring them to their ultimate goal of sharing in God's own life. The God of the Bible has affective and emotional states, inward movement, and dramatic development in inner life.[1] The living God of the Hebrews is not a mathematical and abstract infinity, but an infinity of inexhaustible life and personal being. Passage after passage in the Bible stresses God's great delight in creation; there is no Manichaeism in Scripture.[2] Also, it has often been said that the biblical god is a God who acts in history and as well that the Acts of the Apostles might be called "The Acts of the Holy Spirit."[3] Thus, the biblical God is an agent, the initiator in a genuine relationship between Self and creatures. The main contribution of process theology to pneumatology is to stress this fact that the Spirit is God as supremely sensitive. The Spirit exercises its power lovingly, so that its influence is never undue but persuasive rather than all-determining and coercive. God is not aloof, an unmoved dictator, but He is supremely and emphatically aware of our sufferings. In certain process circles this is understood as the central meaning and testimony of the Incarnation. Thus, Hartshorne and Reese observe

> that the biblical authors certainly had no intention of giving up the spiritual or psychological predicates of deity, such as will, knowledge, and love, in order to exalt some mere monopolar category of Being or Infinity. Quarrel if you will with metaphorical expressions like "the wrath of God," of his "pity," as wholly nonliteral concessions to the weakness of the human understanding; still, it may be suggested that the minimum to be expressed by such metaphors is this: that God is not blankly neutral to the happenings in the world, not simply absolute with respect to them, but rather evaluatively sensitive to the differences in all things in a way analogous to "pleasure" and "displeasure" in us.[4]

However, as will be shown, classical theists, especially Anselm and Aquinas, do not share this interpretation of Scripture.

Indeed, this concept of mutual reciprocity was truncated by certain philosophical prejudices of classical theism that were heavily loaded in favor of a onesidedness or monopolarity, such as the classical attributes or perfections of God—aseity, immutability, impassibility, and so forth. "As if," notes Watts, "the suppleness of movement implied some imperfections, perfections being identified with the finished, the complete, the symmetrical, which is again dead."[5]

Classical theism, in its formal definition of God, affirmed that God is a statically complete perfection and therefore incapable of any further self-realization. As in all respects immutable and absolute, God could not be thought to enjoy real internal relations with other beings, nor could God's nature be understood to involve temporal structure; rather, God is the antithesis of our temporality. God's love (the Spirit) is said to be so sensitive that it marks the fall of a sparrow; yet, God is also acclaimed as the Unmoved Mover, totally unaffected by the motions of the world. There is furthermore an unresolved tension in the classical concept of divine omnipotence. At first it is introduced as purely arbitrary, that is, God can do anything. Yet, God is also granted a specific character qualified by love, which is the Spirit. A classical theist probably would contend that it is the unfathomable mystery of God that confronts us here. But, as Ogden notes, this contention is no longer plausible to many modern thinkers. To some of the best western minds, this so-called "mystery" has been unmasked as merely confused, contradictory thinking on the part of classical theists, which makes their views all the more incredible as a reflective account of our experience.[6]

For example, Aquinas evidences a strong sense of God as present and active in the world (for instance in his doctrine of processions and his affirmation that God is the Lord of history). However, he seems to truncate immanence at the expense of God's radical transcendence. Certainly he was not indifferent or insensitive to the problems incurred in denying the reality of an intimate two-way relationship between God and the world. That is amply demonstrated by the first thirteen questions of the *Summa*, which are devoted to the pros and cons of attributing mutability, temporality, contingency, and so forth to God. However, his insistence upon the divine absoluteness, self-sufficiency, and independency of God led him to deny God's relatedness to other beings:

> Since therefore God is outside the whole order of creation, and all creatures are ordered to Him, and not conversely, it is manifest that creatures are really related to God Himself; whereas in God there is no real relation to creatures, but a relation only in idea, inasmuch as creatures, are referred to Him.[7]

Nevertheless, a relativistic or relational concept of God is implied here in Aquinas. Suppose, as in the above quotation, that one asserts that God is external to or outside of or above and beyond creation. These are all assertions of relationships. Is God then related? Aquinas asserts God to be the Creator, which is an implicit admission of a genuine relation of God to the world, especially since creation is assumed to be deliberately willed.

Since God, in classical theism, is a self-contained, immutable being that could neither be increased nor diminished by what we do, it follows that God must be wholly indifferent to our sufferings and actions. Completely unaffected by the world, the supreme cause but never effect, God is, as Camus has charged, the eternal bystander whose back is turned on the world. It is then impossible to speak of the paraclete; for this unmoved deity can give neither comfort, consolation, nor love. Though it is my contention that process theology presents a more viable alternative, it is fair to say that classical theism did not ignore this problem. For example, it is precisely this problem that Anselm wrestled with. In *Proslogium*, the solution he proposes is that God's great compassion is mere appearance only:

> For, if thou are passionless, thou dost not feel sympathy; and if thou dost not feel sympathy, thy heart is not wretched from sympathy for the wretched; but this it is to be compassionate. But if thou art not compassionate, whence cometh so great consolation to the wretched? How, then art thou compassionate and not compassionate, O Lord, unless because thou are

compassionate in terms of our experience, and not compassionate in terms of thy being.

Truly, thou art so in terms of our experience, but thou art not so in terms of thine own. For, when thou beholdest us in our wretchedness, we experience the effect of compassion, but thou dost not experience the feeling. Therefore, thou are both compassionate, because thou dost save the wretched, and spare those who sin against thee; and not compassionate because thou art affected by no sympathy for wretchedness.[8]

In other words, God helps those in misery but does not suffer emphatically with them. Not to suffer is better than to suffer; and since God by definition is that of which none greater than can be conceived, then God must have the better of two possible predicates. Although the effect of God is as though God empathized with people, really God does not do so. Certainly Anselm was not negligent in presenting a highly intricate, sophisticated line of argument. My objection, however, is that this is an effect that human experience fails to illuminate and even contradicts. It seems untenable that a being would ever know what wretchedness is, if that being never experienced the least shadow of disappointment, suffering, or unfulfilled desire. Furthermore, Hartshorne and Reese observe that Anselm might be faulted for having "only shifted the difficulty"; the claim that God beholds us in our wretchedness and consequently that the Spirit "dost penetrate and embrace all things" puts God in relation to us. God, then, is relative in some ways, rather than purely absolute.[9] Therefore, classical theism, which is his doctrine, is contradicted.

As a further explication of these remarks, in the remainder of this chapter I will move from the general to the specific. That is, first I will present a critique of the classical concept of God as a whole as a Spirit and holy and demonstrate what improvements are found in process theology regarding this subject. Essentially, I will address the classical metaphysical concept of God as pure Spirit and therefore without body, parts, and passion. Why is this assumed to be true of God? How might process theology provide a more satisfactory alternative? Next I will focus upon the Spirit in a Trinitarian context. In the next chapter, I will follow a similar strategy, but I will present a more detailed discussion of the relevance of the Trinity to process theology and also try to illuminate the problems and costs incurred in developing a process pneumatology. At present, however, the goal is to show that the difference between process theology and classical theism is that each handles polarities such as the following differently.

That is: static-dynamic, being-becoming, eternal-temporal, unchanging-everchanging.

My contention is that these two kinds of theology place a different emphasis on the terms of these polarities. Classical theism tends to ascribe only one side of the polarity to God (the monopolar prejudice, see the next chapter). However, I shall present evidence regarding a struggle for a dual concept of God in classical theism, one that anticipates the later development of the dipolar model of God in process theology.

The Spirit in Cosmological Context

Theologians have struggled for a long time with the meaning and definition of the Spirit in relation to the temporal-material order. Their appreciation of the complexities of this difficult question is amply illustrated by the ambiguities and inconsistencies of their attempted answers. Calvin, for example, points to the numerous inconsistencies and obscurities in the doctrine of man in the early fathers.[10] Nevertheless, in this section I will demonstrate that a distinct trend does emerge historically. From earliest times it was assumed that God as pure Spirit was the antithesis of the mutability, multiplicity, and temporality of the spacio-temporal world. This made it difficult if not impossible to speak of the one true God as literally present or penetrating throughout the universe. To keep God wholly separate from and exclusive of any direct substantial contact or unity with the material order, a pervasive subordinationism came to the fore, of which residuals have persisted in even the most astute Trinitarian thinkers down through the ages. It is not accident that historically a hierarchial concept of ecclesiastical authority was connected with this emphasis upon the transcendental aloofness of God. Nevertheless, numerous inconsistencies allow for the emergence of certain elements later to be emphasized in process theology. As noted in chapter 2, the *via negativa* and its program or negative or world-negating attributes of deity could not be consistently carried through. On the one hand, the fathers insisted upon the divine absoluteness and utter independence of God. On the other, they also insisted that God must have a full concrete awareness of the universe, and they at least implied that the universe is the body of God in the sense that the whole of creation is a tangible expression of the will of God. It is this double insistence, which both affirms and yet denies a genuine relatedness of God to other beings, that makes for the ambiguities and complexities of classical pneumatology. To illustrate this claim, I want to turn to a historical survey of the literature.

THE PRE-AUGUSTINIAN PHASE

The situation up to the time of Augustine was summarized by Augustine himself in *De Fide et Symbolo*, where he observed that while the Father and the Son had been treated in many books, there had been no thorough discussion of the Holy Spirit.[11] A few years earlier (circa 380), Gregory of Nazinazus spoke of a great confusion that reigned over that Spirit. He noted that "some consider it energy, others a creature, others God; still others are uncertain what to think of it, out of reverence to Scripture, which makes no clear statement."[12]

I contend that this confusion reflects a deep-seated insecurity over the relationship of God to matter and consequently a vacillation between a Stoical or materialistic view of Spirit as a material reality and a Platonic or nonmaterial view of Spirit. This latter view was probably the more dominant one and tended to emphasize transcendence at the price of immanence.

H. B. Swete has observed that the place of the Holy Spirit in Christian life and thought was so little emphasized and explicated that the early Christians were attacked for being ditheists rather than tritheists. No early hymn was called the Holy Spirit of God, and no writer before the third century sought to investigate systematically the relationship between the Spirit and the Father and Son.[13]

Apostolic and Post-Apostolic writers for the most part made few references to the Spirit and made no explicit claims for the Deity of the divine presence on earth. They tended to confine the activities of the Spirit to the inspiration of prophecy, thereby obscuring its sphere of operations in the natural order. This would seem to be a very attenuated concept of Spirit. In Scripture, Spirit denotes much more than mere prophetic insight; it is also that which intensifies life, life-giving energy, the very breath of life itself. It is true, however, that the emphasis Apostolic and Post-Apostolic writers placed upon the subjective pole of revelation leads to the experiential dimensions of pneumatology and to the concept of Spirit as that which produces experiences with reference to Scripture. This concept evidences a major affinity with certain aspects of the Whiteheadian aesthetic as applied to mysticism.

In what is probably one of the earliest apologies for Christianity, written to Hadrian's successor (circa 138 A.D.), Aristides mentioned the Holy Spirit once.[14] The *First Epistle of Clement* makes few references to the Holy Spirit, only ten, which refer solely to the Holy Spirit inspiring prophecy in the Old Testament. *Second Clement* makes only one reference to the Holy Spirit.[15] Ignatius of Antioch (martyred in 110 A.D.) mentioned the Holy Spirit only once and that solely in connection with the inspiration of preaching.[16] Origen raised more than one question about the Spirit, which shows how little was then known, how much remained to be determined.[17]

The Montanists confined the activity of the Spirit to the inspiration for wild, orgiastic prophecy. Quite possibly this continuing emphasis upon the subjective pole of revelation was a reaction against the early institutionalization of the church, that is, a plea for a greater and more direct sense of God's presence than is generally possible in institutionalized settings.

To Hippolytus, who makes no claim for the Deity of the Spirit, the latter is confined to the intellectual sphere as that which enables us to grasp and understand divine prophecy. He evidences a subordinationistic theme in his contention that the Father commands, the Son obeys, and the Holy Spirit grants understanding. Cyprian spoke of the Holy Spirit exclusively in terms of baptism, so as to seriously delimit the Spirit to a ritual, an outward sign performed by a priest.[18] Hilary nowhere calls the Spirit God; nor does Novatian, who was in fact against any discussion or speculation on the nature of the Spirit, claiming "I possess its reality, though I comprehend it not."[19]

Irenaeus of Lyons explicitly denied that the Holy Spirit was the giver of life or the principle explanatory element of nature. He claimed instead that "the breath of life which renders man alive is one thing, the quickening spirit that renders him Spiritual is another."[20] he never called the Holy Spirit God, though he seemed to see it as some sort of genuinely supernatural entity. Despite the fact that he wrote a strong polemic against gnosticism, some see a deeply subordinationistic theme implied in his contention that the Son and Spirit are the two hands of God. Yet a proto-process theme is implied here: The metaphor of the hands suggests that the Spirit and the Son are two modes of activity by which the Father actualizes himself. However, he says little about the relationship between the two hands, save that the Spirit seems subordinate and inferior to Christ. Thus, Christ is said to be the Samaritan, and the Holy Spirit the servant who does his bidding.

However, certain aspects of Irenaeus' thought evidence a concept of divine immanence later to be developed in process theology, namely his so-called "process soteriology" with its cosmic Christ. Indeed, his refutation of gnosticism suggests that he at least attempted to transcend any sort of spirit-matter dualism and to affirm the innate goodness of the material order. He strives to synthesize or to unify nature and spirit, body and soul, creation and redemption. The Incarnation seems to include the whole of nature. The universe was created through the Son, in the Son, and finds its ultimate fulfillment in the Son. Reality then appears to be dynamic, not static. Christ signifies God ever on the way to restoring the entire creation by absorbing it into himself. Irenaeus writes:

> It is the Word of God, the Son of God, Jesus Christ our Lord, who appeared to the prophet in the form described in their oracles and according to the special disposition of the Father; (the Word) by whom all things were made; and who, in the fullness of time, to recapitulate and contain all things, became man, in order to destroy death, to manifest life and to restore union between God and man. . . . He recapitulated in Himself the long history of men, summing up and giving us salvation, in order that we might receive again in Christ Jesus what we had lost in Adam, that is, the image and likeness of God.[21]

Something analogous to the process notion of redemption by means of initial aims is evidenced in Irenaeus' view of salvation as maturation and fulfillment. Adam is likened to a child who does not realize what he is yet to be. The Son is the full image of human fulfillment and maturation: "For this reason the Son appeared in the fullness of time to show how the copy resembles Him." The Son exerts a perpetual influence upon us by possessing the most intimate relationships with all people and things, by passing through all the stages of life in order to sanctify them.[22] This is very suggestive of the process notion of an empathic bond between God and the world and also of the Holy Spirit (consequent nature) as creative transforming love.

There are, however, certain crucial points in Irenaeus' thought that process theology might find in need of qualification. It is clear that in Irenaeus, cosmic sanctification entails a return to or feedback into God. However, it is not at all clear whether God is changed or enriched by this cosmic sanctification. A central tenet in process theology is the actualization of brand-new possibilities. The future is the explanatory principle of the present. This reflects Whitehead's doctrine of God as final cause. Irenaeus, however, tends to absolutize the past, the restoration of a lost perfection and glory. However, there is some affinity here with Whitehead's concept of God as the preserver and representer of the past, as noted in chapter 1.

Process theology centers upon an evolutionary concept or reality; Irenaeus presents a seemingly deevolutionary concept of reality, with God reversing the direction of this deevolution. Furthermore, Irenaeus evidences a static concept of human nature, so that Christ seems to become a Perfect Pattern Man to be imitated by all. Finally, there is more than one passage that speaks strongly in terms of a spirit-matter dualism. His concept of divinization or deification seems to be one in which we are stripped of the body, of all our finitude and humanness. He writes:

> We blame Him because He did not make us gods at the beginning but men first and gods afterwards. . . . He was aware of the results of human infirmity; but in His love and power He shall subdue the substance of the nature He created. For it is necessary that nature should be exhibited first and afterwards that man should be made after the image and likeness of God, having received that knowledge of good and evil.[23]

Thus, God's saving grace appears antithetical to nature. We mount up to God, we become sharers in the divine nature, by cutting all ties with the natural order. Here he tends to confound or identify the soul with the essence of God, which is not Whiteheadian.

Origen made very confused pronouncements on the Holy Spirit. It has been said that he "tried and failed to build a Platonic hierarchial order in the Trinity."[24] In many passages subordinationism seems to dominate, so that strictly speaking the Father and Father alone is God, who is "free of all matter . . . altogether monad."[25] Thus, the Deity of the Spirit is highly questionable. It is said to be "associated in Honor with the Father and the Son . . . ever with the Father and Son." Yet, it is also depicted as highly inferior to the Son. The Spirit is not deity but something "made" by the Father via the Son. It is not a principle explanatory of nature; its sphere of activity extends only to the saints, whereas the Son's activity extends to all rational creatures.

There is, however, an interesting inconsistency in Origen. As a rule his concept of God as immaterial and immutable compels him to deny that genuine affection can be ascribed to God. Nevertheless, there is at least one passage in which he adopts a solution to the problem of divine compassion opposite from that of Anselm, noted in the introduction. Here some major process thinkers find an important contribution in this nonprocess thinker, Origen. For example, Hartshorne and Reese observe that "the following . . . is one of the rare genuinely dipolar utterances in all patristic theology":

> The father Himself too, the God of the Universe, long suffering and of great compassion, full of pity, is not He in a manner liable to affection? Are you unaware that, when He orders the affairs of men, He is subject to the affections of humanity? The very Father is not impassible, without affection. If we pray to him, He feels pity and sympathy. He experiences an affection of love. He concerns Himself with things in which, by the majesty of His nature, He can have no concern, and for ourselves He bears the affections of men.[26]

However, Hartshorne and Reese also point out that Origen could not stem the tide of being-worship and etiolatry sufficiently to work out a doctrine of the divine Becoming and Effect.[27] Indeed, his spirit-matter dichotomy leads him to conclude that souls preexisted in heaven and were placed in the material order as a punishment for rebelling against God. Thus mutability, passibility, finitude, and physicality become the symbols par excellence of sin.

The spirit-matter dualism is also central in gnosticism, which failed to find any real place for the Holy Spirit. There were many confused utterances in gnostic works on the subject of the Holy Spirit. Generally, it was depicted as only one of many intermediaries between God and the world, the number of which were multiplied in proportion to the gnostics' abhorrence and horror of physical reality.[28] Thus gnosticism, like traditional theology, was primarily a theology of transcendence, of God's radical otherness. Gnosticism understood Spirit and matter to be sharply conflicting, antithetical realities, which made it impossible to speak of a real internal relatedness between God and the world. The material order was believed to have been created by a demiurge, an evil God. Plotinus, then, speaks "against the Gnostics, of those who say that the Demiurge is evil and the world is bad."[29] All evil and corruption was assumed to result from the union of Spirit and matter. Salvation, then, involved the complete and total separation of these conflicting elements. The goal of gnostic spirituality was to become static and immutable as they assumed God to be, and this meant to become free of all corporality. Vice, the breaking of the laws of the evil demiurge, was assumed by some gnostics to be a source of spiritual liberation for the pneumatic person. Thus, Eusebius writes of the gnostics:

> In accordance with these things they taught that it was necessary for those who wished to enter fully into their mysteries, or rather into their abominations, to practice all the worse kinds of wickedness, on the grounds that they could escape the cosmic powers (archons), as they called them, in no other way than by discharging their obligations to them all by infamous conduct.[30]

The Arian controversy was a direct result of the pervasive influence of dualistic metaphysics within the early church. An examination of this Christological discussion contributes to my theme because it shows that the early Christian community was alert to and struggled with the problems of reconciling transcendence with immanence, which by the monopolar tenets of classical metaphysics had become mutually exclusive categories. Is the Divine that made its presence felt on earth identical with the Divine that rules heaven? Did the Divine that appeared on earth enter into a close and permanent union with human nature? Arius (d. 336), a Presbyter in Alexandria, was educated in the school of Lucian of Antioch. The latter was a follower of Paul of Samosata, Bishop of Antioch, who was excommunicated in 269. Paul contended that the one God cannot appear substantially on earth and consequently cannot have become man in Christ. Lucian, however, held that the Logos became man in Christ. But because he also shared the beliefs of his master, he was compelled to see in the logos a second essence, created by but distinct from God. This was the idea that Arius took up and interpreted. From the scattered excerpts that remain of his writings, it is obvious that his primary objective was to establish firmly the unity, simplicity, and radical aloofness of the immutable Godhead. Though the Son may surpass other created beings, He himself remains a created being, to whom the Father gave an essence formed out of nothing. To identify ontologically this creature with God would be a serious violation of the most fundamental point of his radically dualistic metaphysics: It would destroy the divine aloofness of the Creator by attributing to Him the characteristics of change and suffering.

This point merits restating. To the Arians, change and suffering demote and degrade God. Change implies corruptibility. For this reason, the Arians showed a special sensitivity to those passages of scripture that emphasize the suffering and as well the human characteristics of Christ, as arguments against the Deity of Christ.

Thus, according to Bishop Alexander of Alexandria, these blasphemers and troublers of the church (the Arians) are obsessed with biblical passages describing Christ's passion, sufferings and human limitations:

[The Arians] remember all the passages concerning the Savior's passion, both the humiliation, the emptying (Phil. 2:5–11), and what is called his impoverishment (2 Cor. 2:9), and what acquired things (that is, the opposite of essential or natural things) the Savior took to himself for our sake's, as a demurrer of his sublime and eternal divinity; but of those sayings (in the Scriptures) which are indicative of his nature and glory and nobility and union with the Father, they are forgetful.[31]

He devotes a major portion of his *Letter to Alexander* (his namesake bishop of Constantinople) to refuting the Arian concept of the Son's moral changeability or improvability, by which they denied the Deity of Christ. The Arians claimed that Christ, "having a changeable nature, on account of the diligence and exercise of conduct did not undergo a change for the worst."[32] Athanasius makes a similar point: "Because of his coming down . . . and looking upon him as having suffered . . . they do not believe in him as the incorruptible Son of the incorruptible Father."[33] Athanasius also reports that the Arians, in rejecting the concept of God's own empathetic participation and suffering, ask: "How do you dare to say that the one having a body is the proper Word of the Father's essence, so that he endured such a thing as this (i.e., the Cross)? How is he able to be Logos or God who slept as a man, wept, and had to learn by inquiry?"[34]

Arius absolutized the absolute simplicity of God, who was said to be a monad: "as monad and beginning of all so God is before all. Wherefore he is also before the Son . . . the monad was, but the dyad was not before it came to be."[35] Arius's reference to God as a simple monad and his obsession with attributes proper to God "alone" led T. E. Pollard to surmise:

There can be no doubt that the compelling motive of Arianism was the desire to preserve a strict monotheism, but that does not mean that its monotheism was "biblical." The God whom the Arians declared to be "One" is not the Living God of the Bible, but rather the Absolute of the philosophical schools.[36]

Arius's statements on the Trinity are quite vivid; their purpose is to rule out any sort of plurality in God and therefore to prohibit any substantialist connection between the Persons, so as to maintain God's radical aloofness from the world:

There is a Triad not in equal glories; their subsistences are unmixed with each other, one infinitely more estimable in glories than the other. The essences of the Father and the Son and the Holy Spirit are separate in nature, and are estranged, unconnected, alien, and without participation in each other. . . . They are utterly dissimilar from each other with respect to both essences and glories to infinity.[37]

These difficulties are also reflected in pneumatology, which suffered accordingly. At the Council of Nicea, the Spirit remained a vague, ill-defined entity, possibly Deity, possibly not. Whether or not the Spirit denoted a direct ontological unity between God and the universe was undecided. The inferiority of the Spirit was not pressed by the Arians. However, they did deny the Deity of the Divine Presence on earth on the basis of Amos 4:13, which they understood to claim that the Spirit was a creature. The Deity of the Spirit was not pressed at the Council of Nicea, but it was pressed years later at the Council of Constantinople. No attempt was made at this Council to define the concept of the procession of the Spirit. Later, in *Contra Arius*, Augustine admitted that the question of the procession of the Spirit was a difficult one and claimed that he could not define such a concept.[38] This suggests that quite early there was a dynamic concept of Spirit in the offing, but that it was prevented from having any real meaning by the inability of the fathers to break away from the monopolar prejudice of classical metaphysics. My assumption is that the early fathers were unable to explicate the procession or going forth of the Spirit because the ascribing of movement to God was repugnant to their concept of divine immutability. If, for example, God is truly immutable, then God cannot move out toward something not previously attained. Therefore, motion may not literally be ascribed to God. (For a later discussion of this point, see Aquinas, *Summa*, Pars Prima.)

The original version of the Nicene Creed said nothing about the Holy Spirit, save that it was to be believed in. That portion of the Nicene Creed that is at present devoted to the Holy Spirit is a much later addition that may not have been generally adopted until 500 A.D. [39]

While it claims the Spirit is to be worshipped and therefore Deity, it is quite guarded and confusing in this area, a slipshod definition at best, according to scholars such as Hendry.[40] It says little about the work of the Holy Spirit, beyond inspiring prophecy. It initially lacked the filioque; no mention was made of the Son as the bearer of the Spirit; thus, it did not clarify the relationship of the Spirit to God as incarnate. This was a serious omission, one implying the possibility of a genuine relationship with God exclusive of the God incarnate. Perhaps their dualistic metaphysic, in which God is a wholly immaterial being and in which spirit and matter are seen as antithetical foes, led them unconsciously or otherwise to seek for a relationship with God exclusive of all flesh and therefore to bypass the fact of the Incarnation.

Another problem is that the Creed lacks the ascription of the divine essence to the Holy Spirit. It does not state that the Holy Spirit is the very God of God or of one essence with the Father. Indeed, a subordinationistic theme is strongly implied in the Nicene concept of the Father as the *principium* and *fons*, the source from which all else derives. Accordingly, Harnack has suggested that it represents a concession between the Orthodox, the semi-

Arians, and the Pneumatomache, and therefore it is questionable if the Creed's real intent is to affirm the Deity of the Spirit.[41]

In this respect it is important to remember that the subordinationism of Arianism with its static, otherworldly Deity was a very pervasive influence. St. Jerome once remarked that, alas, the world awoke and groaned to find itself Arian. Constantine apparently had no real theological interest other than trying to unify a divided church. His son and successor, Constantinus, was a devoted supporter of Arianism and frequently exiled Athanasius.[42] Arianism lived to flourish anew during the time of the great German tribal migrations, but it did perish before the advent of Medieval Catholicism.

The Cappadocians, though opponents of the Arians, shared with them the common monopolar conviction that Spirit and Matter are antithetical realities. Therefore, they were reluctant to affirm that the Divine present on earth enters into a genuine relationship (a direct, substantial union) with humankind or that it could even be called God.

Gregory of Nyssa and his brother Basil the Great each wrote a separate treatise on the Holy Spirit. In neither case was the Holy Spirit explicitly called God (*Theos*) nor was there any affirmation that the Holy Spirit is cosubstantial or of one essence with the Father.

The spirit-matter dualism and consequently the identification of the temporal-material order as the source of all sin is a pronounced theme in these writers. According to Niebuhr:

> It is unnecessary to make an exhaustive analysis of the writings of the Greek Fathers to establish the conclusion that the tendency of Greek thought to attribute evil to animal passion has tempted hellenic Christianity to a fairly consistent identification of sin with the love of pleasure, with sensuality and lust and prompted it to make sexual life the particular symbol of this lust.[43]

According to Basil, the Holy Spirit is the name of "the corporeal, most simple there is." We are admonished not to think when we say Spirit "of a limited nature, subject to change and variation." The union of the Holy Spirit with the soul "excludes passion, which comes from the flesh and turns one from God." To be truly spiritual is to put nature ruthlessly underfoot as the enemy, to be "free from the flesh."[44]

According to Gregory of Nyssa, to be free of sin is to be purged of all flesh.[45] It is no surprise then that Gregory defines sin as primarily sensual or animal pleasure:

> It is not allowable to ascribe to our constitutional liability to passion to that human nature which was fashioned in the divine likeness; but as brute life first entered the world, and man, for the reason already mentioned, took something of their nature (I mean their mode of generation), he accordingly

took at the same time a share of the other attributes contemplated in that nature . . . thus our love of pleasure took its beginning from our being made like to the irrational creation.[46]

In his work *De Virginitate*, all sexual activity is seen as inherently wrong, bisexuality being attributed to mankind as a consequence of the Fall.

Yet, in the Cappadocians and also in Athanasius a distinct protoprocess element enters the picture: They contend that the singular and distinct characteristic of the Holy Spirit is procession, a moving forth (*ekporeusis*). There subsists then a highly qualified recognition of a dynamic side of God, of God as outgoing relationship. But their overall commitment to an essentially static concept of the Deity prevented them from accomplishing a thorough working out of this concept. (Of course, this is also true of process thought.) They were unable to define this "procession of the Spirit," a point openly admitted by Gregory of Nazianzus. According to Basil, "the Spirit proceeds from the Father and through the Son." But that sheds no light on the matter. It might mean that the Son is merely the vehicle of its communication or that the Son is of joint origin.[47] Athanasius pronounced inquiries into such matters to be quite foolhardy, "the audacity of madmen."[48] Thus, Spirit and its relationship to God as incarnate remained to be defined.

Classical theologians' comprehension of God as dynamic was greatly attenuated and obscured by their inability to integrate it with the concept of change. Modern science, for example, has found that when heavenly bodies emit light, this depletes their store of energy. A significant change, then, has taken place in that heavenly body. But the metaphysics of the early centuries offered a contrary model. Until the Renaissance, heavenly bodies were credited with possessing an unchanging permanence. Light was generated or radiated from them without changing them. Similarly, God, through the Spirit, was assumed to generate beings without being affected or changed in any way by this process.[49] For example, Gregory of Nazianzus, like Basil, distinguished the Holy Spirit from creatures on the grounds that the Holy Spirit does not change.[50] Athanasius also proclaimed that the Spirit is incapable of change or alteration, because it is incorruptible.[51] This means that it is not justifiable to assume that elements analogous to process theology are in operation any time that classical pneumatology applies an action verb to God.

One of the most striking inconsistencies of classical pneumatology is its tendency toward emphatic scorn and abhorrence of the physical or corporeal, which must be denied of God in any sense, along with a preference for analogies drawn from the physical world in order to explicate the Spirit.[52] Plotinus, for example, likens the emanations or processions of God to light radiating from the sun. This is to illustrate his contention (the monopolar prejudice) that God is a cause whose effects contribute nothing to the cause itself nor diminish it. The radiation from the sun is less than the light and heat of the sun itself;

and the sun, he assumes, is neither increased nor decreased by its shining.[53] Certainly one cannot fault Plotinus for relying upon the cosmology of his day. The problem with such analogies today is that they are rendered untenable by modern scientific advances that reveal the complex evolutionary character of the universe. What is light? What is the sun? What is matter? Contemporary science tells us that the sun is a complex process, the total reality of which is more than just the sun itself. Also, the sun is found to be slowly changing, wasting away. If the sun does not seem to receive anything in return for its effects, it is precisely because it, unlike God, is blind and unconscious.[54]

Athanasius is quite interesting in this regard. He, like Irenaeus before him, is an early representative of the strikingly different intellectual climate of Eastern Orthodoxy. Unlike Western Orthodoxy, which was inclined to reject anything tending toward pantheism, the East stressed the fact that somehow God literally contains the entire universe. This, however, was treated as a mystical rather than a philosophical truth.[55] Some scholars have contended that in confronting Arianism, Athanasius threw against it a cosmic Christology of the divinization of all things. His fundamental conviction that "God became a man that man might become God" suggests the intensity and intimacy of God's direct substantial union with the world, which in a Christian context can be justified only by the doctrine of the Incarnation. For Athanasius, grace appears to be a comprehensive term for the innate goodness of all material reality. Writes Jarsolav Pelikan:

> One of the most persistent themes of Athanasian apologetics was this defense of the intrinsic goodness of reality against its detractors. If one accepted the proposition that the Logos of God was present throughout the universe, one would likewise have to grant that the entire universe was both illuminated and moved by the Logos.[56]

However, Athanasius's texts suggest some qualifiers here. A sharp spirit-matter dualism is evidenced by the fact that he seems to contrast God and change as enemies. He agrees with the monopolar prejudice that God is immutable and impassible. Indeed, all corruption is ascribed to the fact of changeability. Materiality, corruptibility and changeability are nearly synonymous terms in his thought. His soteriology centers upon Christ fighting changeability and thereby elevating us from the realm of the changeable to the inchangeable. The universe is offensive to God's goodness because it is perishing, dissolving.[57] God becomes incarnate not because materiality is intrinsic to God's very being (as it is assumed to be in process) but because this will stabilize the universe by purging it of all change. To become immutable was the goal of his spirituality.[58]

Of historical note is the fact that the pantheism of Athanasius evidences a parallel to that of Philo of Alexandria, centuries earlier. Philo also stressed the immutability, immateriality and impassivity of God; yet, he also contended that God is the soul of the universe. The problem is that his monopolar prejudice led to an arbitrarily onesided conception of the soul. What is missing is a sense of mutual reciprocity between the soul and the body. Genuine relationships are always two-way relationships. For example, the soul can hardly be an impassive ruler; if the soul rules over the body, then the soul, like any good ruler, reflects changes in the "subjects," and it responds with appropriate reactions. The better the ruler, the more versatile this receptiveness. To rule a body as to rule a kingdom, is to enjoy and to suffer what goes on in it. Only an inhuman ruler would be unmoved by the sufferings of his or her subjects or be undelighted by their joy. Certainly, it is true that the soul responds to injuries of the body with grief and likewise experiences intense delight in healthy bodily functioning.[59] In the pages that follow, I will expand this analysis of the prejudice against change in classical theism.

Augustine

As with his predecessors, the problem of God's own involvement in time and change did not become acute for Augustine; in fact the problem did not become acute in philosophy until the beginning of the nineteenth century with Hegel. Thus, the immutability, atemporality and immateriality of the God were central and unquestioned tenets in Augustine's pneumatology. Nevertheless, Augustine is not without deep appreciation of the fact that there are numerous perplexities and difficulties in reconciling his notion of an immutable, immaterial Spirit with the facts of human experience, and most especially with his yearning for a responsive God. Augustine is in many respects openminded on metaphysical questions, which anticipates Whitehead's disdain for metaphysical dogma. For example, on more than one occasion Augustine is quite specific that speculation on the nature and structure of the cosmos is quite beyond his skill and as well beyond the needs of the faithful.[60] Yet, it must not be assumed that he did not take metaphysical speculation seriously or that he was without appreciation of the deep contradiction between the abstract, immutable Deity of classical metaphysics and the biblical vision of a loving, responsive God. Some of the deepest, most profound theology written by Augustine is devoted to this topic. He takes time seriously, in the sense that his discussion of its relationship to God, or the lack thereof, has stimulated much subsequent intellectual speculation, even though one may not agree with his conclusion. It is true, however, that Augustine is dominated by monopolar prejudices. He is not satisfied merely to affirm that God is a strictly atemporal being, but also wishes to show in precisely what sense time or change is applicable only to the created order and not to the Creator.[61] In the *Confessions* and in *Genesis in the Literal Sense*, the problem Augustine seeks to address is how to understand the Genesis account of creation on the assumption that God is a wholly immutable, atemporal entity. At the very beginning of the latter work he asks: "How can it be shown that God, without being afflicted in himself by any mutability, created mutable, temporal beings?" Despite his otherworldly concept of Deity, the intent of much of his thought is to deny all forms of metaphysical dualism, that is, to affirm that there is only one being or principle that is the necessary ground of whatever exists or is possible. (This is of course also a central tenet of the philosophy of organism.) This point was very much emphasized in the rediscovery of Augustine by Calvin, who even claims that God is nature.[62]

Is, then, the universe the body of God in Augustine? Does Augustine affirm the all-inclusive or world-inclusive nature of God? Does God have all things as constituents? The answer, as we shall see, is yes and no and neither in a very clear sense.

On the one hand, Augustine seems to suggest that we are all sharers and participants in the very being of God. Something analogous to the consequent nature of God is implied here. Because Augustine contends that the very essence or nature of God is love, it is the nature of God to be dynamic, that is, to move toward and self-relate to us. That is, the Holy Spirit is God as self-sacrificing love (supra-abundant charity); and far from suggesting self-sufficiency, this sacrificial love implies the need to go forth and pass into the other. Spirit is God in an important sense as a relational being, because relationship is said to be the very meaning of the Spirit.[63] The true character of the Spirit is said to be better revealed by defining it as a gift (*munus*), because the "relations" do not appear in the name Holy Spirit. There is an ontological unity between God and the universe implied here: It is the Spirit that makes it possible for us to share in the very essence of God; for the essence of God is love, and the Spirit is the gift whereby that love is shed or infused onto our hearts.[64] The giver, the giving, and the gift are one: "For as God's gift He (i.e., the Spirit) is given in such a way that He Himself is God the giver."[65] The significant aspect of the Spirit is its personal, relational, or relativistic dimension: God has a reciprocal relationship to the world; for God, in self-communicating and self-relating to the world, places Himself in a state of gift. There is a physical aspect to the Spirit in the sense that God as self-relating to the creature, to spirit-flesh, makes the temporal-material order valuable. The paradox that Augustine recognizes in God is that because since God freely wills to give self in personal love, the Incarnation is intrinsic to the very being of God. God's autonomy from the world, God's free grace transcends any sort of spirit-matter dualism. The fact of the Incarnation denoted that God is essentially committed to fulfilling creative responsibilities within time. Thus, God's self-giving has true meaning and relevance only in the context of God as incarnate, as a living reality within time and history.[66] Here Augustine anticipated process theology in the sense that his concept of

Spirit is not an abstract, impassible, disembodied ghost. Rather, to Augustine, the Incarnation is the basis of God's love. God loves us so much that God becomes one of us, taking on all our suffering. The Incarnation shows that God entered into a genuine reciprocal relationship with us so deeply that God is humbled before us and even placed at the mercy and the control of human beings.

On the other hand, serious ambiguities exist in Augustine's concept of Spirit. Spirit is God as dynamically related to the world. Yet, his doctrine of God characterizes God as wholly separate, distinct and independent of the universe. Creation, then, is wholly external to God and therefore can be of no essential concern to God. Augustine, like theists traditionally, stresses God's liberty or indifference, that is, the fact that God is a statically perfect, self-contained incommunicable supposit rather than a personal entity in outgoing self-relation to others. Augustine assumes that the being of God is something withheld and completely inaccessible to humankind. God reveals His will without revealing His being, as if the divine volition is not in but outside or extrinsic to the Deity. Augustine is careful to emphasize that creation is not a self-manifestation or self-actualization of God: The being of God is unmanifest, unrevealed, and so remains totally unknowable. God is the abstract, predicateless Divine Nothing of Negative Theology. Accordingly, Augustine claims that God must not even be described as unspeakable, for by the very use of the term something is spoken.[67] Yet, even here there is an implicit appeal to a dynamic, relativistic understanding of God: Augustine was primarily interested in who God is for us and not in who God is in Himself, which he assumed to be a question impossible to answer. Yet, he is certainly not adverse to some very deep speculation on the nature of God the Spirit in itself, and it is the unresolved tension between his concept of Spirit in itself and Spirit for us that is in focus here.

Must the Spirit be incarnate or possess a physical aspect to be truly relevant to us? If matter is eliminated from the nature of the Spirit, is not its relationship to the material order seriously constricted, rendered remote and unintelligible? These are, of course, questions posed by process theology, not by Augustine. However, it does seem fair to say that he at least implies an affirmative answer, although he is not cogent concerning exactly in what sense the Spirit is incarnate. He evidences some appreciation of the fact that the concept of a wholly disembodied entity is too different from our most fundamental experiences of reality to be tenable. In his *Confessions*, for example, Augustine seems reluctant to disavow a materialistic concept of Spirit. In 7, 1, he views the Spirit as a wind or material breath in the manner of the Stoic materialists. In *The City of God*, the dynamic office of the Holy Spirit in creation is represented by a material manifestation of God, the breath.[68] He acknowledges that he was unable to conceive of an immaterial substance and that he held to a purely materialistic concept of the Spirit prior to his conversion. In seeking to ensure the oneness or unity of Spirit and matter, he seems to evoke something analogous to the substance-attribute dichotomy as a concession to the conflict between his monopolar tenets and the dynamic, physical aspects of the Spirit. The result is metaphysical incoherence. The dynamic, physical manifestations of the Spirit are said to be mere attributes of an otherwise immaterial, static substance and therefore must not be confused with the true reality of the Spirit. Thus, he is careful to emphasize that in no way must our experience of the Spirit as dynamic be allowed to challenge the notion that it is changeless. Whatever changes or is corporeal dies; thus, the Spirit cannot be incarnate. Its physical manifestations are not part of its essence.[69] What we experience of the Spirit, then, is an illusion, mere appearance only. The Holy Spirit seems superfluous; it corresponds to nothing in our experience; it is purely an inner procession within an essentially static Deity. Indeed, his pneumatological formulations seem to impair any sense of God's ontological unity with the world. God and the universe, the human and the divine, are mutually exclusive categories that must be kept separate. Therefore, he rejects the notion that the Holy Spirit is implanted within us on the grounds that this would be a claim for the divine nature and origin of the human spirit. In creation, then, God did not breath into man the Holy Spirit but a created, material breath.[70] Augustine finds the metaphor of the universe as the body of God to be particularly abhorrent. The Spirit appears as a kind of moral energy and therefore exclusive of any cosmic significance. If evil be truly evil, it cannot be part of an absolutely good being. Either we give up God's goodness or his all-inclusiveness.[71]

Augustine here evidences a crucial instance of his monopolarity, which prevents him from seeing God as the categorically supreme analogue of the soul's relationship to the body: God the Spirit cannot have a physical aspect, cannot be the soul of the universe; God is impassive and incorruptible, whereas a soul in a body is mutable and corruptible. His claim here is congruent with the spirit-matter dualism evidenced in many passages that tend to blame the fact of sin on the body. For example, he makes frequent references to Wisdom 9:15, "The corrupted flesh weighs down the soul."[72] The complexity of Augustine's thought is that he also affirms the innate goodness of materiality, the oneness of soul and body, as in his polemic against dualistic modes of thought such as those represented by Platonism and Manicheanism, which make matter an antispiritual principle and the body the cause and source of all sin.[73] Furthermore, it may be argued that Augustine's affirmation of God as sovereign ruler of the universe, of the Spirit as God's *modus operandi* with the world, is given fuller meaning and impetus in a dipolar context.

Though an ordinary soul in an ordinary body may be corruptible, the issue here concerns a categorically supreme soul in a categorically supreme body. This categorical supremacy means that the soul (God) is superior in its ability to integrate the diverse activities of its body (the universe) and consequently to dominate and rule them. This reign cannot be overthrown, not because the soul is impassible, but because of its unique flexibility to improvise and cope with any situation produced by the body. In other words, the higher the being, the more versatile is its capacity for responding to influence. Perception, all knowledge of the concrete and actual, requires passibility, empathic sensitivity, the capacity to reflect the individuals and forces around oneself. Thus, the soul or personality is the most passive aspect of the physiological system, echoing most sensitively everything going on in that system. The unique power of the soul over the body is a direct result of its unique sensitivity and passibility. The same is true of a ruler: The receptiveness of the ruler to the beings over which it rules is the very source of that ruler's responsibility and the capacity to use power rightly.[74]

Another way in which divine passibility is implied in Augustine emerges in the fact that his rejection of the all-inclusiveness of pantheism seems motivated by religious feeling that rejects a wholly neutral or impersonal deity. If he had more assiduously followed out this conviction, he would not have had to reject the all-inclusiveness of God at the price of divine goodness.

Augustine seeks to ensure the goodness of God. What makes the pantheistic option unacceptable to him is its alleged denial of a distinction between character and act, such that of two mutually incompatible acts, either one would express the same character of God. That is, if God literally includes all our sins, then God is both sinful and virtuous and neither one wholeheartedly.[75]

However, my claim, based upon Whitehead, is that the concept of the all-inclusiveness of God by which God can be said to suffer our evil does not limit the perfection of divine power, but rather it is the ideal case of what all supreme power is, a participation in the self-creation of others, partially determining the self-determination of others. In some respects this seems congruent with Augustine's own position: God in creating the world consented to accept the tragedies of life. In the omniscience Augustine ascribes to God, the latter foresaw all the fatal consequences, the great evils and sufferings of the world, and yet consented to create a world under these terrible conditions. Also, God in His redeeming and salvific activity is a suffering, incarnate God who takes up the sins of the world.

As noted in chapter 1, within the experience of God there is the contrast of God's goodness and the evil of various individuals, but not in such a way that God could be called wicked. The total reality of God is more than God's character. All forms of suffering and evil are in God, in the divine experience, but having something within is not the same thing as "being wicked."[76] The properties of parts are not necessarily properties of their wholes. For example, Hartshorne and Reese note that a round stone may be within a square building. However, I find that this particular metaphor is weak and overworked, because it borrows from what is traditionally understood to be the realm of inanimate physical things. A better analogy is that of the mind-body interaction; that is, not everything happens according to God's will, just as our own inner experiences are not all willed by ourselves.[77] For God to have a body of self-deciding parts is not for God to decide for the parts, but for God to suffer or enjoy their own self-decisions.

Augustine, especially in his Trinitarian formulations, speaks of God as a divine personality and also of the Spirit as the mystery of love; yet, he contends that God cannot suffer. Process theology would contend that the concepts of love and personality would not even have a metaphorical meaning were we not to speak of tragic elements in God. Sin, evil and wickedness are essentially insensitivity, the exclusion of others from empathic appreciation. Suffering is not exclusion. The unimaginable scope of divine suffering is due to God's all-inclusive empathy with all creaturely feeling. God's love does not immunize itself from the sufferings of others. It is we, not God, who, in our weakness and finitude, cannot afford to get infected with the pains of others.[78]

Augustine seemingly derides pantheism for presenting an impersonal Deity, but personality would have no meaning if it were totally devoid of all temporality and possibility. God as supreme personality can be achieved only through empathic suffering, because personality to a large extent consists of the capacity to share in the sorrows and joys of others.[79]

There is strong implication of the divine passivity in Augustine in at least two other ways. First, there is some indication that the concept of the universe as the body of God might be acceptable upon purely aesthetic grounds. The immanence of God guarantees a preestablished harmony that cannot be undone by sin. Indeed, evil may be necessary to the perfection of the whole.[80] Nature, then, is hardly a "dis-graced" realm, void of all Spirit; rather, it appears as the vessel of God's grace, the gracious icon of God's face.

However, the danger here is that Augustine's God might be understood to exploit the sufferings of others for personal self-aggrandizement. A comparable problem is encountered in Whitehead's equating of evil with the aesthetic value of discord. Yet, the concept of the consequent nature makes it more obvious in Whitehead's case that any good God derives from our sufferings is not sadistic but tragic. God is torn within by creatures who, in tormenting one another, also crucify God. That is, God emphatically shares in our sufferings and therefore internalizes them. Thus, the kind of goodness that God reaps is roughly analogous to the kind of good or benefit we derive from our own suffering when we achieve perspective upon it, as in tragic drama. Furthermore, Whitehead emphatically denies that evil is required just as it is for the overall perfecting of the whole. Because reality is dynamic and indeterminate, there is no final completion, no finally perfect whole; nor is there any reason to assume that a more perfect, harmonious whole would be impossible at any given moment.[81]

Secondly, according to Augustine, the Father is order, call, demand, in an important sense a principle of divine unrest and longing. Creation implies a dynamism, a movement of God toward the other. It is a dramatic event in the Divine Life. There is powerful movement within the Divine Life: The Father commands, the Son obeys, the Holy Spirit sustains and perfects. Creation is no mere accident but is essentially an aesthetic receptiveness on God's part, that is, a positive prehension or evaluation of the other. God creates the world because He sees that it is good; and this appreciatory sensitivity toward the world is identified with the Holy Spirit. Thus, the Holy Spirit signifies that God's creation is a creation of love, which means that God continues to relate to creation. The Holy Spirit is testimony to the fact that God is not unconscious or insentient, not neutral toward the universe but evaluatively sensitive to differences in things, in a way analogous to states of pleasure and displeasure in ourselves.

In Augustine, then, God's immanence is displayed in a warm, loving spirituality. The Holy Spirit points to a distinctively feminine aspect of God and with that the feminine qualities of cherishing love, hence the preservative, receptive aspect of God. Thus, Augustine likens the Holy Spirit to a mother hen.[82] In a sense, then, creation is continuous, a dynamic process by which God's immanence keeps us in being by successive acts of will. There is, in Augustine, a strong recognition of the Spirit as the presence of a loving, vital will rather than of an abstract will.[83] There is strong appeal here to the contingency and interdependency of all reality: The universe continues if it continues to please God. So there is novelty in nature. Were all things predetermined, nothing would be contingent. Indeed, the emphasis that Augustine places here upon the Spirit as perfecter suggests that it is best thought of as the creative Spirit and that its activity is continuous. Thus, Spirit is a dynamic reality: It is the radiation of life-giving, creative energy. The redemptive role of the Spirit is an extension of its creativity. The Spirit is continually at work in history as Creator and Redeemer, so that the Spirit is concerned with all of life, not only with those aspects specifically seen as spiritual or ecclesiastical. It is to be noted that a comparable theme is to be found in a magnificent passage in Calvin's *Institutes*.[84]

In many respects, Augustine sees reality as static, fixed; according to him, before God created the world, He "completely fixed," "immovably unalterably" spoke all that was, is, or ever will happen.[85] The Spirit maintains the cosmos as a fixed, rigid pattern, the heavens likened to the vaulted roof of a cave. Whether or not there is any movement in the heavenly bodies is a question that Augustine confesses to find uninteresting. Accordingly, if the truth persuades us that the sky is immobile, then the alleged movements of the heavenly bodies should not block us from thinking that it is so.[86] Thus, creation is seen as a finalized, once-and-for-all, instantaneous event. The chronological sequence in Genesis is said to be merely a narrative procedure, a concession to beings who think in incurably temporal modes of thought.[87] When God creates, He creates something full and perfect, so that it is sacrilegious to assume that anything can be later added to creation.[88]

Yet, Augustine's thought provides certain significant dynamic qualifications to this static view of reality. As noted earlier, he recognizes that creation is in an important sense openended, the realm of unmeasured possibilities that await realization.[89] He speaks of the Spirit of God's "benevolent, creative will" as giving form and structure to unstructured being, so that the Spirit appears analogous to a sensitive sculptor who always works with the grain.[90] Although classical theists such as Augustine may speak of God's providential action or will as immutable; nevertheless, God, undergoing an internal change from conflict to resolution, is implied here: God's providential action presupposes indeterminacy in the very being of God, for decision is always the resolution of indeterminacy.[91] This contingent aspect of the Spirit is further emphasized by Augustine in his concept of the all-inclusiveness of God's being, by which the universe must, in some sense, be God.[92] Here Augustine's thought rules out immobility as a divine attribute, because immobility is an imperfection, implying a lack of the dynamic quality of life.

Certain process writers share with Augustine an emphasis upon the New Testamental concept of the all-inclusiveness of God. For example, Ogletree[93] observes that Paul's statement that Christ "is before all things, and in him all things hold together" has distinct affinities with Whitehead's concept of God as the "supreme result" of process. Also, there is the assertion in Ephesians 1:9–10 that God's purpose in Christ is a "plan for the fullness of time to gather all things together in him, things in heaven and things on earth." The key term is *anakephalaiosasthai*, a recapitulation or summing up. (Note a distinct parallel to the process soteriology of Irenaeus, mentioned earlier.) All things share in Christ, and therefore the reality of Christ cannot be spoken of apart from the actualities that have their being in him. Ephesians also speaks of the church as the "fullness of him who fills all in all" (1:23), which suggests that all things contribute to the fullness of Christ. The assumption, then, that the Spirit is immutable and wholly independent cannot be held without severe qualification if Christ is taken as the paradigmatic event upon which our understanding of pneumatology is based.

The paradox of Augustine is that his concept of Spirit implies sensitivity and even vulnerability not allowable in his formal definition of God, in which he capitulates to an abstract, immutable Deity. The Absolute or Divine Nothing of Negative Theology becomes mistakenly identified with God the Creator. Thus, the universe proves to be purely accidental, unnecessary, without any relationship to the inner life of God. It is axiomatic in Augustine that God is the supremely unaffected one. God is " . . . the cause which is cause only and not effect."[94] With God "there is no alteration, or shadow of movement."[95] God, atemporal and immutable, a statically complete perfection, is said to be the complete and total cessation of all need, desire, and longing. Thus, God, wholly self-contained, can neither be fulfilled nor diminished by what we do, free as God is of all need, necessity and contingency.[96]

But if, as Augustine says, God is the God of love, then God must be in some sense consequential to the world; for love means at a minimum to be deeply affected and moved by the human predicament. The concept of love is then irreconcilable with an Unmoved Mover. The concept of God implied in a God of love is intrinsically dipolar. Indeed, creation would have no meaning or significance unless God were deeply affected by it. That is, the reason for denying that the absolute pleasure or bliss of the self-contained Unmoved Mover is possible is that to such a deity the real world of variable, concrete particulars would contribute nothing. The world would be a matter of unqualified indifference to a deity lost in such contemplation. Aristotle, for example, accepted this consequence. His deity is indifferent to nature, does not even trouble himself to stop and contemplate it.[97] The minimum condition of our life is that it have ultimate significance, that it make a difference to God, that God be genuinely affected by all that we say and do.

The monopolar prejudice of classical theism denies that God is the end or consequence of the world. This means that the only concrete ends realized by the world process are purely the selfish ends of the world itself. The fatal weakness of classical theism is that it obscures the meaning of New Testament passages speaking of a "restoration of all things" (Acts 3:21) in which God is "all in all" (I Cor. 15:28).[98] Nor can it give meaning to the traditional affirmation of classical theists that the chief end of humankind is to serve and glorify God. What could we possibly contribute to a God who has everything? A totally perfect, self-sufficient deity would not require our services. The most that can be said is that we admire this deity. These problematical implications of an immutable deity have been emphasized by Hartshorne:

> Really it must, on that assumption, be only the creature who is to be served or benefitted. God would be the cause or protector of value; but the value caused and protected must be simply ours. On this time-hallowed view, God has the mine and the miner from and by which the wealth was dug; but the ultimate consumer was ourselves. God was the policeman and judge and ruler, but man was the citizen, for whose sake the commonwealth existed.[99]

Put another way, implicit within the classical conception of God as the supreme cause is the affirmation of God as the supreme effect of all things. Logically, cause and effect are inseparable realities. For example, we know of no active relations without passive ones. Furthermore, classical theists, I believe, would agree that we know of God only in relation to creation in terms of what is in it for us; that is, we know of God only in relation to having or producing certain effects. Thus, the concept of God cannot be abstracted from the concept of effect. Yet, classical theism contends that the world contributes nothing to the wholly self-sufficing being of God. But at the same time it must be admitted that if God had not made the world, then God would have had it as effect. The contradiction Hartshorne and Reese see in classical theism here is that God-as-having-a-certain-effect and God as not having it are assumed to be one and the same entity. The world has God as its maker, but God does not have the world that God made.[100]

But this is not to claim that Augustine is completely indifferent to the problem of divine change and contingency either. The question he seeks to answer is what status can be assigned to the relations between God and the world without renouncing his monopolar prejudice that God is wholly immutable and noncontingent. His solution is that God is a thoroughly nonrelational being, an unchanging substratum that, paradoxically, undergoes adventures of change without thereby being changed and takes on relative qualifications without thereby being qualified. Creatures change when they receive the Spirit, but this is a purely one-way or nonmutual relationship in which God the Spirit does not change. Because God alone is eternal and because temporality has no relevance to eternity (that is, time is merely a dimension of the created and does not apply to the Creator), God is not subject to temporal qualifications, though temporally given.[101] Relativistic attributes may be predicated of God by reason only of a change in the creature, not by reason of any change in God.

In making this point, Augustine likens God to a piece of money. It can receive relative qualifications by becoming the price of this or that, yet the very being or form of the piece of money is not altered in the face of these prices. Likewise, God can receive qualifications relative to creation without thereby being changed or altered in any way.[102]

But Augustine fails to get at the core of the problem. A piece of money remains unaltered by its relationships because it is insensate, unconscious. Is this, then, how God escapes relation to us? Is God unconscious rather than the supremely rich and conscious being Augustine takes him to be? There is also an implicit affirmation of the divine relativity in his money example: Money does not exist as a value apart from its relationship to other persons and human society. The same is true of the Spirit as God's great gift: To be a gift presupposes the receptivity of the other in mutual love and intercommunion.

Since, in Augustine, the Spirit denotes the fact that God takes pleasure in creation and also that God has a direct, concrete, immediate awareness of all things, there is some suggestion that the world serves to enrich God's experience. However, his capitulation to an abstract, immutable deity compels him to obscure this theme, to disclaim God's relatedness to the object of knowledge. Since God's knowledge is immutable, no change could be made to it as a result of creation.[103]

All this entails an unqualified negation that God has a real internal relationship to anything beyond God's own wholly absolute being. The whole notion of God's evaluative sensitivity to the world is truncated. The actual fact of creation cannot enrich God's experience, because God would fully experience in imagination any world God could completely determine.[104]

It is true, however, that Augustine's concept of God as in his own nature rest (*quies*) might be interpreted as an affirmation of God's perceptual receptivity to the world, that is, God as the categorically supreme form of effect. Augustine contends that the biblical account of God resting on the seventh day must be understood figuratively, not literally. That is, it must not be understood in the childish sense that God toiled at his work, for God is in his own nature rest.[105] Though it may appear foolish to think of God as needing to rest after "working" to create the world, it does not seem foolish to think of God as first performing an act and then pausing, as would any great artist, to aesthetically contemplate its results. The inference would be that we too should stop to appreciate accomplished actualities and not merely immerse ourselves in the production of new ones.[106]

The dilemma here is, in short, the tension between Augustine's affirmation of human beings as free moral agents and the thoroughgoing determinism of his doctrine of predestination, by which God cannot experience anything He does not already know.

The idea of God rewarding and punishing suggests that our future is openended, indeterminate; that is, God waits upon what we will do in our freedom. Certainly, Augustine demonstates a strong sense of sin and personal moral responsibility. That calls for personal freedom and self-determination. Therefore, I agree with Brightman's point[107] that a God with absolute foreknowledge who had predestined everything may enjoy sovereignty of will, but such a God must forego a world of free beings who are morally self-determining. A God whose purpose is to develop a society of responsible persons must forego some knowledge and some power if this divine end is to be attained. Comparably, process thinkers such as Hartshorne and Reese argue that if God, in eternal decree, knows and wills our free acts as definite, they would not be genuinely free, having been eternally definite and so at no time open for decision. This would be "error, not knowledge," since true knowledge must be of things as they are, hence of the indeterminate and unsettled as having these characteristics. Since genuinely free acts are determinate only after they have happened, not beforehand or eternally, the only way God can know the whole truth, can be genuinely omniscient, is for God to have two forms of temporal knowledge: first, the knowledge of what may or may not take place; secondly, the additional knowledge of what in fact does take place or has taken place.[108] In other words, God's knowledge must embrace the contingent if it is to be valid knowledge of the acts of free moral agents. Either God is consequent to the world, or God has no valid knowledge of the world.

Put another way, Augustine's concept of the church as the mystical body of Christ presupposes God expecting an answer to his call through the Spirit to persons endowed with freedom. If, however, God already knows the answer ahead of time, then God is merely expecting an answer from himself and so is "only playing with himself."[109] The richness of the divine experience is frustrated in this fashion. Indeed, creativity seems meaningless; God is void of the intuition of genuine novelty.

If, however, in Augustine we explore more fully the question of whether God is an atemporal being, the answer appears to be a complicated yes and no. Though Augustine says much about the insoluble mysteries of an atemporal eternity, he also evidences a mystical-like affirmation of the paradoxicality and ineffability of time.[110] In a sense Augustine approximates the process conception that God as the chief exemplification or supreme form of temporality is no less sublime than a nontemporal actuality. Indeed he is also quite close to the deification of temporality in his trinitarian metaphor of the Father as memory.

It is also the case that Augustine seeks God through the mystery of time, so that there is a particularly intimate relationship presupposed between temporality and divinity. Time is the foundation, the very essence of the flowering of the human spirit; our capacity for self-transcendence resides in and through our temporal modes of thought. Self-transcendence is not the abolition or negation of time, but means that we may more thoroughly embrace the temporal structure of our being. To transcend temporality, to be outside or beyond time, is in essence a supra-temporal process by which we gain deeper perspective on time by viewing it from a transcendental vantage point. Thus, in Augustine, memory is a particularly important aspect of self-transcendence.[111] To be time-oriented, capable of assimilating the past and appropriating it for the future, is the source of the capacity to become a creative self in personal history. Thus, memory is not the mere preservation of fixed occasions; rather, memory is a dynamic energy, our investment in living experience. Indeed, memory is the power of transcendence that places one so far beyond everything else that one can find a home only in God.[112]

Augustine ensures that God is temporal in the sense that God is the measure of all time, the guarantee of the integrity of time. God's experience of time is far more profound than that of creatures, for only God is capable of embracing the past, present and future as an integrated whole, within a unity. We, however, are too absorbed in the present or too anxious about the future to achieve such integration. Thus, God is correctly said to be "atemporal" or "not in time" only if that means free from the disintegration and atomism that characterize our modes of temporal perception.[113] Here Augustine makes an important discovery that was not fully appreciated for over a thousand years. He anticipates the consequent nature of God in his contention that in God nothing perishes, that the past is a living, ever-present fact.[114]

Augustine, however, appears to contradict himself by a capitulation to his concept of God as wholly immutable. He is compelled to eliminate all temporality from God's nature and therefore seriously to invalidate any sense of God's own internal relatedness to our world of time and change. Indeed, time or change seem purely illusions, for to the immutable God all is merely present. Events do not become, they just are.[115] For God there is no past or future; God knows all things without memory or anticipation; all is simply present for God. Thus, God's experience is void of all temporal content, for God is not conscious of succession. Although Augustine is quite specific that God is the Lord of History who has been disclosed through the history of Israel, he contradicts himself on this point, claiming that temporality has absolutely no relevance to the acts of God.[116] The problem Augustine fails to address is how God's *modus operandi* with the world can be genuinely coordinate with and relevant to the spacio-temporal world if God is not temporally qualified. As noted in chapter 1, a God outside of time would have no relevance to history: Induction would be impossible, because nothing would refer to the past or future. Indeed, Augustine's conception seems to make any statement about God's acts within history impossible. In fact, it completely rules out such statements by representing God's acts as timeless and unhistorical.

Yet, it must not be overlooked that process thinkers recognize an important sense in which there is great merit in Augustine's emphasis upon the seemingly miraculous dimensions of God's activity. This can be understood as expressing the superiority of creativity over mere law and order. This concept of supralegal creativity points in the direction of the doctrine that in Whitehead is seen as the highest possible pinnacle of philosophical-religious speculation.[117]

As a further explication of some implicit parallels between the classical, or more specifically, Augustinian concept of God's activity in the world and that of process theology, I now turn to the Spirit in a Trinitarian context. I shall focus upon how the concept of the divine immutability of God as pure spirit relates to Trinitarian problems concerning the Spirit as an item in the complexity of God. At the same time, I am interested in how Trinitarian thought may be interpreted as an attempt to qualify monopolar prejudices in an era when they could not be expressly abandoned.

The Holy Spirit in Trinitarian Context

Trinitarian thought has a distinct affinity with process theology because the former's appeal to the complex unity of God anticipates the aesthetic model of God to be discussed in the next chapter. The Trinity suggests that there are elements of relativity, complexity, or multiformity and change within an otherwise simple, immutable, self-contained deity.

Classical theism exalted the simplicity and immutability of God; yet, the doctrine of the Trinity asserted that within this supposedly simple and fixed deity there were distinct personalities, one of which was conscious of taking flesh, interrelated or connected by a process of eternal becoming. Through the doctrines of the Incarnation and Atonement, Trinitarian thought inseparably bound up the concept of Spirit with that of great suffering and tragedy within the experience and inner life of God.

However, the monopolar prejudices of classical theism greatly obscured this point. One of the divine Persons was somehow identical with the suffering, human Jesus. Since Jesus was changeable and embodied, whereas God is immutable and wholly immaterial, there had to be two separate natures in Christ. Thus, Channing remarked:

> Trinitarians profess to derive some important advantages from their mode of viewing Christ. It furnishes them, they tell us, with an infinite atonement, for it shows then an infinite being suffering for their sins. The confidence with which this fallacy is repeated astonishes us. When pressed with the question whether they really believe that the infinite and unchangeable God suffered and died on the cross, they acknowledge that this is not true, but that Christ's human mind alone sustained the pains of death. How have we then an infinite sufferer?[118]

As pneumatology is rooted in Christology, the doctrines of the Incarnation and Atonement might serve to qualify the monopolar concept of Spirit as immutable. These doctrines supposedly furnish an infinite being suffering for our sins. Jesus is a temporal being; Jesus suffered; Jesus is God; therefore, it follows that the Spirit or divine presence is the presence of a genuinely suffering, temporal deity. The problem, however, is that the fathers, in their struggle to reconcile Christianity with the immutable deity of classical metaphysics, claim that only Christ's human nature suffered, because the divine nature is impassible. Yet, unwittingly, this doctrine of the two natures seems to defeat its very purpose. If God is but one of two natures, God is but part of a particular man. If Jesus is a God-man, then both God and man are elements of a whole that is more than either of them and that, in certain aspects, is temporal and suffering.[119]

In classical theism, God was said to be a simple monad, but not in such a way as would prevent the highly complicated machinery of the Trinity, that is, as would make impossible a complex structure of social relations within the deity.

Put another way, classical theism, especially in the tradition of Aquinas, regarded complexity and diversity in a wholly negative light as the subjection of unity to division and disintegration, and therefore that strain of theism affirmed that God is a wholly simple entity. Yet, classical theism also affirmed that God is the one supreme reality, that no second reality stands over and against God on an equal footing, imposing limitations upon the deity. God is free of all external restraint so that nothing can exclude God. This appeal to the all-inclusiveness of God, also a fundamental theme in mysticism (see chapters 2 and 3), is in fact an implicit appeal to the complexity of God. If God is all-inclusive and nondual, God must include multiplicity and diversity as well as oneness; otherwise, the principle of diversity would stand over and against God. For example, Calvin affirmed that the divine unity of God is manifested in the splendor of the variety of the cosmos.[120]

Classical theism denies that God is a relational being, yet it speaks of the relationships and the ineffable intercommunication (Spirit) among the Divine Persons. Aquinas, for example, denies relativity or contingency within God; yet, he insists that relation constitutes the very meaning of person. The Divine Persons are said to be subsistent relations: subsistent via their identity with God's essence, distinct via their relative opposition.

Nor was God assumed to be without relativity in a way that would make it impossible to speak of ourselves as being loved by God; that is, through the Spirit we become elements of a relationship of which God is the subject. Classical theism exalts the immutability and absolute perfection of God. Yet, since the Spirit was assumed to be the bond that unites us to the mystical body of Christ, the condition that our being contributes significantly to God appears to be met.[121]

Classical theism would not admit to a process of divine becoming or "process towards novelty and enrichment in God," but does speak of a "begetting" of the Son and the "procession" of the Spirit.[122]

The Trinitarian concept of God as Persons has particular relevance to our process interpretation of Spirit as signifying God as an eminently social reality. The Trinity is precisely that by which God is transformed from metaphysical Absolute, from empty, indeterminate abstraction to a living concrete personal reality in history.

The Trinity is the origin of all personalistic metaphysics; it is impossible to conceive of a personal God as an abstract, self-sufficient absolute: Personality is not self-contained but exists in the relation of love and sacrifice to the other. The Trinity is a distinct affirmation of God as a relational being in the sense that the person of the Father presupposes the persons of the Son and Holy Spirit. The classical concept of mutual immanence among the divine persons claims that the Trinity is a Trinity of Persons precisely because they presuppose one another in mutual love and intercommunion, which is the Spirit.[123]

Because Augustine's thought is so fundamental to western doctrines of the Trinity, a brief survey of some of the main points of his formulation will serve to reinforce and render concrete these considerations.

Western pneumatology tended to draw upon analogies based upon physical things or inanimate objects as opposed to spiritual or psychological factors. Note, for example, the predominance of physical metaphors in the mystical accounts described in chapters 2 and 3. Augustine's Trinitarian thought marks a positive contribution to pneumatology because it is an early effort to counteract this trend. In his Trinitarian formulations he relies upon analogies based upon personality, mind, soul and love.[124] This anticipates the priority process theology grants to the idea of God as a genuinely personal, relational being, one who is supremely sensitive. Relation enters into Augustine's model of God, because the predication involved in the key Trinitarian terms such as Father and Son is descriptively classified by Augustine as relative predication. Thus, the Trinity is said to be a Trinity of Persons mutually interrelated: *Trinitatum relatarum ad in vicem personarum.*[125]

Like Whitehead, Augustine rejects the substance-attribute dichotomy as not being applicable to God. The Divine Persons, these three realities, are said not to belong to God, but to be God.[126] That God is the persons of the Trinity means that the deity is not an impersonal reality behind the personal being of God.

The psychological model of the Trinity means that the personality of God and of human persons presuppose one another, for the life of every individual must be interpreted after the Divine Tri-unity reflected in the world. Creation has deep meaning and relevance to God because it is understood as the realization of the Divine Trinity within the inner life of God. Self-sufficiency, self-satisfaction and despotism cannot be ascribed to the inner nature of God; a psychology of the Trinity is possible only in relation to the God of positive theology, not the abstract Divine Nothing of negative theology. This means that, created as we are in the image of God, we are designed with the capacity for genuine relationships. Sin is the breach or the breaking off of relationships, and for this reason Augustine describes the sinful soul as *curvatus*, that is, curved down or away from.[127]

The significant dimension of God's presence in our lives is the personal dimension. Indeed, the Holy Spirit is a personality in the sense of being consciously and intellectually purposive.[128]

However, several major problems arise here. Augustine is apparently using the term Holy Spirit in several conflicting senses. It is applicable to God as a whole because God is Spirit and Holy; yet, it is also an item in the internal complexity of God. It is said to be the relationship, the loving bond and ineffable communion between the Persons, between the Father and Son; yet, it is also said to be a separate Person alongside the other two.[129] This seems untenable because (1) it assumes mistakenly that the relationships between persons can be personified, and (2) that the relationship between persons is exclusive of the realities of the persons involved, so that it can be abstacted out and considered as a separate reality alongside the other two. The next chapter will outline ways in which Whitehead's aesthetic may resolve these difficulties. Essentially my claim is that these problems disappear in process theology because that theology drives the concept of relationship deeper into the nature of God than does Augustine.

However, Augustine also makes a positive contribution to process theology in that his Trinitarian thought approximates a concept of persons as *causa sui*, which is a central tenet in Whitehead's metaphysics. In the development of his Trinitarian thought, Augustine identifies the concept of Person as outgoing self-relation with the concept of personal autonomy, the individual's power of self-determination. A Person is at once constituted by self-relating to the other (that is, by mutual immanence) and yet is self-subsistent in the sense of being free from external coercion.[130] Later, I shall address a serious ambiguity in these passages in the way Augustine attempts to harmonize the interdependence of the persons with their self-differentiation.

Once God's creative activity is understood on the analogy of genuine interpersonal relationship, it may be understood as a call to the creature to create itself. Because God's presence in life, the Spirit, is conceived by Augustine as a personal rather than a mechanical force, the creature's own autonomy is not threatened but in fact strengthened by it. The more a purely mechanical force acts upon a thing, the more its autonomy is diminished. But in genuine interpersonal relationships, the causal efficacy of one person upon another does not necessarily lessen the autonomy or freedom of the person acted upon, but can actually intensify it. In this way there is nothing that does not depend upon God's initial causal activity, yet, at the same time, everything depends upon the creature's creative response.[131] Since God the Spirit is self-giving, self-relating, personal love, then chance, risk and indeterminacy become necessary elements in creation; only free self-giving creatures can genuinely receive love and give God love in return.

Of historical note is that fact that Calvin, in his rediscovery of Augustine, also sees the Spirit as the source of our self-transcendence, and sees, in human efforts to create culture and beauty, the presence of the Spirit in human consciousness. Thus, the presence and activity of the Spirit is seen as the instigator of the whole of culture. Though the origin of the practical arts is attributed to the sons of Cain, they are not to be demeaned; their validity is not undone by sin. Indeed, Calvin, as Wencelius has emphasized, gave far greater weight to the spiritual value of aesthetic experience than many interpreters have allowed.[132] Even though Calvin tended to overemphasize the cognitive characteristics of faith (for instance, *Ins.* 1, 15, 7–8; 2, 2, 12), he did not neglect to emphasize also that unity with God through the Spirit involves the whole person. Like Whitehead's concept of concrescence, the unity of physical and conceptual feelings, Calvin stresses that faith involves not only the illumination of the intellect but also the fortification of the heart.[133] Therefore, he is quite clear that those who neglect the aesthetic contemplation of God are remaining insensitive to the works of the Spirit and are in fact discordant with the Spirit in an important part of their souls. The chief work of the Holy Spirit may be the bringing of faith, but the Spirit is also the creator and preserver of all beauty. Calvin speaks of the spiritual life as a "melody" that exists between our life and God.[134] He says at more than one point that beauty is not just to delight the senses, but to raise the soul up to God; for in contemplating the beauties of creation, we are humbled before and ravished in admiration of the creator.[135] There is no reason why we should not recognize in God the beauty that we perceive in nature and create in art.[136]

However, a major difference here between process and the Augustinian-Calvinist tradition is this: In process theology, God neither causes freedom, nor creates in us some capacity for freedom, nor creates our free acts. It is not the divine freedom alone that delimits and structures freedom but the freedom of all creatures acting upon God. God as consequent cherishes and fosters the influx of free creaturely acts into his inner life, but they are solely the creatures' acts.[137]

This emphasis upon freedom, autonomy, and with that multiplicity, Augustine attempts to reconcile with the concept of the divine unity or harmony of the Persons as God. God in Augustine is no simple monad, because there is sociality in God.[138]

Here Augustine also anticipates a model of God sensitive to aesthetic values. Since unity among diversity is the basic principle of aesthetics (in the Whiteheadian sense of the term), the mystery of the Trinity is primarily aesthetic. God is the richest possible synthesis of contrasting elements, a kind of meta-or supra-personality, a supraorganic individual constituted by unique personalities. God is dynamic and fluid in the sense that the Spirit, the ineffable bond between the Persons, signifies the flowing forth of personalities into one another. This is unlike anything on earth because we never encounter human personalities that work together so harmoniously as to constitute one metapersonality.

Of historical note is the fact that the Cappadocians approximated such an aesthetic comprehension of the Trinity. God is the name of a common essence (*ousia*) shared by three divine persons. As three human beings have in common their human nature, so the three divine persons have in common the nature of Deity. If so, asks Gregory of Nyssa, then why are there not three gods like three men? The answer he provides is that human beings work individually, but that every work of God involves all three working together.[139] In other words, the Trinity can be distinguished from tritheism on the basis of the aesthetic rationale that there is a perfect harmonious unity of will, purpose and action among the divine persons. The Trinity is a mystery not because it is irrational but because we have no comparable aesthetic experience of such a perfect unity or harmony among such a diversity of content.

There are, however, at least two major differences between the Cappadocians and Augustine on this point. First, according to the Cappadocians, the Deity, the principle of unity, appears to be an impersonal essence. Augustine, however, seeks to affirm God as a genuinely personal being. Second, according to the Cappadocians, the Spirit appears as merely a third hypostasis alongside the other two. The danger here is that this concept may easily turn Trinitarian speculation from a serious effort to understand God's activity in history, that is, to know what is known as Son and experienced through the Spirit is to be affirmed as God, to abstract, speculative thought on the inner nature of God, that is, how the three hypostases can have one *ousia* or essence and still be three hypostases. In Augustine, the Spirit is seen in dynamic terms as outgoing personal relation. Augustine, and later Calvin, tended to stress the dynamic offices and activity of the Spirit over the person of the Spirit. Thus, Son and Spirit seem to denote two inseparable modes of God's activity in himself and toward the world. Augustine, in his doctrine of mutual immanence, makes it clear that the Persons are not just separate aspects of God, one doing one thing, one another. Rather, the Persons presuppose one another and are inseparable in their functioning.[140] Thus, the Spirit as loving bond between the Persons signifies that God acts as an organic whole.

However, several major problems arise that suggest that Augustine has great difficulty in explicating God as a complex synthesis or organic whole while holding to the monopolar emphasis upon the utter simplicity of God. On the one hand, when the diversity or inner complexity of God is in view, Augustine seems to subvert his doctrine of divine unity or mutual immanence among the members of the Trinity. For example, he claims that his psychological model of the Trinity is limited because in the human psyche reason, will and memory are all interrelated, but in God all the Persons are self-sufficient and independent.[141] On the other hand, when the mutual immanence of the Persons is in view, he seems to obscure the ideal of divine complexity or diversity among the Persons. Following the Cappadocians, he argues that any predicate attributed to any one Person must be attributed to them all. What any one does, they all do.[142] For example, each is simultaneously the body of the Son, the dove of the Spirit, and the author of the Father's voice.[143]

As suggested earlier, this dilemma may represent Augustine's attempt to harmonize personal autonomy with interdependence or mutual immanence, but it also may reflect a deep-seated vascillation on Augustine's part over the concept of unity provided by classical metaphysics. That is, Augustine seems torn between what Hodgson terms an arithmetical or mathematical concept of unity and an organic or aesthetic concept of unity.[144] The former denotes unity in the sense of undifferentiated unity. An amoeba would be an approximation of arithmetic unity, although even the simplest things in nature evidence some multiplicity; for instance, even a hydrogen atom has components.

An arithmetic concept of God's inner unity would mean that God is free of all multiplicity and internal diversity. This concept of unity would contradict the multiplicity of God. Holding to an arithmetic notion of divine unity, Augustine would have great difficulty explicating any sort of plurality in God. Indeed, the notion that God was in some sense complex or compound was deeply repugnant to classical theism, because of the pervasive assumption that whatever consisted of parts could be otherwise than it is and also could break down. (See, for example, Aquinas, *Summa*, Question 3.)

In contrast, aesthetic or organic unity exists by the diversity of its parts; it is in fact impossible with multiplicity. For example, great art works are not simple, but compound; they manifest a harmonious diversity of components. Also the higher the organism, the more diverse and multitudinous are its parts. In Whitehead, God as the chief exemplification of all aesthetic principles would be the most complex synthesis that there is.[145] However, it is true that Whitehead sometimes obscures this point by his separate treatment of the two natures of God. Cobb's correction of Whitehead on this point shall be addressed in the next chapter. There I will outline ways in which the Whiteheadian aesthetic, because it transcends this dualism of Augustine's thought, may provide a more logically coherent account of the divine complexity, though not in the sense of merely repeating or rephrasing Trinitarian formulations.

However, these criticisms should not obsure the fact that Augustine's psychological models of the Trinity make a positive contribution to process theology by at least implying that in some sense God is contingent or consequent, the Holy Spirit signifying a movement within God toward self-fulfillment through the other. Augustine claims that God is love and uses the Trinitarian metaphor of the lover (Father), the love (Holy Spirit) and the loved object (Son). This suggests that there is in God a deep longing for the other and for sacrificial self-surrender to that other. A solitary lover is a contradiction in terms, for love always demands another. Also, he likens the Trinity to the mind (Father), the mind's knowledge of itself (Son) and the mind's love of itself (Spirit). This is suggestive of the mystical concept of God as a becoming self that must enter into the complexity of its own being, go beyond itself, to find and know itself (see chapter 2). Indeed, in Augustine the mystery of self-consciousness is seen as the key to the mystery of God. There are many passages in which Augustine comes close to the deification of self-consciousness.[146]

All this implies a proto-process theme in Augustine; that is, Augustine's God cannot be the Unmoved Mover or Passionless Absolute, as in his formal definitions; a God thought to be purely external to the conflicts of the world, above and beyond any effect the world might have upon God's own self, would be a God who is mere empty potentiality with no actual experience or consciousness. The dilemma of Augustine is that he failed to develop this most important implication. The same is also true of Aquinas, although contemporary defenders of Thomism obscure this point.

Thomism

Contemporary Thomists have raised vigorous objections against process theology. At this point a succinct summarization of these objections will help to supplement the preceding material. My point is that if Thomists are particularly sensitive to areas in which they think Thomas has been misunderstood by process theologians, process thinkers are also sensitive to areas in which these critics may have misappropriated process theology. Unfortunately, this latter state of affairs is very often the case. More dialogue between Thomists and process people is therefore essential. So far, Thomist objections fall into four major areas.

First and foremost is the objection against the process concept of God needing the world. Hill, in *The Three Personed God*, argues that creation is a totally motiveless act; if God is affected by the world, then God would lose his "true transcendence" and "cease to be the God of Christian experience."[147] The advantage of Thomistic theology is that it safeguards the independence of God by an emphatic denial that God's relations to the world are real "in the precise sense of bespeaking an ontic determination of deity, a passive dependence upon creatures."[148] Process theology is said to be in total opposition to Christianity, because "God's knowledge is determined by creatures, and his love is ultimately Eros, motivated by self-fulfillment, rather than the altruistic agape of the New Testament."[149]

Burrell, in *Aquinas: God and Action*, makes a similar claim. He believes that Hartshorne misread Aquinas by making the illicit assumption that the Thomistic denial of God's real relationship to the world is a denial of God's relationships to creatures *simpliciter*. Rather, Thomas' denial of *relatio realis* is correctly understood as a denial such that "there is no process or property in divinity which demands or results in creatures."[150] Burrell cites the passage in the *Summa* that reads "God's relationship to creatures does not flow from his nature. He does not produce creatures out of the necessity of his nature, but rather by intellect and will."[151] The term "real relationship" cannot be used, because this would suggest a relationship between God's essence and creatures. Accordingly, a more profound concept of divine love is to be found in the concept of a statically complete, self-sufficient creator who has no real need of creatures yet freely creates.[152]

Why then does God create the world? If God could be just as happy, whole, and complete without it as with it, why does God bother to create? These thinkers do not provide a metaphysical explanation for the universe.

Furthermore, if creation is in fact purely an altruistic act, does not that still imply God's needing the world? How could God be truly altruistic without there being an object toward which to be altruistic?

What exactly is the relationship, if any, between the will and the being of God? How does one differentiate them? They seem to be independent, conflicting forces, one calling for a world, one not, one related to the world, the other not.

A serious oversight in these thinkers is that neither made mention of the fact that Hartshorne and other process thinkers have given strong consideration to the tensions between agape and eros. Neither made reference to a key section in *Reality as Social*, for example, where Hartshorne addresses Nygren's similar position.[153] In the process model of God, egotism and altruism, or self-interest and other-interest, are one, are in fact reconcilable. God's love cannot help but gain a value from the other, nor can God help but be deeply moved and affected by the other; the perfect love of God is the enjoyment of the enjoyment of others. Granted, Thomists such as Burrell and Hill may wish to reject such notions, but they still have the responsibility, which they did not exercise, of including their opponents' position in the matter.

Neo-Thomist W. N. Clarke is more sympathetic to the issues raised by process thought. Clarke concedes that the time has been reached for the Thomistic doctrine that "God is not really related to the world to be quietly dropped."[154] He emphasizes that to tell people that God is "truly personally related" to the universe yet "not really related," that the personal relationship of God with us is not "real," appears so counterintuitive, contradictory and in conflict with the Christian revelation of a personal Savior that it is simply too difficult to justify convincingly and to explain. He notes that there is in fact a convergence among recent Thomists toward "toning down" Thomas's doctrine on the relationship of God to the world, but that many are still reluctant to go as far as he is: namely, to affirm that God is "truly personally related" to the world.[155]

Although it is clear that Clarke is striving for an intermediate position between Hartshorne and his critics, there are certain ambiguities in his position that leave one uncertain exactly what the implications of his position are. According to Clarke, in Thomism the relations of God's will to the world (intentional relations) are genuine. But these relationships are not real in any definitive sense of the term. In the theoretical framework of Thomism, such relations cannot be called "real relations," because all "real" relationships for Thomas require some change or difference in the real intrinsic being of God. This is incompatible with the divine infinity, which allows of no increase or diminution in perfection.[156] Clarke's advance on traditional Thomism, then, is to distinguish sharply between the relational consciousness of God, which is genuinely affected by creatures, and the intrinsic perfection of God's "real being," which is simple, immaterial and unaffected by creatures.[157] But there is a serious problem here, for this distinction seems to create a false dichotomy within God, who is truly one, not two, separate beings. Recognizing this problem, Clarke proposes that the inner being of God is affected by the world but not in such a way as to alter its perfection.[158] However, this seems merely to reinstate a false dichotomy, because surely the inner being of God is one with its perfections.

A second line of Thomist attack is that the rationalism of process theology fails to appreciate the fundamentally mystical orientation of Thomas. According to Burrell, Aquinas is not a classical theist in the Hartshornean sense of the term because Aquinas does not provide "descriptive propositions" about God. Rather, Aquinas follows the mystical route of the *via negativa*, which allows us nothing more than "to show what we cannot use our language to say" about God. Thomas's denial of *relatio realis* is a crucial instance of the *via negativa* showing what cannot be predicated of God, namely, that there is no necessity in God for creatures. Aquinas does not conceive of God as having any properties, characteristics, or attributes whatsoever. God is simply to-be and the to-be cannot be described or circumscribed.[159]

This criticism, however, overlooks certain important points made by members of the process camp.

It is Hartshorne's position that if human concepts must ultimately be denied of God, then too must such concepts as God's love, Creativity, will, causality and intelligence. Such simple denial is no way to arrive at the uniqueness or transcendence of God. For example, God's relationship to goodness is unique, but it does not consist in God's being simply nongood. God's relationship to time is special and unique, but it does not of necessity consist of God being outside of time or atemporal.[160] Unless we can say something positive and affirmative about God, then the whole notion of God becomes philosophically absurd and meaningless (as the positivists claim) as well as religiously sterile, for none can worship a huge, dark, apophatic void. Such knowledge of God is possible only because there is a genuine continuity between our existence and God's.

The problem Hartshorne has with Thomas's method of analogy is that it violates this continuity by shifting the meaning of terms when applied to God as compared to when those same terms are applied to humans. What we can understand of these terms applies only to ourselves, whereas what applies to God in the radical new usage we cannot understand. Consequently, God remains an empty, indeterminate abstraction.[161] Let us examine this contention in more detail.

Aquinas's theory of knowledge is realistic. In ordinary cases of knowing, it is the knower or subject who is really related to the object known, not vice versa. The object's relation to the subject is not real but logical, something purely external to the reality of the object. For example, the relation "on the right" is not applied to the column, unless it stands on the right side of the subject. This relation is then "not really in the column but in the animal." It is the subject that takes account of relations because of its superior subjectivity, its sensitive awareness.[162]

Presumably then in the relation (in the Spirit) that constitutes God's sensitive knowing of the world, it is God as subject who is really relative, whereas the world as object is nonrelative and absolute. If the known or object is the nonrelative element, then it would seem that God as omniscient is supremely relative. But Aquinas draws precisely the opposite conclusion: God's relationship to creatures is in him only by means of our way of thinking about him. God cannot be genuinely related to the world because that would make God essentially dependent upon the world.[163] It is the world as known that is related to God as its wholly absolute knower. Thus, there is nothing to prevent these names that import relation to the creature from being predicated of God temporally, not by reason of a change in Him, but by reason of the change in the creature, as a column is on the right of an animal without there being any change in itself but because of the change in the animal.[164] The problem is that although Aquinas assumes that there is a common analogical meaning of knowing in both cases, he has arbitrarily inverted the logical structure of the analogy, giving the subject (God) the status of the ordinary case of the object.[165] This means that God, supremely absolute, is in fact the most abstract and objective factor, or the least concrete and subjective one. The world is known by God, but it would be incorrect to assume that God knows the world because to know is to be in relation to.[166] Because God can be in no sense relative or temporal, God can be said to "know" or "love" the world only by contradicting the meaning of these terms as they apply to our experience; therefore, these claims for God become hollow and seem to lack authenticity, if we take seriously the notion that God is the affirmation, hence, the supreme exemplification of our humanity.

Pneumatologically, the problem is: Are there two separate and mutually exclusive levels or forms of knowledge or evaluative sensitivity, human and divine, or are such metaphors to be completely invalidated by maintaining that the Spirit is love without any analogue to the responsiveness, empathy, and deriving of value from the other that are essential dimensions of human love.[167]

All our experience suggests that knowing and loving constitute the nature of the knower or lover. Yet classical theism contends that God's knowledge and love are an enormous exception to this rule. Divine knowledge and love may make a real difference to the creature, but they make no difference to an essentially immutable, noncontingent deity. It is true that classical theism maintains that God in knowing and loving himself knows himself as creator of the world. But because God is not really related to the world in knowledge and love, it follows that God does not know or will us, his creatures.[168]

Hartshorne, however, admits that there is a genuine conceptual transcendence of God, that no simple, fool-proof affirmations can be made about God. The issue between process people and Thomists such as Burrell is not whether or not God transcends the world but where this transcendence lies. A major oversight on Burrell's part is his identification of the transcendence of God in Hartshorne with the abstract or absolute nature of God.[169]

This is incorrect, because Hartshorne's position is that the abstract or absolute nature of God can be known absolutely. The baffling mystery is the relational nature of God or God's radical sensitivity to and empathic participation in all things. Of this, creatures have a merely "infinitesimal" awareness.[170] Hartshorne writes:

> The concrete or actual individual is referred to by an indexical sign (Peirce) which points to, rather than describes, him. Description of any individual in its actuality always falls infinitely short of completeness and accuracy. A fortiori God transcends conceptualization.[171]

This marks an important affinity between process theology and mysticism. As noted in chapters 2 and 3, the *via negativa* of mysticism ultimately takes on a positive meaning because it places God's transcendence in the context of God's radical immanence. The mystery of God is not God's absoluteness or aloofness from the world but the fact that God is all things and therefore comparable to none.

A third line of objection on the part of Thomists has been that process theology falsely depicts the Thomistic God as a static, enclosed, metaphysical absolute. Hill states, for example, that the deepest meaning of the Trinity in Thomas is that the finite order exists only "in" God. In the creative act, understood Thomistically, "God empties himself out . . . making room 'within' for the non-divine."[172] That God and the world enjoy a mutual immanence is the fundamental theme of Thomas's participation metaphysic, for perfection as it exists in the creature is contained in God.[173] The divine power, according to Thomas, is extended to other things by the very fact it is the first efficient cause.[174] Thus, Clarke sees in the Thomistic concept of efficient causality a very rich sense of divine immanence. God is present in every creature as a concrete creative power.[175] He emphasizes that efficient causality establishes a "bond of community" between the effects and the cause. Since all the effects have come from the cause and since the cause imparts its reality into the effects as a gift, there is an ontological unity between cause and effect, creature and Creator. For Thomas, then, every act of efficient causality is self-communicative and self-expressive of the cause. God is in God's effects. In Thomas, "the world takes its origin from God as His self-expression."[176] It would appear, then, that for Thomas the universe is the incarnation of God. Thomas might be closer to process thought than one would suspect. Or is he?

These defenders overlook crucial instances where Thomas, like Augustine, is blocked by his monopolar prejudice from further developing these insights.

When Aquinas takes up the question of "God's existence in things," he emphasizes that God is not literally present in all things. Neither *ubiquitas* nor *immensitas* are used by him to signify God's immanence. Presence in a place can mean bodily contact (*circumscriptive*), as water in a bucket; it can also mean the interior quickening of a thing (*per informationem*), as the soul is related to the body, and operating in a definite place (*definitive*), as when a spirit operates at a certain spot. Because God is neither body nor soul, the first two usages do not apply to God. Because God's actions do not tie him down, the third does not apply either.[177] Thus, his claim that "God exists by presence in everything" has no real special significance. Rather, it means only that God's providence oversees everything. Strictly speaking, God is not in the world but in a unidimensional causal relationship with "outside things," said to be analogous to a prince ruling from afar.[178] Indeed, it is for Aquinas an utter impossibility for God to share and participate in the world; for then God would be a component of the world; but that is strictly ruled out, since then the world would qualify God.[179]

The immanence of all things in God is severely truncated by Thomas's concept of divine knowledge. Because God is the sole cause of all things and because in the knowledge of a cause its effects are known, God, merely in knowing God's own essence, knows whatever will be and therefore needs no further relationship to the actual reality of creation.[180] The universe contributes nothing to God's knowledge.

In process theory, however, to know a cause is to know only a range of possible results, because causes are always openended as to their effects. No matter how hard we may try to pre-image an event, the actual reality of the event always transcends the pre-imaging. Merely in knowing God's own essence, then, God would not know the actual world.[181]

Clarke concedes this point. He states that between God's knowledge of a creature as merely possible and the knowledge of it as actually existing there is in fact a new addition to God: the knowledge of the real act of the creature, which was not possible in the knowledge of it as merely possible.[182] Now, my point is that here Clarke has deviated radically from Thomas himself. In Thomas, there is no future, no novelty in God, because God is the changeless being from whom all creatures proceed.[183] As all creatures are merely unfoldings of powers or perfections that God already has, the conservation of energy, not creativity, is the key. Furthermore, Thomas is quite specific that God is without emotion, body, or parts, as these would subject God to change.[184]

This radical duality of God and the world in Thomas means that there is no explanation why either God or the world is present, or why there is a positive affinity, if there can be such, of one for the other, or how God can be truly present in a universe that is the complete and total negation of God's own being. Why should one wish to be united with something lacking any affinity or resemblance with anything truly human? Why should God wish to be united with anything so totally in conflict with anything truly God? Total heterogeneity allows of no true union.

Clarke thinks that his concept of the relational consciousness of God puts a human face on God and therefore permits a reconciliation between God and the world. God is "infinitely Higher" not "totally Other."[185] But unfortunately, Clarke is wrong. His concept of the "real inner being" of God as wholly simple and immaterial means that all the ontological similarity between God and creatures vanishes into thin air. Also, his concept of efficient causality is the subject of suspicion, at least in process circles. Whitehead understands causal efficacy or causal feeling as very deep bodily feeling, far beneath the veneer even of sensation. To associate causality with immateriality seriously jeopardizes the whole concept.

The problem with Clarke, as with Aquinas, is that we have a model of God based on an analogy to human consciousness but without any analogy to the human body. Now the oneness of mind and body, the fact they are inseparably bound together, compels us to seek for a better analogy. Process thought provides such a model precisely because it understands the universe as the body of God.

A fourth line of objection emanating from Thomists has been that the true Christian faith in God as Creator necessitates belief in the absolute beginning of the universe created out of nothing.[186] God is the sole source of all creative power. This concept of God, argues Clarke, has distinct advantages over that of Whitehead, because the latter keeps appealing to ultimates of an independent origin from the divine mind. God is not responsible for the primordial potentiality to be ordered. God is not responsible for the existence of the world. Nor is the world responsible for the existence of God.[187] Creation is the voluntary self-limitation of God's power whereby a share is given to each creature. God creates agents, but these agents are free to choose their own acts. For Thomas, every creature is *dominius sui* and therefore self-creative. Process thinkers, then, should not have the difficulty they do in reconciling the fact of a genuine autonomous power in creatures with the concept of creation out of nothing by the all-powerful God.[188]

This view, however, both omits and seriously distorts key aspects of process theory. It is true that God does not create or "think up" eternal objects (abstract possibilities) because they are eternal and therefore uncreated. But they have no existence whatsoever outside of or independent of the primordial mind of God, any more than imaginative ideas have any existence outside of the imagination (see chapter 1). God certainly does have the power to order them by means of God's primordial envisagement. This means that creativity has no reality exclusive of God because God is the sole source of all relevant novelty, by means of initial aims for occasions. It is true that the earlier Whitehead allowed creativity a reality exclusive of God, but that is not the case in *Process and Reality* (see chapter 1).

Another way in which God is the sole source of creativity is that only God is the synthesis of all feeling in the universe; only in God do the many become one; thus, only God can serve as the source of harmony or unification for creatures.

A large part of Clarke's difficulty with process thought stems from his insecurity over the process concept of causal efficacy. He is very attentive to certain process thinkers such as Ford and Sherburne, who seem to deny the efficient causality of entities by placing all causal efficacy in the birthing subject. This can create the impression that there is no causal connection among actual entities or between actual entities and God. Reality then disintegrates into a heap of unrelated monads. He is seeking to ensure the causal influx of God and is not quite sure this is readily available in process theory, although he does find it in Nobo and Suchocki.[189] My own analysis of Whitehead, as in chapter 1, compels me to agree with Suchocki. I can see no way the principle of relativity would have any meaning aside from the causal influx of the past. Furthermore, I understand *Process and Reality* as Whitehead's attempt to rescue the concept of causal efficacy or the transmission of emotive energy from past to present. This certainly is obvious in his polemic against Hume and Locke. It is true that Whitehead tends to imply that there is no cause-and-effect relationship between God and contemporary entities, because contemporary entities cannot prehend one another. Are God and God's own contemporaries in total isolation from one another? Does God know only the past and do entities then know only a God in the past? In chapter 1, I proposed the solution that the Holy Spirit, as the all-encompassing matrix of sensitivity, was the ground for all true community. This is based upon Hartshorne's contention that God as the chief exemplification of the principle of relativity is omnipresent, unlike all other entities, and therefore can directly prehend or experience entities *formaliter*, that is, as they exist in their subjective immediacy.[190] There is then an immediate influx of God into creatures and visa versa in the strongest sense of the term influx. This point was unfortunately omitted by Clarke and also by Hill.

At best, Clarke seems to propose a free will defense of God. Freedom itself is such a grand idea that God voluntarily limits God's own self to permit the creature's autonomy, but this defense fairs poorly. For one thing, it implies that God is holding back, not doing all that God can do. For another, one must ask whether freedom per se is such a noble idea.

Because it is in and through our freedom that we sin, perhaps it would have been better for God to have created a universe of perfect programmed robots. The loss of freedom would be a small price to pay for the abolition of all sin, suffering, evil. Some more astute defense of freedom is required other than saying it is a value in itself. This is accomplished through Whitehead's aesthetic (see my next chapter). Finally, process thought understands the distinction here between act and agent as a false dichotomy. What something is, is what it does (see chapter 1). If God creates the agent, then God also creates the acts of the agent. So, there is no real autonomy or freedom.

In process theory, God's relationship to creativity is no on-again, off-again matter, but exists from all eternity. It is the nature of God to be creative. Creativity is an essential dimension of God. God could not be God without being creative.

Thus, God's creativity cannot be confined to any one order of reality. That God has created eons of worlds before this one and eons after it simply means that God's creativity is on an unimaginatively larger scale than that permitted by the arbitrary dictates of church fathers who would unduly restrict God's creativity to the present order.

The fact that God has created before makes God no less an object suitable for veneration and worship. The fact that truly great artists do not create out of nothing but out of something preexistent does not render them any less creative, any less worthy of reverence. What value is affirmed in imagining God having refrained from creating until the beginning of this universe?

If God does not create, has not God done the worst possible thing, that is, let the divine creative power lie idle?[191]

5
Summary

In this chapter, I will show how process theology may help to solve some of the outstanding problems of contemporary pneumatology. I argue that process theology maintains the traditional emphasis on the omnipresence of divine love, while Whitehead's aesthetic includes affective connotations of "love" that were lost to traditional theories of God's relation to the world. As noted in the last chapter, traditional formulations have stressed the unchanging perfection of God at the cost of God's relationship to and interaction with creatures. Transcendence has been affirmed, to be sure, but at the expense of immanence; sovereignty has been exalted, but with the loss of presence. No sound pneumatology can treat immanence and presence so lightly. In contrast, process theology provides the conceptual resources to formulate God's relation to the world in a way that upholds the intimate interresponsiveness of God and creatures without losing sight of the fundamental differences that govern their relationship. This reformulation comes with a price of its own, of course: Spirit, in this view, is not impassible, but sensitive and even vulnerable to the contingencies of nature and history. In the pages that follow, I will show why this consequence is more to be welcomed than it might at first appear, and why it is worth the cost.

The following explication of these points will proceed from the general to the more specific. First, I shall outline some significant implications for the concept of Spirit that logically follow from the doctrine of God in process theology. Second, I will describe implications for the soul-God relationship that follow from the centrality of the human spirit or self-transcendency in process theology. These two sections are largely a summation of the preceding chapters; they are also preliminary to the final section, which will focus upon the concept of Spirit experience that follows from Whitehead's aesthetic.

God as Spirit

In this section I will focus on how process theology might resolve a serious ambiguity in classical pneumatology. On the one hand, Spirit is identified with God as a whole, that is, God is Spirit and holy. This was a major theme in the previous chapters. On the other hand, there has also been a traditionally Trinitarian concept of Spirit as a separate or distinct item or person within

God. That is to say, God as pure Spirit was traditionally assumed to be wholly simple and immutable. This is the extreme doctrine of transcendence, well represented by Aquinas' concepts of *immutabilitate Dei, Dei simplicitate.* (But how can such a radically transcendent God ever be truly immanent?)[1] In contrast, when faced with the problem of God's relationship to the world, classical thought introduced the complicated machinery of the Trinity, which allows for highly complex social relationships within an otherwise simple and nonrelative deity. The dilemma of classical pneumatology (especially in Augustine) was the yearning for an immutable yet essentially responsive God. We may resolve this tension if the Spirit is identified with the consequent nature of God.

It is Whitehead's contention that the concept of mutual immanence or real internal relations that is central to his philosophy of organism was presupposed by early Christian discussions of the Trinity in order to ensure the full and direct immanence of God in the World.[2] By this doctrine of mutual immanence among the members of the Trinity, "these early Christian theologians have the distinction of being the only thinkers who in a fundamental metaphysical doctrine have improved upon Plato."[3]

While Whitehead understands himself to be in accord with the basic intent of Trinitarian thought, his aesthetic vision of reality marks a significant modification of the latter. The notion of multiplicity or differentiation in God is founded on the doctrine of two natures whose mutual relations constitute one center of consciousness. This enables us to more clearly affirm that the divine reality present as Spirit is fully God, not a separate, subordinate or derivative aspect of God.

This was the intent of traditional Trinitarian thought. However, the problem is that the use of the term person, denoting as it does a separate and distinct entity, tended to undercut any sense of mutual immanence among members of the Trinity. It obscured the personal presence of God by implying that the Deity is an impersonal essence shared by three separate selves, or that one of the persons, the Father, as *principium* and *fons* of all the rest, is more truly God than the others, who are merely subordinates or lesser Gods sent down to earth. In classical thought, nothing must challenge the transcendental aloofness of the Father. He always remains at a distance, enthroned above and beyond us. He does not descend to earth and therefore does not suffer. For example, Calvin writes: "le Pere n'est pas descendu en terre, mais celuy estoit sorty de luy; il n'est pas mort, ne ressusscite, mais celuy qui avoit este par luy enyoue." (The Father did not descend to earth, but He who was sent by Him. He did not die, was not resurrected, but He who was sent by Him.)[4] One is also reminded of Aquinas's argument that the concept of a motion or movement of God toward ourselves can be applied only figuratively, not literally, to God, who remains enthroned on high.[5] Another problematic implication here is that the essence of the Deity is other than love. God is not revealed in the Trinity but is an impersonal essence hidden behind it. Indeed, theologians of the past made this point quite explicit in their distinctions between the "revealed will" in Christ and the "hidden will," which ultimately ruled the world. But the whole doctrine of incarnation and revelation insists that the one true God is revealed in Christ, who is then normative for God's *modus operandi* with the world. Christian faith affirms that Christ is God's decisive act, which expresses the ultimate truth about our life before God. We are created and redeemed by God's love, so that in God we realize our true humanity. God, then, is not the negation but the chief exemplification of our humanity. Now, I contend that the Trinitarian insistence upon three persons obscured this point by shifting the discussion from the way Christ is normative for the divine activity in the world to the way certain otherworldly concepts of divinity explicate Christ and in turn the Spirit, as was emphasized in the last chapter. This dilemma is well represented by the fact that, traditionally, Christology has had great difficulty achieving a balance between the human and the divine, often tending toward docetism. (For example, still popular in many circles is the ancient doctrine of *anhypostasia*, the theory that Christ had no distinct human personality.)[6] The difficulty of reconciling the human and the divine does not exist in process theology. It overcomes this dilemma by internally relating God to the universe. God is no disembodied Spirit entering the universe from without; rather, incarnation throughout the entire universe is essential for the very being of God. This is the special character of the incarnation as it is understood in process theology.

As noted in the last chapter, a social theory of the trinity has certain implications for process theology. According to Lowry, Augustine took the first step toward sociality in the trinity by contending that God is love, for love always demands another, an object to love.[7] Illingworth contends that if we are to think of God as personal, we must invoke some kind of plurality, for personality implies sociality. A solitary personality is a contradiction in terms.[8] The obvious implication here is that God and his creatures are mutually interdependent. However, certain theorists have failed to develop this point. Both Hodgson and Lowry champion the claim that the social theory of the trinity, which is seen in a rudimentary form in Augustine, enables us to see how God can be truly personal, without falling into the so-called error that the universe is necessary or contributory to God. Indeed the social model is said to be decisive in affirming that God is wholly independent of all creation and therefore in no way organic to it. Thus God obtains fulfillment through self-differentiation into a purely divine society of beings exclusive of all social intercourse with humankind.[9] Their interpretation seems to reflect the monopolar prejudice and is not necessitated by the concept of sociality within God. The advantage of process theology is that its concept of the mutual interdependence of God and the world overcomes this omission and therefore presents a viable alternative to the limited interpretation of these thinkers. The meaning of mutual reciprocity as applied to God is fully developed in process theology. For example, the bipolar deity enjoys relationships with itself that creatures do not. However, this internal complexity is neither transcendental aloofness nor remoteness from the world. Rather, it is the ground for all relevant novelty in the world and as well the ground of God's internal relationship to creation, as we shall see.

Bracken, in *The Triune Symbol: Persons, Processes and Community* and in several articles, has proposed a processive social theory of the Trinity to advance beyond the point where Hodgson and Lowry left off. The Trinity is a democratic society of three coequal persons (three psychological selves), each of which has unlimited empathic awareness of the other two. They experience no tension or contradiction among themselves and therefore constitute a perfect harmony.[10] The Father is identified with the primordial nature, for it is the Father who proposes the possibility best suited for their conjoint existence at any one given time. The Son is identified with the consequent nature; for it is he, who by saying yes to the Father's proposal, actualizes that particular possibility for all three persons. The Holy Spirit is identified with the superjective nature; it is he who is the "vivifying principle" of nature and therefore inspires or "prompts" the Father to offer a new possibility. Likewise, he prompts the Son to say yes to the proposal. His activity within creation is the same—he inspires or prompts each of the occasions to say yes to the Father's aim for it.[11]

Bracken's claim is that this personification of the three natures gives new-found impetus to the Christian affirmation of God in three persons. However, I find that it can create some severe problems within a process framework. Strictly speaking, the primordial nature in itself is not an actuality; rather, it is the necessary precondition for the concrete actuality that is God. Only in this sense can it be thought of as the Father/Mother/Source of all being. In chapter 2, I drew out parallels between this and the mystical concepts of the *Gotheit* or *Ungrund*, which denote a dynamic but unconscious, indeterminate source of all being. The mystical contribution to process Trinitarianism warns us not to collapse the Trinity into the concrete actuality of God. I will say more about this later.

The personification of the consequent nature as Christ seems to reduce it to being merely one person or nature among three. In Whitehead, it represents much more than this, because it is the concrete reality of God as a transcendent, all-inclusive subjectivity. The consequent nature is the concrete reality of the personal God, not merely a member or item in the Godhead, as Bracken would have it. Furthermore, Bracken's notion that Christ (the consequent nature) constitutes a subjectivity distinct from that of the Father (primordial nature) is simply not possible in Whitehead's model; for the consequent nature is the conscious state of awareness attained by the primordial nature. It is the primordial nature, the divine imagination, having become self-conscious. This point was developed in chapter 1, and in chapter 2, it was shown to have a distinct mystical pedigree.

This conception renders the Holy Spirit, identified with the superjective nature, entirely superfluous. There is clearly no need to introduce a third nature as the principle of unity or the prompter for the togetherness of these two. Whitehead did not have a three fold nature of God in mind. He made only one reference to the superjective nature,[12] and in the context of the last pages of *Process and Reality*, it appears redundant with the causal efficacy or objectification of the consequent nature in the world.[13]

Bracken seems to have confused Christ, in whom God was present, with the total reality of God's incarnation. He stands in tension with process Christology, which emphasizes a richer, more radical sense of presence than that allowed by his Christocentric bias. The Christ event is a special case, a rising into consciousness, of the all-pervasive incarnation of God throughout all of the universe. As such, this incarnation transcends the Christ event or any other particular event. Pittenger, for example, in updating his *Christology Reconsidered*, recently observed that Jesus is a way of focusing upon the way in which God is present and active everywhere and always.[14] The Christ event always points beyond its own parameters, back to a subconscious prereflective awareness of God in all persons and things. In *The Divine Triunity*, he speaks strongly against the "christological error" and the "uncharitable imperialism" of Christians who fail to recognize the fact of God's massive presence apart from the specific instance of Jesus.[15] I believe that the term Spirit is the best one to designate this all-pervasive immanence because it denotes a deep, subliminal source of divine inspiration, unity and empathic responsiveness.

Bracken himself admits serious ambivalence as to the strict consistency of his process orientation. He notes that it stands in tension with Whitehead's explicit statements that every subjectivity (every actual entity in concrescence) is a distinct actuality. He also refers to Ford's claim that "any doctrine suggesting three subjectivities within the Godhead automatically degenerates into tritheism."[16]

Bracken's solution is that Whitehead should be radically reinterpreted to include the possibility that a Whiteheadian nexus or society is a fundamental reality and therefore can exercise a corporate agency that transcends its constituent subjectivities.[17]

But, in fact, does Whitehead make such a sharp distinction between nexus and actuality in the first place, such that Bracken is justified in claiming to be a making a significant reinterpretation of Whitehead?

I share Wallack's interpretation of Whitehead to the effect that an actual entity is simply any concrete existent whatsoever. Because a nexus is really a togetherness, it is also an actual entity in the Whiteheadian cosmology. It is a set of actual entities constituting another actual entity. Since every entity is itself a composite of other entities, it is also in the Whiteheadian perspective a nexus.[18]

Bracken emphasizes that the divine society does not exist apart from but not in and through the interaction of its members.[19] This appears identical with Whitehead's claim for the concrescing process as exemplified in The Category of Freedom and Determination, which states that the unified whole, although it enjoys an autonomy of its own, always arises out of the decisions and determination of its parts.[20] Bracken's denial that the divine society is a "super-entity" or "super-individual" is puzzling.[21] Is it his intention to claim that the unity that is God is merely an impersonal essence, devoid of its own unique subjectivity? Has he reduced the unity of God to mere unanimity, a kind of collective spirit analogous to the unity attained by the cells of our body when we are asleep? If so, how can we speak of a truly personal God? Is he not in violation of the principle of relativity? This principle calls for God to be the subjective synthesis of all feeling. Thus, there must be a synthesis of the feelings of the Three Persons, which would constitute a more ultimate reality over them. Bracken, then, should have proposed a Fourth Person, a metapersonality that is the synthesis of the other Three and to which these Three are subordinate.

Unlike Bracken, I am not interested in formulating distinctions in God solely to conform to principles of traditional Trinitarian thought. There is no need to posit separate persons in God and no need of a doctrine of Spirit separate from a doctrine of God. Nevertheless, process theology parallels Trinitarian thought in the sense that God is understood as a complex synthesis of contrasting elements. God as one does not deny the rich inner complexity of God, as we shall see below. In this way, process theology may place stronger emphasis upon the Trinitarian concept of a plurality of distinctions within God than did the dualistic concepts of God, by which the divine immutability was ensured by the utter simplicity of God.[22]

Whitehead, however, does speak of God's relationship to the world in terms of "a threefold creative act composed of (i) the one infinite conceptual realization, (ii) the multiple solidarity of free physical realizations in the temporal world, (iii) the ultimate unity of actual fact with the primordial conceptual fact."[23] In other words, there is first God's primordial appetition to become, to actualize the infinite wealth of abstract potentiality; second, the incarnation of God in the universe through the physical actualization of some of these possibilities; third, the concrescence or harmonization of the divine experience of actual fact with that of potentiality. This latter is the consequent nature of God, that is, God as concrete, actual and real.

Process thinkers such as Ford and Cobb believe that this threefold distinction correlates with the Father, the Logos, and the Spirit of Trinitarian belief. The Father signifies the primordial ordering or envisagement of all possibilities. The Logos signifies the temporal objectifications of the primordial nature; it is God entering into finite reality; it is God present as the initial aims for occasions. The Holy Spirit or consequent nature signifies God's intimate responsiveness to creation, that is, God as the supreme effect.[24]

However, this distinction between Logos and Spirit proves to be artificial. It tends to imply that God is present merely as an aim rather than in a more concrete way. The principle of relativity, however, calls for the concrete reality of God as an experiencing subject to be present in every occasion. All entities feel the subjective feelings of the datum occasion, so there is a flow of God's own subjective feelings or consequent experience into every occasion. Because God is the chief exemplification of relativity, this flow is not indirect, as it is in the case of other entities, but it manifests the full, warm, subjective immediacy of God's own feeling.

In Whitehead's aesthetic vision of reality, an actual entity is a complex synthesis and therefore not fully analyzable into its components. Actual entities are actual by virtue of the integration or interweaving of their physical pole (physical feelings or prehensions of actual fact) and their mental pole (mental or conceptual feelings, prehensions or proximate novelty). Taken alone, then, either pole is less than the actual thing. Thus, God as an actual entity functions as an organic whole in the world, not as two separate poles or natures that stand external to one another, one doing one thing, one another. As noted in chapter 1, the consequent nature is rooted in the primordial nature. In my view, Spirit is identifiable with the unitive experience of God, because the latter signifies God as present and efficacious in the world. The Spirit is not a separate aspect of God alongside others; rather, it is the synthesis of physical and conceptual feelings by virtue of which God is actual. In this view, Spirit is the union of supreme actuality with supreme potentiality. The relationship of Spirit to God is analogous to the relationship of my thoughts and feelings to myself. God is the unity of God's thinking and feeling, just as I am the unity of my thoughts and feelings. These have no existence apart from God, just as I do not first exist and then begin to think and feel. The meaning of the unity or interaction of these aspects of God can be stated more fully in the following analysis. This conception can be reduced to a kind of binitarian concept of deity. Roughly speaking, in highly pictorial terms, we might conceive of God as a circle without distinct boundaries, open at the periphery. Certain mystical conceptions of God call for such a notion, as we noted in chapters 2 and 3. Schelling, for example, speaks of God as "the out-flowing, out-spreading, self-giving" and as "selfhood, of return unto self, of being-in-itself."[25] These highly poetic terms are given sharper analytical meaning in process theology.

On the one hand, the problem is the reconciliation of permanency with flux. The completion or actualization of God occurs by the derivation of the consequent nature from the world. There is also the completion or salvation of the fluent temporal world as it acquires everlastingness in the consequent nature, and also as God floods back into the world as a new lure.[26] In God, permanence is primordial, flux is derived from the world. In the world, flux is primordial, permanence derives from passage into God. God, then, is one and many; the world is one and many. God is one because God is the "primordial unity of relevance of the many potential forms." God is many because in the process of self-actualization, God acquires a multiplicity through experiencing the multiplicity of finite actual entities. God is both one and many because the divine experience receives or absorbs the multitude of the world into the harmonization of God's own self-actualization.[27]

This conception resolves the tension between traditional Trinitarian thought, which claimed an inner complexity or diversity of elements within the deity, and the classical doctrine of the utter simplicity of God. This resolution becomes possible only by relating God to the world. Such double predication is not contradictory, provided that it refers to different aspects of God. God is many in the sense that there is a diversity or multiplicity of factors within God. God is one, is sheer simplicity, in the sense that this multitude is a concrescent unity of experience.

On the other hand, the problem is also the relationship of actuality to potentiality. This area of controversy brings out a most crucial difference between process theology and classical theism. The latter, to stress the radical transcendence or aloofness of God from the world, depicted God as an *actus purus*, the actualization of all possible perfections. For example, the central theme in Aquinas is that God must be denied the imperfection of potentiality. Aquinas is quite specific that "since God is infinite, comprehending in Himself the plenitude of perfection of all being, He cannot acquire anything new."[28] In sharp contrast, Whitehead speaks of the primordial nature of God, which is pure, abstract potentiality yet to be realized. The actuality of God resides in the fact that the consequent nature makes determinate certain of these abstract possibilities or conceptual feelings to specific actualities in the world. God's actuality resides in the synthesis of physical and conceptual feelings, in the harmony of the primordial nature and the consequent nature. Thus, in process theology Spirit denotes the unitive experience of God. But, unlike creatures, there is in God a residual of pure conceptual feelings, feelings of potentials or eternal objects "with the definite extrusion of any particular realization."[29] Spirit, then, is God, yet it is also an item in the complexity of God. The latter consists of the fact that God as actual is not a full description of God, for God is also pure potentiality yet to be made determinate.

Both of these problems are dealt with in the "Law of Polarity," which also serves to emphasize that this dipolar model of God represents aesthetic ideals. This law states that two seemingly irreconcilables are in fact reconcilable into a harmonious unity. What traditionally appeared to be ultimate contraries or dichotomies, like static-dynamic, necessary-contingent, being-becoming, are in fact mutually interdependent elements. According to Whitehead, "opposed elements stand to each other in mutual requirement."[30] Nothing real, including God, can be described with reference to only one pole. Classical theism and also mystical pantheism erred in attributing only one side of the polarity to God. This is the monopolar prejudice, mentioned earlier. I shall present a viable alternative based upon two points of Hartshorne's analysis. First, neither pole in the various sets of contraries is intelligible without the other. It is a sad mistake to deprecate the contingent and temporal to a status unworthy of God. Rather, these serve to emphasize God's sensitivity or loving responsiveness to the world. If God truly loves the world, certainly God must be deeply affected by it. Moreoever, love is essentially empathy, sharing in the experience of others. As finite creatures we empathize, but only imperfectly. God, however, enjoys a full and complete empathy with all actualities. Thus, God as the chief exemplification or "categorical ultimate" of relativity transcends the world just as decisively as the traditional notion of God's absoluteness: The actualities of the world are absorbed with such adequacy and completeness into God that the significance of all things is fully appreciated and preserved forever *in God*.[31] (I underscore *in God*, since God is bifurcated into two natures only for purposes of analysis.) The Spirit as the divine relativity denotes the perfection of God, because the divine experience is enriched to the extent that God maximizes relationships to other creatures. God does not respond merely to the "bare facts" but enjoys a real internal relatedness to all things. In a sense, this is God as absolute. That God is ever-changing, ever-enriched by the world is an eternal fact without beginning or end. It is, as Ogden has observed, "the absolute ground" of all relationships.[32]

This conception gives a new-found emphasis to the biblical notion of Spirit as represented in the phrase: "And God saw that it was good" (Genesis 1:10). As an alternative to Augustine's interpretation (noted in chapter 4), I suggest that the value of things is not due to God's arbitrary acts but to something intrinsic in things. This is a concept of value arising through reciprocity and interaction. Everything has intrinsic value because everything has extrinsic value, that is, contributes to the enrichment of another. Thus both creatures and God are cocreators of value, a point to be explicated in the next section.

Hartshorne, however, uses a slightly different terminology in speaking of the two poles or natures of God. There is the absolute nature of God, which is unchanging, eternal, unconditioned. (Note, then, that process theology does not neglect the importance of divine absoluteness or immutability.) This absolute nature, like the primordial nature, signifies God's abstract identity and moral fiber. It denotes the characteristics of God's action at every moment in every situation. For example, God is always omniscient, loving, appreciative. It is also God's fundamental aim, which is to promote the creatures' enjoyment of life. (Again note the concept of value arising through interaction.) There is also a relative nature of God or God as concrete actuality. In this sense, God is temporal, relative and contingent. Each pole requires the other for completion, as was the case with Whitehead's model. For example, although God is always omniscient and therefore knows all actualities, God's knowledge of the world is dependent upon the world and is therefore ever-changing. This ensures that God is truly relevant to the world. Hartshorne's dipolar concept of God has much the same meaning for pneumatology as does Whitehead's: The togetherness of creativity and sympathetic responsiveness is the essential defining characteristic of the Spirit.

Spirit, then, is essentially the presence of what Cobb and Griffin define as creative-responsive love. This makes clearer the transcendent-immanent character of Spirit. Transcendence and immanence are not exclusive but complementary categories. The primordial nature is creative love. It is "the active entertainment of all ideas, with the urge to their finite realization, each in its due season."[33] In chapter 1, I argued that it is the lure towards novelty in the universe, stimulating all creatures to actualize new possibilities to enrich their enjoyment. It is, therefore, immanent as an initial aim, the principle of unrest. This creative purpose is always loving, because it seeks to promote the creatures' enriched experience or enjoyment of the world. Thus the primordial nature is in an important sense divine agape.

The primordial nature, however, cannot function alone. God's creative purpose is not based upon an inflexible vision. Although they are in a sense distinct, the two natures are inseparable. Apart from the consequent nature, pure potentiality would have no real relevance, "for effective relevance requires agency of comparison, and agency belongs exclusively to actual occasions."[34] Creativity and sensitivity are inseparable in God. God's creative activity in the world is based upon empathic responsiveness (agape at its best), and this responsiveness is always in light of an intended creative influence to lure the world to higher forms of realization.[35] Thus, a more "active" meaning can be given to God's love than is sometimes the case in process literature. For example, Ogden argues that God is love in that God can perfectly sympathize with or participate in the being of creatures.[36] Now, his emphasis appears to be totally upon God's receptivity, that is, upon God as redeemer. However, God's love also has a creative, active dimension, since it provides initial aims for occasions. This is God's active "good will" toward creatures. God's love is not only a full appreciation and empathic understanding of creatures but also an active influence upon them.[37]

In this, Whitehead evidences a strong parallel with the mystical tradition. The Spirit, God's consequent nature, signifies a process in God whereby God completes "the deficiency of his mere conceptual actuality," a process whereby God's infinity acquires realization.[38] According to Whitehead, "abstract possibility and unlimited creativity can produce nothing."[39] Now, the mystical tradition, especially German speculative mysticism, has argued that the divine nothing or absolute of negative theology cannot be the Creator of the world. This is central in Eckhart's doctrine of the *Gottheit* and in Boehme's doctrine of the *Ungrund*, as was noted in chapter 2. Out of the divine nothing or *Gottheit* or *Ungrund*, God the creator as living personality is born. The creation of the world by God the creator is a secondary act rooted in the appetition of the nothing or *Ungrund* to become something.

Because God is fully present in these two interrelated ways, as creator and as responder, life in the Spirit is not world-flight but the fullest possible actualization of our capacities for creaturely existence. Because God is responsive, God always acts in and through creatures. Indeed, to be effective, relevant, the initial aim must be conditioned by the feelings of others. This gives renewed emphasis to the biblical concept of God's acts in history. Furthermore, life in the Spirit means more than merely acting in harmony with or in obedience to the will of God. Because God is not beyond or exclusive of the world but is its receptacle, we are in direct contact with God, hence capable of entering into a mutual relationship with God. This point is central to the mystical tradition, for mystical knowledge of God is not an affair of abstract speculation but of going into the world and directly experiencing God as present and active.

Accordingly, there are serious implications here for our concept of love. Process theology can call upon a more accessible notion of divine love than can classical theists like Aquinas. Because God serves as an ideal model (see Matthew 5:48), the monopolar prejudice of classical theism by which Spirit is depicted as an impassive absolute in our lives tended to promote a harsh, cold notion of love as purely active good will minus any degree of empathic sensitivity. Classical theism saw the Spirit as a purely creative influence, totally unmoved by the world. In Anselm and also in Aquinas (ST,1,21), God's love is argued to be purely creative, minus any degree of sympathetic compassion. Indeed, in Aquinas, God is a "cold" deity totally void of all emotion. He argues that the great emotions Scripture attributes to God must be taken figuratively, not literally.[40] In *Agape and Eros*, Nygren is quite explicit is asserting that the true Christian love is purely unmotivated, outgoing, having nothing whatsoever to do with the intrinsic value or the sympathetic appreciation of the loved one.[41] My point is that this is precisely why "charity" and "do-gooder" have become words of reproach. It is not that we should fault people for wanting to do good; but too often the "do-gooders" impose their own will upon others without communicating any real degree of affection for or sensitivity to the other. The concept of Spirit as creative-responsive love is an attempt to correct for this onesided conception of love. According to the law of polarity, if there is an impassibility or absoluteness that is admirable, there is also a relativity or receptivity that is equally admirable. Neither has any meaning without the other. For example, certainly we would not admire a God who observed impassively from without, who remained in absolute bliss while creatures were in great agony. Indeed, we know from our own experience of love that it entails in the fullest sense a sympathetic responsiveness to our loved ones. Our moods are in part a reflection of theirs. We feel their feelings, hurt with their pains, rejoice in their joys.[42]

There is also the question whether or not the monopolar concept of love is congruent with Scripture. Certainly, Anselm recognized that there was a serious tension between this concept and the biblical emphasis upon God's great compassion. While it is not my purpose to deal in detail with the biblical concept of Spirit, nevertheless it is helpful to provide a brief sketch of certain biblical themes to which a process pneumatology may give renewed emphasis. In no simple, convincing way does the Bible affirm monopolarity; many passages imply a dipolar concept of God. For example, if one objects that the highly anthropomorphic images of God in Scripture, by which great feeling and compassion are attributed to God, are merely a concession to our weak intellects and have nothing to do with the divine reality itself, then the objector is challenged to show what possible meaning and utility, philosophically and religiously, these images would then have. At the very least, it would appear to be the intent of the biblical writers to affirm that God is intimately related to historical events. Moreover, because in our humanity we are created in the image of God, we are creatures with whom God can communicate. Indeed, the divinity of Christ is revealed not outside of but through his humanity.

Thus, the ontological dualism of the human and the divine is swept away. Over and over again in scripture (for instance, Psalm 8) Spirit appears as the feminine affirmation and glorification of our humanity. We are made in the image of God; so, even though we are small, God takes us seriously. God always works with us in and through our humanity. The saving act comes through a human being. The innate goodness of creation and the fact of the incarnation demonstrate that matter is not to be rejected or devaluated as an antispiritual principle. Temporality, mutability, and materiality are not antithetical to God. Indeed the ancient Hebrews knew of no immaterial being or Spirit. Mind- or spirit-stuff as opposed to body-stuff are later Hellenistic concepts that are not part of ancient Judaic thought.[43] Persons are seen in a nondualistic light as animated bodies or psychosomatic unities, as represented by the claim that *nephesh* or soul is in the blood.[44] The visionary experiences of God as reported in the Old Testament suggest that the Hebrews thought of the deity itself as embodied (see Exodus 33:17; Ezekiel 1:26–27). The prohibition against idols or images of the deity is not an obvious rejection of the universe as God's body, as classical theism falsely assumed.[45] If the entire universe is the body of God (as argued in chapter 1), then it is unlikely that any representation would be anything other than a gross oversimplification or caricature of it. It is highly problematic how one could image the entire universe. If, for example, the cells of our bodies could see a few of the cells around them, still they would be unable to see the whole physical person to which they belong.[46]

Yahweh is not an impersonal force, but rather is characterized by dynamic personal qualities: The voice from the whirlwind that awed Job; the God who is momentarily angry and can even change his mind, "repenting himself" (Genesis 6:6). Yahweh is not quiescent and detached but deeply involved in the politico-social world. Yahweh is not a static Being but a Doer.[47] H. W.

Wolff has observed that "the appropriate expression for history in the prophetic books is, therefore, 'the work of Yahweh.' "[48] Yahweh feels, knows, wills and acts in the here and now:

"Am I a God near at hand and not a God far off? Can any hide in secret places that I cannot see him? Do I not fill heaven and earth? It is the oracle of Yahweh." (Jeremiah 23:23, 24)

All these biblical descriptions of God as conscious and perceptive at least imply divine passivity, for only a deficient perception of others can remain indifferent and serene.[49] Yahweh is righteousness in action, but this righteousness can be realized only through human behavior. Thus, God's personal presence was discerned in the choices and decisions a person must make in order to be a responsible human being. According to von Rad, "men . . . have become persons because God has addressed them, and they had to make a decision in his presence. This was something new in Israel."[50] As we shall see, this concept of decision making is very analogous to the function of the initial aim in the concrescing moment.

The prophetic encounter with God's presence evidences items central to Whitehead's concept of aesthetic experience, as described in the following section. Intensity of feeling through inner unification appears to be the distinctive theme of the prophetic experience of God. Possession by the Spirit marks an intensity and exaltation intimately related to the concentration of the mystic and the artist. For example, of mystical ecstasy, Rufus Jones writes that "when the powers of the mind are fused and unified, overbrimmed and revitalized by intense concentration, the whole interior self becomes an immensely heightened organ of spiritual apprehension in correspondence with the real world to which it belongs."[51] Mowinckel sees that kind of apprehension as a factor in prophetic experience. He observes that "it is quite clear that the prophets speak and act in a state of mental high tension . . . (in which) the ideas, thoughts, etc., which in one way or another have been created in a person will rise above the threshold of consciousness, and in a flash attain sudden clarity."[52] Indeed, the prophets were neither theologians nor metaphysicians; God was something concrete to them, the subject of a direct personal encounter, not the object of abstract thought or reasoning. According to Deuteronomy 8:5–18, the true prophet is personified by Moses with whom God spoke "mouth to mouth, plainly and not in riddles" (Numbers 12:7–8). Thus for prophets the divine encounter is a reciprocal relationship, "as a man speaks to his friend" (Exodus 33:11; Jeremiah 23:18, 22). The reciprocity of this relationship is highlighted by the fact that the intensity of feeling may alter the operation of Yahweh's will, so that he changes his mind at the prophet's intercession (as in Amos 7:1; Hosea 11:8, 9.) Malachi 3:5–7 is understood by some process thinkers to be a typical example of a biblical passage that appears to be monopolar but in reality denies this principle. God persists in certain attitudes ("I, the Lord, change not") and, in this consistency, does not change. But rather than affirming divine immutability, the passage speaks of divine change. "Return to me, that I might return to you" implies that if we change in a certain direction, God will change in an appropriate way. In process theology, God is not deflected from a commitment to seek the greatest beauty in all situations (primordial nature), but to promote the greatest beauty, God must be informed by the feelings of others.[53] The question, then, is whether or not the many biblical passages that seem to assert the otherness of God from temporality and mutability occur in the context of a genuine metaphysical discussion of the nature of God. Hartshorne and Reese, for example, argue that on the contrary the context of these biblical passages is generally a discussion of a specific form of mutability, namely a vacillation of purpose or lack of adherence to a resolution once formed.[54] It is also to be noted that in my process pneumatology, the Spirit always expresses a certain fixity of God's character (primordial nature, absolute nature). Because God is always loving and cannot help but love, God's actions in the world cannot fail to express love. Thus, there is also a relative notion of God implied here—God as deeply involved with the world, not aloof from it. God loves, so God cannot help but be deeply involved. God can feel, can be hurt. Here the Christian affirmation of a suffering savior achieves technical metaphysical expression.[55]

The Holy Spirit and the Human Spirit

Mysticism centers upon a strong affirmation of the human spirit, of our higher side or the so-called apex of the soul. However, the problem is that this conception tends to confound the human spirit with the Holy Spirit and thereby equate the soul with the very essence of God. (This is especially the case in Eckhart.) Ecstatic unity was generally assumed to be an infusion of the divine nature into the human soul. This meant a complete and total surrender to the controlling domination of God, until the mystic is purged of all humanity. Moreover, the pantheistic side of mysticism fails to do justice to creativity. As all is an emanation of God, there can be no creativity, novelty or accidents; for all is merely the unfolding of another form. The conservation of energy, not creative elan, is the key. Accordingly, there is no freedom in the world.

On the other hand, classical theism tended to deny the reality of the human spirit. Classical theism creates a need or appetite for a sense of divine presence, then quickly frustrates it by overemphasizing God's radical transcendence at the price of his immanence. (This was a logical consequence of the spirit-matter dualism, which emphasized the absolute ontological gulf between God and the world and therefore failed to integrate the human and the divine.) For example, Augustine speaks of a human spirit or an unspoiled capacity for self-transcendence in human beings by which we may attain to God.[56] Yet, in his doctrine of *infirmitas humana*, or original sin, he is quite specific that the mystical quest for the vision of God is the "sin of sins," a vain, prideful attempt at self-salvation.[57] No one, not even Moses, ever saw God face to face.[58] God is never to be apprehended directly.[59] Also, Luther evidences a similar inconsistency. On one hand, he describes the human spirit as "the highest, deepest, noblest part of man, by which he is able to grasp eternal things." On the other, in his *Smaller Catechism*, he denies this spirit—"I believe by my own reason and power I cannot believe or come to Jesus Christ."[60]

Though classical theism explicitly denied determinism, I contend that doctrines such as original sin, predestination and the divine immutability all assert that human freedom is merely apparent. The concept of divine omnipotence meant that God must determine every detail of the world and must be wholly noncontingent and independent of the world, lest something happen that was not known or willed by God. Power as controling domination was the essential definition of the Spirit. This concept reflected the ancient oriental attitude toward the absolute potentate projected to infinity. It is the human adoration of power writ large. God's will alone is sovereign and all-determining; He has total dominion over all creatures, to do by them, for them, and upon them whatsoever He pleases. Before Him, even the mighty, who serve solely at His pleasure, must tremble and abase themselves. Nothing is uncertain to Him, for He is wholly immutable, independent, active.

As a representative example to support my claim, I turn to certain aspects of Calvin's thought. In more than one passage, Calvin emphasizes that God must not be thought of as a tyrant.[61] Calvin asserts freedom in that he puts forth a strong sense of personal moral responsibility and sin. However, Calvin also assumed that God's sovereign control over creation includes each and every event right down to the smallest detail. Because there are no exceptions to this sovereign control, the problem of free choices arises. Calvin unsuccessfully attempts to resolve this dilemma by arguing that we do in fact make free choices, even though God has predetermined what choices will be made. But if God makes all our choices for us, how can we be responsible? How can there be genuine freedom if God predetermines all that shall transpire in our freedom? We are said to sin inevitably and by necessity, yet freely.[62] Sin is by definition against the will of God, yet by predestination nothing can happen against God's will. Calvin then posits two wills of God. When we sin we go against God's will, yet support God's secret or hidden will.

The Spirit, or God's will power, is said to be the "absolute" power of God by which he executes all his decrees.[63] God is the supreme cause, never the effect. Indeed Calvin is quite specific that the will of God is not subject to any causal influences, that the cause of the will does not appear outside of itself.[64] It is the cause of all things and therefore cannot be preceded by any cause.[65] The "secret counsel" of God, by which all things are deposed, depends upon nothing other than itself.[66] It is difficult to see how God's will is anything other than purely arbitrary. Calvin himself claims that since we cannot search for any cause of God's will outside of itself, we can give no reason for God's election.[67] If then we asked why God did such and such, the only answer is that God wished it. If we continue and ask further why God wished it, the reply is that no answer can be given. The secret will of God exceeds all human understanding, and furthermore, God is not accountable to us to render reasons for what he does.[68] Everything depends upon and has no rationale other than God's own good pleasure, which is exclusive of any obligation on God's part toward us.[69]

In other words, there is no cause for election, because that would violate the absolute gratuity of election. Rather, election occurs according to the eternal decree of God's will, which is purely self-determining. Calvin admits that this is tantamount to claiming that God thinks only of himself, for God thinks of nothing outside of or beyond himself in making his decisions.[70] Whatever happens is the will of God, and nothing can happen save that God wills it. The will of God, then, is defined as the necessity and inevitability of all things.[71] Things have absolutely no power in their own right, for God governs such that nothing happens save that it was determined by his secret will.[72]

One problem here is that empirically we know of no things that have no power of their own. To be actual is to have some degree of power. Therefore, God cannot be all-powerful. Furthermore, in this thorough-going determinism, the possibilities of freedom, creativity and spontaneity in things is strictly ruled out. The universe appears very unappetizing in this regard. It is intrinsically static, inert, dead. Indeed, Calvin argues that beauty is essentially the admiration of the fixity of the universe, governed by the immutable laws of God.[73] God created the world in an instant, and complete and perfect, so that it is sinful pride for human beings to imagine that through their efforts any further beauty can be actualized in the world.[74]

A greater problem is that evil does in fact appear to be the will of God. Since nothing happens save that God ordains it, then logically evil is part of the eternal decree of God. For example, Calvin is quite clear that God did not merely foresee or permit the Fall but ordained it; for God would not foresee things save that His almighty will predetermined that they should occur. Though the reason for the Fall eludes us, it cannot be denied that God predetermined to what end man must come.[75] Elsewhere, in attacking the concept that things happen by chance, he specifically contends that God is the author of evil misdeeds and criminal activities. He provides the illustration of a helpless man whose throat is cut by robbers, and he claims that this tragedy did not happen by chance but was foreseen and ordained by the secret will of God.[76] Larceny, murder and other such evil deeds are all said to be the instruments of God's providence.[77]

Calvin provides no real solution to the problem of theodicy. If anything, he tries to deny that there is such a problem in the first place. Why, for example, did God predestine there to be reprobates? In answer, he refers to Romans 9:20—the pots must not complain or talk back to the potter.[78] Calvin also claims that evil is only apparent. All works for the best, because whatsoever God ordains is just and fair. There is no cause for complaint. Moreover, like Augustine, Calvin stresses that evil is necessary to serve the purposes of God's own self-aggrandizement through the exaltation of His almighty power.[79] Interestingly enough, there is here an implicit appeal to God as contingent; for a truly perfect and supreme being does not need greater glory.

Whitehead argues that in the traditional and pervasive concept of divine immanence, God's influence is mistakenly understood as the "supreme agency of divine compulsion."[80] God traditionally appears as "the archetype of the dominant, inflexible, unemotional, completely independent (read 'strong' male)."[81] However, it would be a mistake to assume that this "masculine" image of God is completely insensitive to aesthetic ideals. Whitehead himself notes that one can take great joy in the creative energies of a supreme ruler, in the glorification of magnificent and barbaric power (see Psalm 24). Such joy might be interpreted as an affirmation of the Spirit as the bearer of the past, for example, a people choosing what it wants from its past, keeping traditions alive. This is central to aesthetic experience in the Whiteheadian sense of the term. Nevertheless, a serious problem arises: Whitehead recognized that this worship of power, this thrill we get from dominating others, is the difficulty haunting the modern world.[82]

The world has learned much since the days of the absolute monarchs. Through the centuries there has been gained a hard-won intuition that there is another, better concept of ruling power in which the personal dignity of the governed is protected and in which rulers interact with the governed, limited by the intrinsic rights of the latter.[83] Humankind has had enough of despotic rulers in history not to warrant a supreme despot in the Spirit. In the last two centuries there has been an enormous shift, promoting the value of freedom over the value of order. It is unlikely, then, that we can return to the traditional concept of divine omnipotence. Some have argued that the solution is to affirm that we are totally free yet totally determined. Others have denied causality. The relevance of process pneumatology is that it offers an effective alternative whereby we can speak of both freedom and causality without contradiction. Here Whitehead's deep appreciation of Christ is paramount. He understands Christ as the supreme revelation of God's agency in the world as persuasive power.[84]

Process theology strives to reconcile the human spirit with the Holy Spirit, or one could say divine immanence with the concept of ourselves as free creators. While all persons, indeed all entities, have the power to shape their own destinies and to realize a full and ideal selfhood, the fulfillment of this creative potential is grounded in the presence of God's creative-responsive or persuasive love. Thus, as Come has emphasized, the Holy Spirit is not a

miraculous supernatural energy overwhelming and filling up persons. That
would depersonalize and dehumanize our relations with God, for our human
condition would then not be rooted in God. In contrast, Spirit denotes the
fullest expression of the potentials for creaturely existence. As the supreme
organ of all relevant novelty, God opens up the future by luring us beyond
the tyranny of the given. Thus, Spirit is the key to understanding how the
world is stimulated to actualize those possibilities relevant to it. To Whitehead,
God is no mere element in an abstract scheme, but a concrete presence in the
dynamism of life and growth. The mutual immanence between God and the
world means that we are no longer forced to choose between the dignity of
the human spirit and the Holy Spirit. All creatures are responsible co-creators
of the universe.[85] In other words, we, as constituents of a dynamic, relativistic
universe, are part of the vast drama of creative advance that involves ourselves
and much more. However, God is not the sole lure for novelty. We are all
lures to one another, so that we are caught up in competing lures. This point
is analogous to that of theologians such as Moltmann: Unless we define
ourselves in terms of God, we absolutize some aspect of present reality (we
actualize lures other than God's). Everything is cut short, tied down, and so
we stagnate.[86] For example, human beings tend to divide themselves against
one another by defining themselves exclusively in terms of nation, race or class.
God's love, however, transcends these narrow definitions; it takes hold of
persons who are black or white, Jew or Gentile; all are one in their misery.[87]

God governs persuasively, not coercively, because God's role is to initiate
the process of self-creation. Because each entity creates itself by the realization
of an aim, this aim must be initially established by God; otherwise there would
be no self-creation, since by the ontological principle nothing can come from
nothing. Thus, God must initially define what is best for the situation. As
the principle of concretion, God's role "lies in the patient operation of the . . .
rationality of his conceptual harmonization."[88] God is "the ideal harmony,"[89] "the measure of the aesthetic consistency of the world."[90] Spirit
as creative-responsive love might be thought of as serving the purposes of
providing an effective role model (the image of God). The goal of all creatures,
the aesthetic quest for beauty (for depth and breadth of feeling), has been
described as the imitation of God.[91] Spirit as the union of supreme
potentiality and actuality manifests the richest possible harmony of the infinity
of contrasts between actuality and potentiality; its goal (initial aim) for each
of us is that harmony of contrasts relevant to particular individuals on
particular occasions.[92]

This initial aim is never negligible. It is always felt conformally by the subject
and therefore is always actualized to some degree. Because the *telos* of the
universe is beauty, all creatures are receptive to God's initial aim for the richest
possible concrescence or harmony of feeling possible at that particular time.
All feel an impulse to do the best they can. Thus, the Spirit has a power of

its own such that it shapes our character and elicits an appropriate response from us. The effects of God's presence cannot be totally effaced and are reflected even in those who may espouse, for example, atheism or nihilism. Therefore, I would not completely reject a monarchic concept of God. Hartshorne has emphasized that if there were no cosmic ruler, then absolutely anything could happen. That is, the universe would be chaos, analogous to a human society without centralized control. For example, true democracy is impossible without a monarchic dimension. Freedom is impossible without some form of determinism, and God structures our freedom so that we do not destroy ourselves.[93] God "stacks the deck," so to speak, so that the chances for good are greater than chances for evil. Nevertheless, chances for evil overlap with chances for good, as I shall show.

Although there is an ontological relationship between God and creatures, there is as well a distinction between them. By the doctrine of mutual immanence, the world transcends God just as decisively as God transcends the world.[94] The initial aim does not fully determine the subject's own aim (its subjective aim). Because all entities are *causa sui*, subjective aims are always products of their own decisions. Freedom is meaningless and arbitrary unless we have a goal. Initial aims provide us purpose, but we can and certainly do modify our goals. Therefore, we may fail to conform to the aim offered by God in the context of the total situation. According to Whitehead, "so far as the conformity is incomplete, there is evil in the world."[95]

God cannot predetermine all the world, because freedom is presupposed by beauty. The relationship between freedom and aesthetics is a necessary one. That is, freedom is not something granted to us by God's arbitrary decree in order voluntarily to limit divine power. It is not dependent upon divine choice. I am not undertaking a "free will" defense of God, arguing that freedom in itself is such a great thing that God deliberately limited divine power to allow us genuine freedom. Rather, freedom is a logical requirement for the realization of all beauty. This point becomes clear if we remember that the intensity or depth and breadth of experience, which is beauty, requires complexity. Increased complexity means increased freedom; as creatures become more advanced, they have more data to synthesize in the concrescing moment. The experience of lower actualities is primarily physical, that is, it takes place primarily in terms of conformity to elements received from the past. Lower actualities have some but very little capacity for conceptual or mental experience, the ability to imagine beyond the given, to entertain novel possibilities. Higher organisms are capable of more beauty or more enriched experience because they have a more developed mental pole and, as well, an increased capacity for physical experience. Thus, they have more data to synthesize in the concrescing moment of self-actualization. There is then an increased capacity to deviate from God's initial aim in favor of some other possibility at the time. That God lures us toward a more complex world necessarily means that the more advanced creatures will have more and more freedom to reject as well as to conform to divine aims. However, this rejection or deviation from God is not necessary; thus, evil is not necessary, but the possbility of evil is necessary.[96] God, then, is the Cosmic Adventurer who takes great risks; and this risk-taking is necessary if there is to be any opportunity for enjoyment or beauty.[97]

While it is not my purpose to provide a doctrine of evil, it should be noted that this aesthetic orientation has significant implications for the problem of theodicy. I contend that in the context of process theology, the value of freedom justifies the sufferings risked and the sufferings actual. The perfection of experience cannot be had without the possibility of evil, for to avoid trivia is to risk evil in the sense of discord. According to Whitehead, discord "is the half-way house between perfection and triviality."[98] In other words, beauty is the maximum harmonious intensity of the experience possible for a particular creature, given its context. Now, the greater the intensity of experience, the more elements to be unified, hence the greater the possibility for disharmony or discord. For example, a highly complex body and nervous system is the required context in which evolutionarily advanced beings such as ourselves are capable of producing greater beauty in one another than are relatively less complex beings. Yet, the body can be the source of great suffering, as when it is invaded by elements it cannot absorb. Thus, increased complexity, while it makes greater enjoyment possible, also makes greater suffering possible. Indeed, it might lead to discord so great that the positive enjoyment of experience is eliminated completely.[99] Thus, many may argue that intense enjoyment is not at all worth the risk of suffering, and they may choose a far more trivial existence that is possible for themselves, to avoid being hurt. But if the absence of suffering or discord were the sole criterion of perfection, then the logical conclusion is that God should not have created a world at all.[100] God, then, is in part responsible, but not indictable, for the evil of discord; for had God not lured the universe in the direction of increasing complexity, no suffering would have occurred. Had God not lured the world on to the creation of highly complex entities such as human beings with a capacity for conscious self-determination, human forms of evil would not have occurred.[101]

Moreover, if the universe is the body of God such that God has self-deciding parts (as was argued in chapter 1), then it is up to God to suffer or enjoy these parts' own self-decisions and not decide for them. Evil is not incompatible with the existence of a benevolent Deity; and the possibilities of great tragedy and suffering are inescapable, because they come from our freedom. The possibility of a holocaust or even of a worse tragedy is a live one. Like Niebuhr and Come, sin is understood not as lost innocence or innate corruption but as frustration over our high destiny. Sin affects the whole of our being, body and soul together, and so is not merely a question of emotion predominating over reason. Sin affects even the best of us because it is precisely our strengths, our transcending capacities, that can be used for evil ends. We misuse our greatest accomplishments, which is what makes us a most dangerous animal. There is something about our freedom that suggests that we are completely self-sufficient. We, therefore, often refuse to acknowledge our finitude. Most specifically, we sin by denying the relational nature of our being. Consequently, we become selfish, isolated and destroy all unity within and between ourselves.

This conception does not mean that God is impotent. In this aesthetic framework, God's power is the finest exemplification of what power should be: power over powers, emphathically participating in the self-creation of self-determining entities.[102] Power effective over free beings, sinful as they may be, requires greater talent than would the mere manipulation of programmed robots. Because we are intrinsically free so that the future is indeterminate, God does not know ahead of time what will happen. God, then, must improvise. Unfortunately, many take an overly dim view of improvisation. For example, it is often assumed that only the poor and needy must improvise. But, in point of fact, it takes great talent to improvise. So, if God has to improvise to elicit or lure order out of chaos, and does so, then God is strong, not weak.

Critics might argue that a deity unable to predetermine, hence guarantee, a certain outcome lacks the essential power of a deity. Indeed, I believe that a major reason why Christianity has clung so long to the notion of the Spirit as an all-controlling power is that this conception provides assurance that God's will is always victorious. But, as noted earlier, this concept of God's sovereign control over every detail of creation has led historically to some serious problems; that is, it denied human freedom and responsibility, denied the reality of evil (evil is only apparent, since all things work for the best) and made God as the supreme cause of it all the author of terrible human sufferings. This is a major reason why we have had the revolt of atheistic humanism. The advantage of a process pneumatology is that it would avoid these difficulties. The Holy Spirit is not the adult version of a Santa Claus who steps in and magically solves all our problems or prevents the destructive consequences of our acts. What would faith mean if all were certain? If the triumph of God is inevitable, what room is there for our own initiative? In a process pneumatology there is no assurance that God's will is always done or that the total destruction of the human race can be prevented. But it does affirm that whatever the case may be, God's creative-responsive love acts upon the wreckage to elicit whatever beauty is possible under the circumstances. Thus, the immanence of God does in fact guarantee that complete chaos is intrinsically impossible. Complete destruction of life is possible, however.

The superiority of God's power in this aesthetic sense may not be obvious to those who hold with a strictly legalistic concept of God as a cosmic moralist or a dispenser of rewards and punishments. In this respect, process theology

has a distinct affinity with the   nnation of our efforts
to extrapolate from our petty s   'or instance, Romans
3). Process theology provides a   our understanding
of the Spirit into harmony with th   experience of love;
if we truly love others, we do not s   hreats of rewards
or punishments. Only as a last resort   ments contribute
to present beauty and only as such ha   pneumatology.
While the presence of the dipolar dei   ie behavior of
creatures, it is remote from a legalistic   irit does not
dispense rewards and punishments, an   e symphony
conductor hands out instruments or music   punishments
rather than in terms of possibilities for op   ..ice. The creature's
present is for the sake of beauty, not for th   or past deserts. In the first
place, the vast complexities of life—the fact that we are all free, that there
is an interplay between our freedom and God and also natural law, and that
we are all interdependent—makes it quite impossible to "blame" the joys and
sorrows of life upon any one entity, let alone ascribe them to divine rewards
and punishments.[103]

Obviously, there are some severe implications here for the traditional doctrine
of *creatio ex nihilo*. Traditionally it was assumed that ordinary creativity
presupposes a preexistent material to be molded, whereas divine creativity does
not. This was a logical consequence of the monopolar prejudice of classical
doctrine, whereby God was assumed to be wholly self-sufficient, unmoved,
and therefore in absolute control. However, on biblical grounds alone, *creatio
ex nihilo* is suspect. It is not at all evident in the Genesis account of creation.
Rather, what is shown is a disordered and chaotic world already before God,
who functions as an orderer: "And the earth was waste and void; and darkness
was upon the face of the deep; and the Spirit of God moved upon the face
of the waters" (Genesis 1:2). Also, Scripture is quite specific that God does
not deal with marionettes who are merely an outward projection of the divine
mind; God has chosen to enter into relationship with free yet sinful persons.
On aesthetic grounds *creatio ex nihilo* is also a dubious way of formulating
God's privileged way of creating. As Ford has emphasized, *creatio ex nihilo*
is essentially *creatio ex deo*; for the world possesses no more independence
than an idea in God's own mind would have. Were it to exist apart from the
divine mind, it could not enrich God's experience, because this doctrine claims
that God must fully experience in imagination anything he could completely
determine.[104] But assume instead that God's love is essentially dipolar, that
is, creative and responsive, effect as well as cause. This would be the grounds
for a pneumatology of human creativity and liberation as opposed to servitude
to an absolute despot. It is by this dipolar love that the world of free self-
deciding creatures and God are mutually relevant to one another. Because God
and the world are mutually immanent, God is deeply moved by our experience

of beauty. For example, the adult is created out of the child, not out of nothing by God's arbitrary decree. The issue here is that of the relevance of divine acts. The Spirit's activities in the creation of Beethoven's symphonies did not overlook the free self-decisions of Beethoven's predecessors.[105] Analogous to a sensitive sculptor, God always works with the grain. God cannot work any faster than creatures will allow. God "can only produce such order as is possible."[106] Whitehead supposes that there is an order or gradation of relevancies of the eternal objects or potentialities for the universe. They cannot be actualized at once or randomly. Some are relevant possibilities only after others have been actualized. In this sense, all things work in a purposive way. God is carrying out a project, so the finite world is openended, unfinished. It is precisely this relationship between order and novelty that enables us to reconcile the existence of God with the fact of a vast cosmic evolution of billions of years.

However, this concept of change as a metaphysical ultimate is in many respects quite threatening to us. What perverts the actualization of the human spirit is the fear that all values are in fact temporal. Why try to do better if it is all going to go up in smoke anyway? A major problem or sickness of modern life is the loss of confidence in the significance of the transitory goods of life. The ancient Greeks depreciated them, so the loss is long established. If we are to secure the worth of life, we must find some sense in which it is permanent. If the perpetual perishing of all things is all that there is to life, then life is ultimately meaningless. All things are ultimately futile. If God is truly immutable, then nothing of ourselves can contribute to God. Consequently, God cannot save our experiences from ultimate meaninglessness. For this reason Indian mysticism seeks release in Nirvana.[107] Whitehead contends that classical theism seriously erred in contrasting the aseity and immutability of God over and against the temporal world.[108] If, however, God's love is responsive as well as creative, if God is present to us as the Final Beauty as well as Eros, then it is a different story. All things are of ultimate meaning and significance because they deeply affect the divine life and are somehow preserved forever in the consequent nature of God. (This is an extension of my earlier point that value arises through interaction.) Thus, the human spirit finds its *raison d'être* in the Spirit or God's unitive experience; the "operative growth of God,"[109] is everlasting or eternal in the sense that it is continually affected and enriched by the world, and yet also preserves the past "with a tender care that nothing be lost."[110] (As noted in chapter 3, Christian mysticism entails such an intuition of permanence and ever-lastingness.) Divine justice resides in the fact that our lives count for all they are worth in the divine life of God. God cannot prevent tragedy but does in fact overcome the evil of all evils: that the past fades, so that we come to doubt that our moments of joy and triumph are of any real significance.

I turn now to a more detailed explication of the implications of these metaphysical concepts for the interpretation of Spirit experiences.

SPIRIT EXPERIENCES

This section is my original attempt to bring further details of Whitehead's aesthetic into relation with pneumatology. Since Whitehead's aesthetic theory reflects back upon his metaphysical system, the following analysis will provide an additional unifying factor in this work. Essentially, I will present evidence that it is fruitful to conduct investigations into the problems of the experience of presence within the framework of Whitehead's aesthetic, thereby further strengthening the relevance of the philosophy of organism for pneumatology. Mystical literature counsels that the experience of presence is rooted in the subconscious, preconceptual realm and therefore entails dimensions of experience beyond what one is capable of consciously analyzing at the moment. For example, Plotinus states that "what sees is not our reason, but something prior and superior to our reason.[111] *The Cloud of Unknowing* states that "thou mayest neither see him clearly by the light of understanding in thy reason."[112] The major theme of St. Teresa's work, *The Interior Castle*, is that to find God we must transcend conscious experience and introspectively explore the subsconscious realms of experience, which she likens to deep, dark antechambers of the soul. Eckhart speaks of the experience of presence as *Unwizzen*, which may be variously translated as unknowledge, unconscious-ness, unself-conscious.[113] Relevant secondary sources on this theme are to be found in the writings of Bergson, Huxley, Mallory and Watts.

Various aestheticians have resorted to the rather inexact notion of a divine madness or inspiration from the unseen (Spirit?) to account for creativity. Beauty has been depicted as a mystical quest by which we push beyond the facts of ordinary conscious experience to the "gates of the Divine."[114] The advantage of Whitehead's aesthetic is that it grants clarity and precision to these conceptions.

If we are to understand how God is present in our experience, God must not be understood as an item of or inference from sensory experience nor as an item of bizarre, extraordinary experiences confined to an elite subset of persons such as mystics and creative geniuses. I believe that Whitehead's aesthetic is helpful in providing an alternative model. His aesthetic theory appeals to a richer, more primal experience than that represented by thought or sensation alone or the more specialized forms of conscious knowing. Cobb notes that the fact that God is not an item of conscious, sensory experience does not rule out God as a definite factor in experience.[115] We experience God by means of our deep-seated emotive tones; we do not see God; we feel God's presence, but we do not necessarily feel our feelings of God's presence. Indeed, the concrete presence of God, although felt by all creatures, may not and need not be consciously grapsed; for the truly important thing is the fulfillment of initial aims via the free self-creative decisions of creatures. Initial aims are directed toward the world, so they need not be explicitly revelatory of the concrete God behind them. However, there is no reason why initial aims in Whitehead should be restricted to this particular context. There may be initial aims whose goal it is to have conscious, conformal feelings with the internal structure of the consequent nature. Process, then, may be able to provide a more satisfying account of the ecstatic experience of divine immanence than did mysticism.

Mysticism, as was demonstrated in chapters 2 and 3, centers upon the notion that it is accurate to envision oneself in an intimate, two-way relationship with God. My claim is that Whitehead's aesthetic provides a coherent philosophical psychology to exemplify this reciprocity in continuity with ordinary experience. Furthermore, Whitehead's aesthetic solves or at least points the way toward solving certain problems of Spirit experiences by reintegrating unities lost through mistaken differentiations and dichotomies in mysticism. To clarify, on the one hand, mystics speak of a mutual reciprocity between God and the world. Yet, on the other hand, in numerous passages they depict God in wholly dualistic terms as other than the world, as atemporal, aloof, changeless. There is a serious contradiction in the mystical literature. If God is genuinely unchanging, hence nonresponsive, then God is present and subject to a direct reciprocal relationship only in a highly fictive sense. If, however, God is genuinely responsive, then the dualistic affirmations are artificial. In process theology, this problem disappears.

The value of process theology is that it resolves this paradox and therefore more thoroughly reconciles divine transcendence with divine immanence. In chapters 2 and 3, I suggested that the dualistic side of mysticism with its experience of nonpresence or alienation may be interpreted as part of a process whereby artificial distinctions are set up and then overcome. For example, I emphasized the transition in Dionysius from the *via negativa*, or Negative Theology, in which God is a huge, dark apopathic void, to the Affirmative Theology, in which God includes the fullness of all empirical reality. The following analysis will further this interpretation by adding that the experience of nonpresence or alienation reflects frustration relative to the divine lure for feeling.

For organizational purposes, I will first examine the connection between aesthetics and the subconscious in Whitehead. Then I will turn more specifically to the role of divine inspiration in aesthetic experience.

The Reformed Subjectivist Principle

The reformed subjectivist principle is the centerpiece of Whitehead's theory of aesthetics. It provides the connection between aesthetics and subconscious experience, which in turn provides the basis for the experience of presence. As noted in chapter 1, this principle is a rejection of the traditional epistemic dogma of western philosophy, the primacy of conscious, sensory experience. According to this principle, sense perception is not the basic paradigm of experience, nor is consciousness. "Feeling," not sense, is the most primary experiential construct, "the primary at the basis of experience."[116] According to Whitehead, "the more primitive mode of objectification is via emotional tone."[117] Thus, the terms "feeling" or "positive prehension" are technical ones to denote the vehicle by which subjects, including God, absorb or incorporate other entities into the unity of their own constitutions.[118] This process of integration or concrescence does not presuppose conscious experience. Rather, conscious experience is only one special form of experience, not a primitive one, as was traditionally supposed, but a derivative of highly complex integrations of feelings. Whitehead's justification here is (1) the avoidance of certain difficulties and perplexities in the sensationalist doctrines of modern philosophy, and (2) the appeal to common sense, or more specifically to common recurrent experience.[119]

In my explication of this principle, first I will note some basic ways in which ordinary consciousness accentuates this notion of nonsensory experience; then I shall focus in particular on aesthetic experience.

Normally our relationship to our bodies is almost exclusively a sensory one. To see what we look like, we look in a mirror, and so forth. The once-exclusive primacy of introspection in psychology lifted "the clear-cut data of sensation into primacy."[120] Thus, ordinarily the relationship of mind to body and also of ourselves to our bodies lacks vividness in consciousness because of the exclusive preoccupation with and reliance upon sensory experience. In point of fact, however, the reason for our instinctive identification with our bodies is the awareness of the derivation of present experience from our bodies. This relationship, upon which our sensory experience depends, is itself non-sensory.[121] Sensory experience is the end-product, a complex integration of a multitude of nonsensory events. For example, when we see green, what happens is that first we feel greenly or have greenly feelings and then by projection we see green. The visual impression of green is the result of the synthesis of countless microscopic feelings or nonsensory events in the body, brain, and nervous system of which we are not conscious that finally culminate in the sensory impression of green. Causal efficacy informs sense data, for the senses represent "qualifications of affective tone."[122]

This conception may provide an explanation for the nonsensory character of mystical introspection. That is, if awareness were fully turned back upon itself, consciousness would then be exclusively preoccupied with a direct apprehension of those nonsensory events from which sensory experience is later derived.

To further highlight Whitehead's point, let us briefly consider the phenomenon of memory. It is not always recognized that memory is a nonsensory process, because much of what is remembered has sensory content. For example, Hume denied that memory is nonsensory by claiming that only a lack of vivacity of sensory images distinguished it from ordinary sensory experience.[123] But Hume may have been wrong. Memory is the interplay of the past upon the present, that is, perception in the mode of causal efficacy. The brute facts tell us that this relationship is not a sensory one, however dominant the sensory element was in past experience. (See for example, the discussion of causal efficacy in chapter 1). For example, the past experience of seeing causes images to arise in present experience and in such a way as to affect the eyes, but the present experience of the past experience is not mediated by the eyes.[124] In other words, we do not see our experience of seeing; we do not see the eye making us see, we feel the eye making us see. Consider music as another example. What is enjoyed is the interplay of the past upon the present, that is, the flow of the melody, the sense of temporal passage. Yet to enjoy music is not necessarily to remember sensorially; one does not take the trouble to conjure up sensory images in the mind's ear of the past notes, immediate or otherwise, of the piece.

To clarify these points, let us turn more specifically to aesthetic experience. At this point in my analysis, I will limit the discussion to perception in the mode of causal efficacy, that is, to unconscious experience or physical feelings of the past. This, however, is only one aspect of aesthetic experience. In the next subsection, I will turn to the role of conceptual feelings.

I believe that the reformed subjectivist principle is Whitehead's attempt to restore us metaphysically to the fullness of human experience. I understand it as in part a protest against the reductionism of the modern scientific worldview by which aesthetic values have been divorced from the rest of life. His "doctrine of harmony," which is a logical corollary of this principle, claims that the exclusive preoccupation with sense perception, important as it may be for scientific and practical affairs, detracts from the richness of experience by obscuring the fact that we always respond holistically.[125] Thus, it is a sad mistake to assume that all communication with reality can be narrowly circumscribed to the sensory pathways. Indeed, sense experience is not paradigmatic of our experience of relatedness. Now full, rich experience is possible only by means of the apprehension of the relatedness of things, which is essentially perception in the mode of causal efficacy. According to the Category of Transmutation, this operation is the prehension of actual entities forming a nexus, not as many but as a unity, so that the world is felt as a community by virtue of its order. Without transmutation we would "fail to penetrate into the dominant characteristics of things."[126]

Some concrete exemplifications of aesthetic experience will help clarify these conceptions. In Whitehead, the aesthetic is not a realm separate and apart from the world, but one indissolubly linked to the depth and complexity of reality; hence he draws his distinction between Appearance and Reality. Sensory perception is defined as "blunt truth" or "clear and distinct Appearance."[127] Aesthetic truths, however, are not sensory truths, but dim, massive ones that well up from far beneath the veneer of consciousness.[128] In other words, reality is a huge, complex sea of unconscious emotive tonal color. Aesthetic experience lifts some of these elements into consciousness. We perceive a brand new factor in our experience that would have gone unnoticed. Aesthetic experience represents a significant enrichment of our emotional lives, by the elicitation into radiant consciousness of this penumbra of feelings surging through relevant realities in a context far less articulate than those factors ordinarily disclosed in sensory awareness. Aesthetic experience is a revitalization of the sense of mystery both within and around us; it is experience cloaked with heavy, shifting, indeterminate meanings.[129]

In an important sense, aesthetic experience is the experience of living faith; it is the experiential affirmation of a depth and complexity to reality that exceeds the grasp of ordinary consciousness. This I believe to be very analogous to the mystical "cloud of darkness" in which thoughts and clear images no longer exist but instead a new dimension is perceived.[130]

Though all are capable of experiencing this penumbra of feeling-tone, normally it is not paramount in consciousness. Indeed, normally the relationship between sense and affect lacks vividness in our conscious experience. Ordinarily we do not relate to our sensory experiences the way we relate to our emotions. We say that we see green, we do not say that we feel greenly; we say that we see a table, we do not say that we feel tablely. Our conscious perceptions are ordinarily abstract rather than concrete because we mostly abstract and classify. Thus, ordinarily consciousness is characterized by the separation of emotional experience from "presentational intuition" or sensation, which is a "high abstraction of thought."[131] We, therefore, have great difficulty eliciting into consciousness the notion that green, for example, is the qualifying characteristic of an emotion. Traditionally, philosophy tended to compartmentalize sense and emotion as two separate processes, with emotionality as a mere byproduct of sensation.

Prall, a noted asethetician, makes an analogous point. The qualitative content of the concrete datum is always felt directly, not merely labeled; it is always felt with some degree, however slight, of affective interest. There is no concrete datum absolutely indifferent to feeling, no sensation without affect; for there is no such thing as abstract discrimination as a separate process devoid of feeling. However, normally and for all practical purposes only the "abstractly discriminating" aspect of experience is relevant, even though pale blue, for example, feels milder than brilliant flaming red and just as definitely as it feels pale blue.[132] Obviously feeling is given, is in fact concrete direct experience, but somehow it manages to get lost. The problem then is this: How can one legitimate feeling? How does one transcend the gulf between subjectivity (the in-here) and everything else (the out-there) so that one can say that the qualitative dimensions of life have an objective basis? Prall laments the traditional philosophical dichotomy between primary and secondary qualities, which renders suspect the validity of aesthetic experience as merely mental, private and wholly subjective.[133]

Whitehead was also deeply aware of this problem. By the dichotomy of primary and secondary qualities, "nature is a dull affair, soundless, scentless, colorless, merely the hurrying of material, endlessly, meaninglessly."[134] His solution rests upon the principle of relativity that transcends the subject-object dichotomy inherited from Aristotle. In short, secondary qualities like all perceived qualities are neither exclusively the property of the object nor of the subject. But they are objective; that is, they are "out there" because they describe a genuine relationship between subject and object. To perceive things is to perceive them relationally, is to enter into a lively dialogue with them. As noted in chapter 1, actual entities enter each others' constitutions through an empathic bond, variously termed conformal feelings, physical feelings, or responsive feelings. Direct experience is not thinking; that is, it is not discriminating and abstracting activity, though it may be conditioned by such activity. Instead, direct experience is concrete feeling. Now, concrete feeling means feeling something that is just there, present to feel and felt as a whole. Feeling is the full perspective of the subject. This conception challenges the sensationalist doctrine, which confines itself to bare sensa.[135] My own interpretation of Whitehead here is that in aesthetic experience the act of seeing, for example, is no longer merely seeing something out there, something that remains fixated in the visual field; rather, seeing becomes an act of empathic participation in the object of aesthetic contemplation. One is no longer inside looking out at the world. This is quite different from ordinary perception. Normally we perceive the world in terms of a rigid subject-object dichotomy. We are conscious of ourselves perceiving objects out there, objects purely external and separable from ourselves. But aesthetic perception transcends this subject-object dichotomy so that we become aware of the relational nature of our being, of our oneness with the world. Aesthetic experience is of a kind of kinetic identity between oneself and the object of aesthetic perception. The seer, the seeing, and the seen, the feeler, the feeling, and the felt all are experienced as one. The principle of relativity states that this experience is true, despite the fact that it violates the tenets of Aristotelian logic.

I believe that this transcendence of the subject-object dichotomy[136] is suggestive that certain basic items of mystical experience were achieved. This emphasis upon mutual interdependence is congruent with my earlier discussion of God as creative-responsive love. As an all-encompassing matrix of sensitivity, the consequent nature or Spirit may be thought of as the underlying sensitive communal ground of our existence, analogous to the hidden land that joins two seemingly isolated islands.[137] Openness to the experience of presence, then, is inseparable from our openness to one another. In this sense aesthetic experience as the perception of things in their relatedness is essentially Spirit experience; for it is in those moments when we become acutely aware of the sensitive communal nature of our being, in those instances of genuine I-thou relationship, that we come to experience the Spirit.

Consequently, I find that there are grounds for a new, positive reinterpretation of the mystical notion of the annihilation of the self or "the dark night of the soul." I am suggesting that from the aesthetic standpoint of process theology, these experiences might be understood as a powerful affirmation of the relational nature of our being or of the inescapable oneness of our lives in God and in one another. My claim is that the period of alienation or the Dark Night of the Soul prior to the experience of presence is unnecessary. A person who holds to a dualistic metaphysic, in which all is seen in terms of separate self-sufficient entities, is committed to this alienation. This period of frustration is reflecting an unnecessary obstacle to the lure for feeling, created by false dichotomies. Worry over personal security and identity drives individuals to lead separate, isolated lives, enclosed within themselves. Many are unable to accept the emotional vulnerability that stems from empathically sharing in the lives of others. Before there can be life in the true community of the Spirit, this narcissistic struggle for survival and the ensuing rugged individualism must be overcome, so that personalities may merge together and flow into one another in the harmony of God. The autonomy of the individual must be transcended. The dark night is the first step in this process of reorientation. It marks the transition from multiplicity to unity. It is not a denial of the self; it is a denial of the narrow, rigid confines of the self. The dark night occurs when the subject finds the quest for personal security too exhausting and too futile to be maintained. For example, James found that a state of total exhaustion in which "we drop down, give up, and don't care any longer" forms part of the conversion crisis underlying certain mystical phenomena.[138] All defenses, all barriers or boundaries that separate the self from others are destroyed. According to law, the self ceases to be its "own center and circumference."[139] Self-isolation is no longer felt to be viable, because self-sufficiency has proved futile. This is the painful awakening to the fact that the harmony of life is not to be found in the self alone but comes from a mergence into a depth and complexity beyond the self. Concrescence, as we shall see, means not only proper depth but also proper width or breadth of experience, which is beauty. Those who live unto themselves are like narrow fissures; they have lots of depth but no real breadth. To obtain proper width it is necessary empathically to open oneself to the lives of others. Thus, concrescence means that the subject in its moment of becoming empathically takes up the emotional lives of its antecedents into a fresh synthesis. This is the measure of its worth for the world. The great intensity of inner feeling generated by the struggle for survival is now released outwardly and enriches the whole. Superficially it may seem that the self has been destroyed; but, as Ford and Suchocki suggest, in the Kingdom or Harmony of God, the self has not been deprived of its own subjectivity; for only the narrow confines of the self have been lost. There is no longer any clearly defined "border" of the personality. There is, however, a center of the personality flowing forth into others in the giving and receiving that is the Harmony of God. (Note that this conception parallels the model of God I introduced at the very beginning of this chapter.) In a way this is self-fulfillment at its highest level. The relational nature of our existence means that there is no true selfhood or personality exclusive of the other. No one recognized that better than the mystics. According to Catherine of Genoa, "My *me* is God: nor do I know any selfhood except in God."[140] Salvation then means more than mere redemption from sin; it means a wholeness of life, an integration made possible through the Spirit, which lifts persons to new relationships. This calls for a clearer description of the role of God in aesthetic experience, which I will describe in the following subsection.

Propositions

According to Whitehead's aesthetic, God serves as the lure for feeling. This lure is technically termed a proposition. As noted earlier, a proposition is "an eternal object made relevant to particular occasions"; it is "a suggestion, a theory, a supposition about things."[141] A proposition is a hybrid feeling or prehension of an actual occasion and an eternal object. Thus, a proposition is God's vision of the potentialities relevant to the subject's concrescence as they are felt in God's hybrid physical experience of the world. The lure for feeling is essentially a vision of what the prehending subject might become. Experience is aesthetic when and if the subject has been lured into successfully recreating the proposition in its process of self-actualization. According to Whitehead, the subjective aim, which controls the becoming of a subject, is the feeling of a proposition with the purpose of realizing it in that process of self-creation.[142] As noted earlier, the subjective aim, however, does not necessarily conform to God's relevant proposition or initial aim. Not all lures are of God.

Whitehead is quite precise on the meaning of the experiences to which these propositions serve as lures. Beauty, the *telos* of the universe, is the way things are felt when they are felt as fully and richly as possible. Beauty is defined as "the mutual adaptation of several factors in an occasion of experience."[143] This adaptation relates to the subjective form. Thus, "the perfection of Beauty is defined as being the perfection of Harmony; and the perfection of Harmony is defined in terms of Subjective Form."[144]

Therefore, in Whitehead's system, terms such as "art" and "aesthetic" are openended concepts. The concept of aesthetics introduced here is far broader than that which can be narrowly circumscribed to the fine arts. In a certain sense all experience is aesthetic experience. Whitehead deplores the fact that logicians, for example, ignore all but the narrow class of propositions that interest them directly.[145]

An aesthetic theory of the experience of presence is both helpful and dangerous. It is helpful because it provides generalities about the divine aims through which God becomes actualized in experience. It is dangerous because these generalities may overlook the concreteness of the prehending subject. No precise statements can be made about which propositions will or will not serve as a lure for feeling; for the self-transcendent nature of aesthetic experience means that any closure would be intolerable. (I believe this to be a rephrasing of the mystical claim, emphasized in chapter 3, that the vision of God cannot be circumscribed to any set of procedures.) Sherburne has provided a "hillock metaphor" to help illustrate this point. Propositions are likened to hillocks covering the plane of possibility. Some sit at the top of very high hillocks; they have great power to determine the subjective aim. These hillocks, however, are in constant flux. Some erode away, while new ones push their way up from the plane. Propositions that may serve as irresistible lures for feeling in one particular situation may be absolute bores in another. Fatigue and cultural advances may impair the power of a proposition to be an effective lure for feeling. For example, one does not find an 'immortal" novel and then read and reread just that novel perpetually. Instead, one strives to keep alive the freshness of literary experience by roaming further and further into literature.[146]

However, Sherburne's metaphor is in many respects inelegant and overworked. My correction of Sherburne would be that his thesis unnecessarily confines aesthetic experience to the perception of art objects. This does not do justice to God's massive presence through each minuscule segment of time. Whitehead's aesthetic has a much broader scope; it refers to the beauty or harmonization attained by the actual entity in its moment of self-creation. When Whitehead speaks of beauty, he is not pointing at some particular characteristic of an art object but at a continual, complex process by which the subject always becomes a new entity.

Earlier God's initial aim was defined as creative-responsive love, or agape, because it provides each entity with a possibility relevant to its particular moment of self-creation. God as the mediator between actuality and potentiality ensures that the initial aim is genuinely relevant to entities in the context of their particular situations. The past informs the present, it helps set the aim for self-creation so that there is a continuity or pattern. As noted earlier, perception in the mode of causal efficacy is central to aesthetic experience. Yet the divine aim is a proposition that lures the subject to transcend the past and become something new. Thus, God is encountered in risk-taking and adventure as opposed to mere maintenance or sanctification of the *status quo*.[147] Such adventuresomeness is the source of the richness and the excitement of the concrescing moment.

The affirmation of self-transcendence is central in Whitehead's protest against evolution in the Darwinian sense of the term. Whitehead, of course, is well aware that this doctrine has "its merit of truth," that it is "one of the great generalizations of science."[148] He argues, however, that the concept of adaptation to the environment does not fully explain why there has been an upward trend toward more complex organisms.[149] Whitehead argues that those species that self-transcend through actively modifying the environment spearhead the upward trend.[150] This modification of the environment is directed by the aesthetic quest for enriched experience.[151] This means that creative transformation constitutes our very existence. When creativity ceases, the organism dies. Thus, the Spirit continually functions to challenge the *status quo*, to jar us out of our complacency. In a sense, this is divine chastisement. But it is essentially God's agape, because it condemns in the world that which would destroy us.[152] This is God's transcendence in the context of immanence. God as the principle of relevance of all genuine novelty transcends any given epoch. Yet God is also immanent or incarnate to the extent that relevant potentiality is actualized, thereby deepening the incarnation. God has efficacity only as incarnate.[153] According to Whitehead, "the world lives by its incarnation of God."[154]

The concept of the temporal subject as a discoverer[155] helps to highlight this self-transcendent character of aesthetic experience and also provides a valid insight into how the activity of temporal subjects can be distinguished from God's infinite conceptual valuation. The temporal subject in its moment of self-becoming actualizes a relevant proposition. But the subject does not create *ex nihilo*. Propositions always occur in a certain, specific context. They relate to preexistents. Without such a contextual relationship, creation would be meaningless and unintelligible.[156]

This point is central in Whitehead's concept of conceptual reversion, for example. A conceptual reversion is a conceptual feeling partially identical with and partially diverse from the eternal objects (propositions) constituting the prehended datum at hand. Hume's famous case of the missing shade of blue would be a prime example of conceptual reversion. Whitehead's point is that, in the final analysis, Hume's contention that "all our ideas, or weak perceptions, are derived from our impressions or strong perceptions"[157] is without exception. Conceptual reversions depend upon the hybrid physical feeling of God that is part of every concrescence.[158]

There is a significant difference between Whitehead and humanistic psychologists such as Maslow. Humanistic psychology tends to assume that potentials are something instinctual or innately possessed by the individual. For example, Maslow finds his hierarchy of needs to be instinctual in that they are "in some sense, and to some appreciable degree, constitutional or hereditary in their determination."[159] Mysticism also evidences a similar tendency. Thus, the concept of a "higher side" or apex or citadel of the soul is generally introduced as something innately given. In Whitehead, however, potentials are not some innate property of the individual but arise in the total situation including God. They are possibilities for relevant novelty and not merely the recapitulation of the past or the liberation of repressed perceptual capacities. It is true, however, that the aim of the occasion is toward a fresh synthesis of the past that will allow maximum incorporation of physical or unconscious feelings. This process of transformation must struggle against habit, anxiety and defensiveness.[160] Whitehead, however, is striving to avoid the extremes of humanism and of the radical transcendence of God in a dualistic sense. I refer to Loomer's point that if God's values or aims bore no relationship to our own, then God would be unknowable and unintelligible. Such a God would be totally irrelevant. Yet, if God merely echoes our present goals, unconscious or otherwise, again we can dispense with God; for there would be nothing worthy of worship except our human ideals. Thus, if God is to be at all meaningful, God must transcend yet be relevant to our present ideals. Whitehead is quite specific that creativity is not merely the expression of our present unconscious wants, desires and aims. God's aim is not merely to satisfy these, but to lure us continually to change our present wants in order to attain a larger, grander beauty, which is depth, breadth and intensity of feeling.[161] Whitehead's aesthetic theory is not a static, backward-looking affair, but centers upon a dynamic thrust into novelty.[162] According to Whitehead, "the type of Truth required for the final stretch of Beauty is a discovery and not a recapitulation."[163] Even discord is of some aesthetic value, because this restlessness can be an aim toward higher degrees of aesthetic harmony.[164] God lures us to avoid both the chaos of discordant feelings and also the staleness of monotony.[165]

Thus, "all aesthetic feeling experience is feeling arising out of the realization of contrast under identity."[166] Hartshorne makes a similar point:

> Let there be as much unity in contrast as possible, both within the new pattern and between it and the old patterns — so that the pattern of ongoing life shall be unified and diversified. . . . This is the aesthetic imperative which the artist feels laid upon him by the scheme of things, and it is the voice of God as truly as any other imperative.[167]

Concrescence, then, is an extremely difficult and complex process of synthesis. It is not unidimensional, not informed by a single feeling. Instead, it is informed by a multitude of physical or unconscious feelings arising out of the subject's past. The subject is new but not wholly so. The future (conceptual feelings) is also multidimensional. There are numerous possibilities, some imposed by the world, some by God. Since the divine aim occurs in the context of the total situation that includes other aims, the divine aim may not emerge with certain clarity. According to the Category of Subjective Unity, the subject seeks to unify or synthesize this variety of discordant feelings so that they intensify one another through compatible contrasts. Thus, aesthetic experience represents the subject's efforts guided by the subjective aim, always to some degree conformal to the divine aim, to synthesize physical and conceptual feelings. Such a harmonious contrast makes possible the breadth, depth and intensity of feeling, which is the essence of beauty. In this way Spirit experience is essentially personal transformation.

Notes

Introduction

1. Donald Sherburne, *A Key to Whitehead's Process and Reality*, (New Haven: Yale University Press, 1961), 33.
2. Alfred Whitehead, *Process and Reality* (New York: Free Press, 1957), 26.
3. Ibid., 244.
4. Ibid., 400.
5. Ibid.
6. Alfred Whitehead, *Modes of Thought* (New York; Macmillan, 1937), 120.
7. Whitehead, *Process and Reality*, 400.
8. Ibid., 26.
9. Ibid., 28.
10. Ibid., 54.

Chapter 1. Divine Immanence in Process Theology

1. Donald W. Sherburne, "Whitehead Without God," in *Process Philosophy and Christian Thought*, ed. Delwin Brown, Ralph James, and Gene Reeves (New York: Bobbs-Merrill, 1971), 313.
2. Sherburne, *Key to Whitehead's Process and Reality*, 222.
3. Jacob Boehme, *Samtliche Schriften*, Bd. I, *Morgen Rote* (Stuttgart: Fr. Frommans Verlag, 1957), 271.
4. Ibid., 9:15.
5. Ibid., 3:271.
6. *The Cloud of Unknowing* (London: J. M. Watkins, 1950), 232.
7. Alfred Whitehead, *Science and the Modern World* (New York: Free Press, 1967), 127.
8. Whitehead, *Process and Reality*, 64.
9. Walter E. Stokes, "God for Today and Tomorrow," in *Process Philosphy and Christian Thought*, 261.
10. Whitehead, *Process and Reality*, 91.
11. Ibid., 39.
12. Ibid., 125.
13. Ibid., 172.
14. Ibid., 407.
15. Sherburne, *Key to Whitehead's Process and Reality*, 26.
16. Ibid., 76.
17. Ivor Leclerc, *Whitehead's Metaphysics* (New York: Macmillan, 1958), 97.
18. Alfred Whitehead, *The Concept of Nature* (Cambridge: Cambridge University Press, 1926), 28.
19. Whitehead, *The Concept of Nature*, 43–44.
20. Ibid., 145.
21. Ibid., 148.
22. Ibid., 147–48.

23. Joseph Sittler, *Essays on Nature and Grace* (Philadelphia: Fortress Press, 1972).

24. Whitehead, *The Concept of Nature*, 27.

25. Ibid., 27.

26. Whitehead, *Science and the Modern World*, 90–91.

27. Whitehead, *The Concept of Nature*, 27.

28. Ibid., 27.

29. Ibid., 159.

30. Ibid., 33.

31. Ibid., 34.

32. Ibid., 35.

33. Ibid., 78.

34. Ibid., 66.

35. Whitehead, *Science and the Modern World*, 51.

36. Whitehead, *The Concept of Nature*, 52.

37. Whitehead, *Process and Reality*, 171.

38. Whitehead, *Science and the Modern World*, 160.

39. Ibid., 171.

40. Ibid., 410.

41. Charles Hartshorne and William Reese, *Philosophers Speak of God* (Chicago: University of Chicago Press, 1953), 13.

42. Charles Hartshorne, *Reality as Social Process* (Glencoe, Illinois: Free Press, 1953).

43. John B. Cobb and David R. Griffin, *Process Theology: An Introductory Exposition* (Philadelphia: Westminster Press, 1976), 27.

44. Whitehead, *Process and Reality*, 413.

45. Ibid., 31.

46. Ibid., 171–72.

47. Alfred Whitehead, *The Principle of Relativity* (Cambridge: Cambridge University Press, 1922), 29–31.

48. Alfred Whitehead, *The Principle of Relativity*, 8.

49. Alfred Whitehead, "Uniformity and Contingency," in *Proceedings of the Aristotelian Society* 23 (1922–1923): 5,7,8.

50. Charles Hartshorne, *Man's Vision of God and the Logic of Theism* (Chicago: Willet, Clark, and Co., 1941), 220.

51. Whitehead, *Process and Reality*, 372–73.

52. Ibid., 407.

53. Schubert M. Ogden, *The Reality of God* (New York: Harper and Row, 1966), 178.

54. Whitehead, *Process and Reality*, 287.

55. Ibid., 280.

56. Ibid., 71.

57. Hartshorne, *Reality as Social Process*, 69.

58. Pierre Teilhard de Chardin, *Oeuvres*, Vol. 1, *Le Phenomene Humain* (Paris: Editions du Seuil, 1955–1976), 77.

59. Rosemary Reuther, "Critic's Corner," *Theology Today* 27, 3 (October 1970): 337.

60. Whitehead, *Process and Reality*, 245.

61. Ibid., 163.

62. Ibid., 164.

63. Ibid., 203.

64. Ibid., 205.

65. Ibid., 204.

66. Ibid., 10.
67. Ibid., 410.
68. Ibid., 125.
69. Ibid., 410.
70. Ibid., 37.
71. Ibid., 37.
72. Ibid., 85.
73. Ibid., 406.
74. Ibid., 284.
75. Ibid., 410.
76. Hartshorne, *Man's Vision of God*, 205.
77. Ibid., 200.
78. Whitehead, *Process and Reality*, 404.
79. Bernard Meland, *The Seeds of Redemption* (New York: Macmillan, 1947), 60.
80. Hartshorne, *Man's Vision of God*, 195–98.
81. Whitehead, *Process and Reality*, 413.
82. Bernard Loomer, "Christian Faith and Process Philosophy," in Brown, James, Reeves, *Process Philosophy*, 70–98, 83.
83. St. Teresa, *Interior Castle* (New York: Image Books, 1961), 194.
84. Hartshorne and Reese, *Philosophers Speak of God*, 15.
85. Hartshorne, *Man's Vision of God*, 193.
86. Whitehead, *Process and Reality*, 200.
87. Ibid., 131.
88. Ibid., 109.
89. Ibid., 41.
90. Odgen, *The Reality of God*, 60.
91. Alfred Whitehead, *Religion in the Making*, 68, 72, 76.
92. Whitehead, *Process and Reality*, 126.
93. Whitehead, *The Concept of Nature*, 162.
94. Harold K. Schilling, *The New Consciousness in Science and Religion* (Philadelphia: United Church Press, 1973), 108.
95. Pierre Teilhard de Chardin, *Escrits du Temps de la Guerre*, Vol. 12 (Paris: Editions du Seuil, 1956) 306.
96. Pierre Teilhard de Chardin, *Le Coeur de la Matiere*, Vol. 13 (Paris: Editions du Seuil, 1958) 105.
97. Pierre Teilhard de Chardin, *Science et Christ*, (Paris: Editions du Seuil, 1955) 151.
98. Ibid., 43; *L'Activation de l'Energie*, Vol. 7 (Paris: Editions du Seuil, 1955) 236.
99. Whitehead, *Process and Reality*, 408.
100. Ibid., 408.
101. William Christian, *An Interpretation of Whitehead's Metaphysics* (New Haven: Yale University Press, 1959), 323–27.
102. Whitehead, *Process and Reality*, 131.
103. Ibid., 279.
104. Ibid., 269.
105. Ibid., 278.
106. Ibid., 286.
107. Whitehead, *Religion in the Making* (New York: World Publishing, 1976), 131.
108. Whitehead, *Process and Reality*, 33.
109. Walter Stokes, "God for Today and Tomorrow," Brown, James, Reeves *Process Philosophy* 244–63, 251.
110. René Descartes, *Meditations 2, The Philosophical Works of Descartes*, trans.

E. Haldane and G. Ross (Cambridge: University Press, 1911) 2 Volumes.

111. Whitehead, *Process and Reality*, 198.

112. Sherburne, *A Key to Whitehead's Process and Reality*, 115–56.

113. Whitehead, *Process and Reality*, 55.

114. Gordon Jackson, "In Search of Adventure: The Aesthetic Project," (draft for forthcoming book, 1981), 105.

115. Whitehead, *Process and Reality*, 31.

116. Ibid., 55.

117. Ibid., 55.

118. Ibid., 188.

119. Alfred North Whitehead, *An Enquiry Concerning the Principles of Natural Knowledge* (Cambridge: Cambridge University Press, 1925), 167–68.

120. Whitehead, *Process and Reality*, 286.

121. Ibid., 238–39.

122. Ibid., 104, 155.

Chapter 2. *Process Theology and Christian Mysticism*

1. Maurice Gandillac, *Oeuvres Completes de Pseudo-Denys*, (Paris: Editions Montaigne, 1943), 189.

2. Ibid., 141.

3. Ibid., 183.

4. Ibid., 162.

5. Ibid., 184.

6. Ibid., 159.

7. Ibid., 160.

8. Ibid., 159–60.

9. Franz Pfeiffer, *Deutsche Mystiker: Meister Eckhart*, (Gottigen: Vandenhoeck, 1914), 515.

10. Gandillac, *Oeuvres Completes de Pseudo-Denys*, 181.

11. Ibid., 182.

12. Ibid., 74–75.

13. Ibid., 75.

14. Ibid., 71.

15. Ibid., 86.

16. Ibid., 278–79.

17. Ibid., 132.

18. Alfred Whitehead, *Process and Reality* (New York: Free Press, 1957), 413.

19. Gandillac, *Oeuvres Completes de Pseudo-Denys*, 185.

20. Whitehead, *Process and Reality*, 412.

21. Ibid., 411.

22. Gandillac, *Oeuvres Completes de Pseudo-Denys*, 108.

23. Ibid., 135.

24. Ibid., 132.

25. Ibid., 109.

26. Ibid., 183.

27. Ibid., 188.

28. Ibid., 191.

29. Ibid., 188–89.

30. Ibid., 183.

31. Ibid., 108.

32. Ibid., 177.

33. Ibid., 118.

34. Ibid., 121.

35. Ibid., 114.

36. Ibid., 118.

37. Ibid., 131.

38. Ibid., 126.

39. Ibid., 107.

40. Ibid., 261.

41. Ibid., 258.

42. Ibid., 223.

43. Robert Blakney, *Meister Eckhart,* (New York: Harper & Row, 1941), xiii–xv.

44. Rufus Jones, *Some Exponents of Mystical Religion*, (London: Camelot Press, 1930), 100.

45. Jones, *Some Experiments of Mystical Religion*, 101.

46. Ibid., 101.

47. Ibid., 229.

48. Pfeiffer, *Deutsche Mystiker: Meister Eckhart*, 308.

49. Ibid., 222.

50. Ibid., 75.

51. Ibid., 239.

52. Ibid., 207.

53. Ibid., 85.

54. Ibid., 304.

55. Ibid., 307.

56. Ibid., 164.

57. Ibid., 117.

58. Ibid., 497.

59. Ibid., 39–40.

60. Ibid., 316.

61. Ibid., 94.

62. Blakney, *Meister Eckhart*, 253.

63. Pfeiffer, *Deutsche Mystiker: Meister Eckhart*, 226.

64. Ibid., 81.

65. Ibid., 95.

66. Ibid., 100.

67. Ibid., 100.

68. Ibid., 305.

69. Ibid., 170–71.

70. Jacob Boehme, *Sex Puncta*, (Stuttgart: Fr. Fromans Verlag, 1957), 95.

71. Jacob Boehme, *Vierzig Fragen von der Seelen*, (Stuttgart: Fr. Fromans Verlag, 1957), 55.

72. Boehme, *Sex Puncta*, 97.

73. Boehme, *Aurora*, 132.

74. Pfeiffer, *Deutsche Mystiker: Meister Eckhart*, 366.

75. Ibid., 428.

76. Ibid., 429.

77. Ibid., 492.

78. Blakney, *Meister Eckhart*, xx.

79. Charles Hartshorne and William Reese, *Philosophers Speak of God*, (Chicago: University of Chicago Press, 1953), 104.

80. Pfeiffer, *Deutsche Mystiker: Meister Eckhart*, 222–23.

81. Jones, *Some Exponents of Mystical Religion*, 234.
82. Pfeiffer, *Deutsche Mystiker: Meister Eckhart*, 284.
83. Ibid., 233.
84. Ibid., 314.
85. Ibid., 292.
86. Ibid., 293.
87. Ibid., 293.
88. Charles Kelley, *Meister Eckhart on Divine Knowledge*, (New Haven: Yale University Press, 1977), 221.
89. Blakney, *Meister Eckhart*, x.
90. Pfeiffer, *Deutsche Mystiker: Meister Eckhart*, 549.
91. Ibid., 547–48.
92. Ibid., 573–74.
93. Ibid., 573.
94. Ibid., 553–54.
95. Ibid., 607–08.
96. Ibid., 484.
97. Ibid., 485.
98. Ibid., 486.
99. Ibid., 221.
100. Ibid., 485.
101. Ibid., 488–89.
102. Ibid., 492.
103. Ibid., 180.
104. Kelley, *Meister Eckhart on Divine knowledge*, 187.
105. Pfeiffer, *Deutsche Mystiker: Meister Eckhart*, 325.
106. Ibid., 327.
107. Ibid., 282.
108. Ibid., 241–42.
109. Ibid., 318–19.
110. Ibid., 320.
111. Ibid., 500.
112. Ibid., 282.
113. Blakney, *Meister Eckhart*, 230.
114. Pfeiffer, *Deutsche Mystiker: Meister Eckhart*, 181.
115. Ibid., 501.
116. Ibid., 632.
117. Ibid., 282.
118. Whitehead, *Process and Reality*, 125, 145.
119. Pfeiffer, *Deutsche Mystiker: Meister Eckhart*, 320.
120. Ibid., 489.
121. Ibid., 487.
122. Ibid., 405.
123. Rufus Jones, *Studies in Mystical Religion*, (London: Macmillan, 1909), 234.
124. Pfeiffer, *Deutsche Mystiker: Meister Eckhart*, 322.
125. Ibid., 622.
126. Ibid., 309–10.
127. Ibid., 605.
128. Ibid., 514.
129. Ibid., 514.
130. Ibid., 197.

131. Ibid., 180–81.
132. Ibid., 254.
133. Ibid., 104.
134. Ibid., 531.
135. Ibid., 614.
136. Ibid., 137.
137. Ibid., 220.
138. Ibid., 620.
139. Ibid., 170.
140. Ibid., 497.
141. Ibid., 269.
142. Ibid., 82.
143. Ibid., 169.
144. Ibid., 83.
145. Ibid., 313.
146. Ibid., 322.
147. Ibid., 531.
148. Ibid., 109.
149. Ibid., 612.
150. Ibid., 497.
151. Ibid., 311.
152. Ibid., 442.
153. Ibid., 618–19.
154. Ibid., 608.
155. Ibid., 608.
156. Henry Suso, *Little Book of Eternal Wisdom, Little Book of Truth*, trans. J. M. Clark (New York: Harper and Bros., 1949), 18.
157. Suso, *Little Book of Truth*, 19–20.
158. Ibid., 192–93.
159. Ibid., 38.
160. Ibid., 179.
161. Ibid., 178.
162. Ibid., 26.
163. Ibid., 27.
164. Charles Hartshorne, *Man's Vision of God and the Logic of Theism*, (Chicago: Willett, Clark and Co., 1941), 147.
165. Suso, *Little Book of Truth*, 25–26.
166. Ibid., 25.
167. Ibid., 173.
168. Ibid., 189–90.
169. Ibid., 185.
170. Ibid., 186.
171. Ibid., 200.
172. Ibid., 199.
173. Ibid., 38.
174. Ibid., 38.
175. Ibid., 37.
176. Ibid., 71–73.
177. Ibid., 55.
178. Ibid., 51–53.
179. Ibid., 161.

180. *Theologica Germanica*, S. Winkworth, trans. (New York: Pantheon Books, 1949), 208.
181. *Theologica Germanica*, 208.
182. Ibid., 205.
183. Ibid., 195.
184. Ibid., 178.
185. Ibid., 117.
186. Ibid., 179.
187. Ibid., 142.
188. Ibid., 185.
189. Ibid., 127.
190. Ibid., 131.
191. Ibid., 177.
192. Ibid., 163.
193. Ibid., 218.
194. Ibid., 168.
195. Ibid., 185–86.
196. Ibid., 168.
197. Ibid., 168.
198. Ibid., 170.
199. Ibid., 169.
200. Jones, *Studies in Mystical Religion*, 160.
201. Abraham Maslow, *Religions and Values and Peak Experience*, (New York: Viking Press, 1970), 84.
202. Jones, *Studies in Mystical Religion*, 169.
203. Boehme, *Sendbriefen*, 77.
204. Hartshorne and Reese, *Philosophers Speak of God*, 164.
205. Ibid., 514.
206. Ibid., 286.
207. Ibid., 287.
208. Nikolai Berdyaev, *The Destiny of Man*, trans. N. Duddington (New York: Charles Schribner's Sons, 1937), 31.
209. Boehme, *Sex Puncta*, 8; *Vierzig Fragen von der Seelen*, 11; *Betrachtung göttlicher Offenbarung*, 80.
210. Boehme, *Sex Puncta*, 4.
211. Boehme, *Mysterium Pansophicum*, 9.
212. Boehme, *Sex Puncta*, 8, 11.
213. Boehme, *Die Drei Principien göttlichen Wesens*, 3.
214. Boehme, *Übersinnlichen Leben*, 49; *Vierzig Fragen von der Seelen*, 11.
215. Boehme, *Übersinnlichen Leben*, 165, 185.
216. Boehme, *Aurora*, 7.
217. Boehme, *Aurora*, 23; *Die Drei Principien*, 8–9.
218. Boehme, *Sex Puncta*, 20; *Vierzig Fragen*, 52.
219. Boehme, *Aurora*, 74; *Die Drei Principien*, 38.
220. Boehme, *Vierzig Fragen*, 50.
221. Ernst Benz, *Les Sources Mystiques de la Philosophie Allemande*, (Paris: J. Vrin, 1968), 70.
222. Benz, *Les Sources Mystiques*, 71.
223. Boehme, *Vierzig Fragen*, 61.
224. Boehme, Sex Puncta, 23; *Vierzig Fragen*, 61; *Ubersinnlichen Leben*, 159.
225. John Stroudt, *Sunrise to Eternity*, (Philadelphia: University of Pennsylvania Press, 1957), 201–02.

226. Boehme, *Betrachtung göttlicher Offenbarung*, 66.
227. Boehme, *Weg zu Christo*, 188.
228. Whitehead, *Process and Reality*, 284.
229. Boehme, *Betrachtung göttlicher Offenbarung*, 7.
230. Hartshorne and Reese, *Philosophers Speak of God*, 514.

Chapter 3. Mystical Ecstasy

1. David Butler, *Western Mysticism* (London: Everyman's Library, 1919), 50.
2. Ernst Arbman, *Ecstasy or Religious Trance* 2 Vols., (Stockholm: Scandinavian University Press, 1963), 2:150.
3. Henri Delacroix, *Essai sur le Mysticisme Speculatif en Allemagne* (Paris: Alcan, 1900), 237; Arbman, 1:346, 385.
4. John of the Cross, *The Complete Works of Saint John of the Cross* (Westminster, Md.: Newman Press, 1963), 305. John of the Cross, *The Dark Night of the Soul* (London: J. M. Watkins, 1922), 116.
5. Arbman, *Ecstasy or Religious Trance*, 2:310.
6. *The Cloud of Unknowing* (London: J. M. Watkins, 1950), 209.
7. Charles Tart, ed., *Altered States of Consciousness* (New York: Doubleday; 1970), 182.
8. Walter Hilton, *The Scale of Perfection* (London: Burns and Oats, 1953), 120.
9. Ibid., 37.
10. John of the Cross, *Dark Night of Soul*, 55–56.
11. John of the Cross, *The Ascent of Mount Carmel* (London: Thomas Baker, 1906), 32.
12. John of the Cross, *Dark Night of Soul*, 66–67.
13. John of the Cross, *The Ascent of Mount Carmel*, trans. P. Lewis (London: Thomas Baker, 1906) 84.
14. Teresa of Avila, *The Interior Castle* (New York: Image Books, 1961), 10.
15. Ibid., 11.
16. Ibid., 11.
17. Jacob Boehme, *Weg zu Christo* (Stuttgart: Fr. Fromanns Verlag, 1957), 72.
18. Henri Delacroix, *Les Grandes Mystiques Cretiens* (Paris: Alcan, 1938), 356.
19. Alfred Whitehead, *Process and Reality* (New York: Free Press, 1957), 408.
20. Plotinus, *The Enneads* (London: George Bell, 1917–1924), iv, 9.
21. Evelyn Underhill, *Mysticism* (New York: Dutton, 1961), 234.
22. Louis Blosius, *A Book of Spiritual Instruction* (London: Burns and Oates, 1955), 57.
23. Ibid., 58–59.
24. Arbman, *Esctasy of Religious Trance*, 2:304.
25. Ibid., 2:304.
26. Ibid., 2:148.
27. Paul Jaegher, ed., *An Anthology of Mysticism* (Westminister, Maryland: Newman Press, 1950), 29.
28. Ibid., 25.
29. Ibid., 247.
30. Catherine of Siena, *The Divine Dialogue of Catherine of Siena*, trans. Algar Thorold (London: Everyman's Library, 1906), 286, cited in Underhill, *Mysticism*, 228.
31. Jaegher, *An Anthology of Mysticism*, 228.
32. Arbman, *Esctasy of Religious Trance*, 2:382.
33. John of the Cross, *The Ascent of Mount Carmel*, 312.

34. Jaegher, *An Anthology of Mysticism*, 94–97.
35. Arbman, *Esctasy or Religious Trance*, 2:35.
36. Ibid., 2:5.
37. Margaret Mallory, *Christian Mysticism: Transcending Techniques*, 73.
38. Ibid., 172.
39. Arbman, *Esctasy or Religious Trance*, 2:340–41.
40. Ibid., 2:341.
41. Ibid., 2:343.
42. Ibid., 2:344.
43. Ibid., 2:344.
44. Jaegher, *An Anthology of Mysticism*, 125.
45. Whitehead, *Process and Reality*, 407–08.
46. Teresa of Avila, *The Interior Castle*, 186.
47. Mallory, *Christian Mysticism: Transcending Techniques*, 166.
48. Underhill, *Mysticism*, 263.
49. A. Symons, in *Contemporary Review*, 1889. Cited in Underhill, *Mysticism*, 89.
50. Underhill, *Mysticism*, 89.
51. Ibid., 85.
52. Ibid., 372–73.
53. Franz Pfeiffer, *Deutsche Mysticker: Meister Eckhart* (Gottigen: Vandenhoeck, 1914), 77.
54. Richard Rolle, *The Fire of Love* (London: F. Comper, 1914), 76, cited in Underhill, *Mysticism*, 354–55.
55. Underhill, *Mysticism*, 58.
56. Surin, *Fondements de la vie Spirituelle*, v, ix. Cited in Arbman, *Ecstasy or Religious Trance*, 1:313.
57. Underhill, *Mysticism*, 88–89.
58. Ibid., 89.
59. Mallory, *Christian Mysticism: Transcending Techniques*, 161.
60. Ibid., 163.
61. Ibid., 161.
62. John of the Cross, *The Ascent of Mount Carmel*, 282–83.
63. Ibid., 283–84.
64. Mallory, *Christian Mysticism: Transcending Techniques*, 170–71.
65. Ibid., 168.
66. Ibid., 168–69.
67. John of the Cross, *Canticle*, 38, 3. Cited in Arbman, *Ecstasy or Trance*, 2:39.
68. Mallory, *Christian Mysticism: Transcending Techniques*, 170.
69. Jaegher, *An Antohology of Mysticism*, 147–48.
70. Mallory, *Christian Mysticism: Transcending Techniques*, 163.
71. Charles Hartshorne, *Man's Vision of God and the Logic of Theism*, (Chicago: Willet Clark Co., 1941), 148.
72. Arbman, *Ecstasy or Religious Trance*, 2:229.
73. Bernard of Clairvaux, *Canticle*, 31, cited in Arbman, *Ecstasy or Religious Trance*, 1:169.
74. Arbman, *Ecstasy or Religious Trance*, 2:102.
75. Ibid., 2:103.
76. Ibid., 2:105.
77. Jaegher, *An Anthology of Mysticism*, 244.
78. Ibid., 51.
79. Arbman, *Ecstasy or Religious Trance*, 2:302.
80. Lyonnard, *L'Apostolat de la Souffrance*, cited in Arbman, *Ecstasy or Religious Trance*, 2:303.

81. Teresa of Avila, *The Life of St. Teresa of Jesus, Written by Herself*, 18:210, cited in Arbman, *Ecstasy or Religious Trance*, 2:306.

82. Teresa of Avila, *Third Spiritual Letter*, 379, cited in Arbman, *Ecstasy or Religious Trance*, 2:308.

83. Arbman, *Ecstasy or Religious Trance*, 2:348.

84. Butler, *Western Mysticism*, 11.

85. Arbman, *Ecstasy or Religious Trance*, 2:348.

86. Teresa of Avila, *The Interior Castle*, 6:4.

87. John Clark, *Meister Eckhart*, (Edinburgh: Nelson and Sons, 1957), 109.

88. Underhill, *Mysticism*, 420.

89. Ibid., 470.

90. Arbman, *Ecstasy or Religious Trance*, 1:78–79.

91. Ibid., 2:228.

92. Jaegher, *An Anthology of Mysticism*, 261.

93. Boehme, *The Threefold Life of Man*, 88, cited in Underhill, *Mysticism*, 307.

94. Underhill, *Mysticism*, 429.

95. Ibid., 370.

96. Teresa of Avila, *The Life of St. Teresa of Jesus, Written by Herself*, trans. David Lewis (London: Everyman's Library, 1903) 78, cited in Underhill, *Mysticism*, 326.

97. Augustine Baker, *Holy Wisdom* (London: Everyman's Library, 1891) 132, cited in Underhill, *Mysticism*, 323.

98. Underhill, *Mysticism*, 324.

99. Ibid., 351–52.

100. von Hugel, *The Mystical Element of Religion* (London: Burns and Oates, 1908), 143.

101. Jan van Ruysbroeck, *De Ornatu Spiritalium Nuptiarum*, (Cologne: Surius, 1652) 234, 66, cited in Underhill, *Mysticism*, 322.

102. Madame Guyon, *Moyen Court*, (Paris: Peirre de Vingle, 1791) 21, cited in Underhill, *Mysticism*, 327.

103. Teresa of Avila, *The Interior Castle*, 97.

104. Ibid 160.

105. Ibid., 149–50.

106. Arbman, *Ecstasy or Religious Trance*, 2:65.

107. George Coe, *The Psychology of Religion*, 277.

108. Teresa of Avila, *The Interior Castle*, 160–61.

109. Arbman, *Ecstasy or Religious Trance*, 2:245.

110. Teresa of Avila, *The Life of St. Teresa*, (London: Macmillan, 1913) 22, cited in Underhill, 351.

111. Arbman, *Ecstasy or Religious Trance*, 2:421.

112. Ibid., 2:639.

113. Ibid., 2:105.

114. Ibid., 2:352.

115. Mallory, *Christian Mysticism: Transcending Techniques*, 160.

116. John of the Cross, *Flame*, in *The Complete Works of John of the Cross* trans. David Attwater (Maryknoll, Maryland: Newman Press, 1953) 401.

117. Teresa of Avila, *The Interior Castle*, 31.

118. Maurice Gandillac, *Oeuvres Completes du Pseudo-Denys*, (Paris: Editions Montaigne, 1943), 64.

119. Madame Guyon, *Justifications* (Paris: Pierre de Vingle, 1791) 126, Cited in Henri Delacroix, *Les Grandes Mystiques* (Paris: Alcam, 1938) 200.

120. Hilton, *The Scale of Perfection*, 231.

121. Teresa of Avila, *The Interior Castle*, trans. E. Aillson Peers (New York: Image Books, 1961) 121–22.

122. Teresa of Avila, *The Interior Castle*, 135.

123. Bernard Meland, *Higher Education and the Human Spirit* (Chicago: University of Chicago Press, 1953), 95.

124. Meland, *Higher Education*, 95.

125. John of the Cross, *Flame*, 4.

126. Suso, *Life of B. Henry Suso by Himself*, trans. Paul Thiriot (London: Everyman's Library, 1896) 422, cited in Underhill, *Mysticism*, 405–06.

127. Suso, *Life*, 575, cited in Underhill, *Mysticism*, 408.

128. Underhill, *Mysticism*, 407.

129. Charles Tart, *Altered States of Consciousness* (New York: Doubleday, 1970), 182.

130. Arbman, *Ecstasy or Religious Trance*, 1:350.

131. Ibid., 1:351.

132. Ibid., 1:314.

133. William James, *The Varieties of the Religious Experience* (New York: Longmans, Green, and Co., 1917), 380–81.

134. R. Masters and J. Houston, *The Varieties of Psychedelic Experience* (New York: Dell Publishing, 1966), 302.

135. A. G. B. Russell, ed., *The Letters of William Blake, and Life by F. Tatham*, 111. Cited in Underhill, *Mysticism*, 259.

136. Blake, "The Marriage of Heaven and Hell," xxii, cited in Masters and Houston, *Psychedelic Experience*, 303.

137. Jacob Boehme, *Dialogues on the Supersensual Life*, (New York: Pantheon Books, 1961), 62, cited in Masters and Houston, *Psychedelic Experience*, 324.

138. *Theologica Germanica*, 135.

139. Ibid., 205.

140. Teresa of Avila, *Vie*, cited in James, *Varieties of the Religious Experience*, 411.

141. Jaegher, *An Anthology of Mysticism*, 237–38.

142. Blosius, *A Book of Spiritual Instruction*, 26.

143. Ibid., 9.

144. Ibid., 52.

145. Ibid., 26.

146. Underhill, *Mysticism*, 255.

147. George Fox, *Journal of George Fox*, ed. Norman Penny, 2 Vols. (Cambridge: Cambridge University Press, 1911) 1:67, cited in Underhill, *Mysticism*, 257–58.

148. Arbman, *Ecstasy or Religious Trance*, 1:295.

149. Ibid., 1:295.

150. Hilton, *The Scale of Perfection*, 370.

151. Ibid., 235.

152. Ibid., 302.

153. Ibid., 296.

154. James, *Varieties of the Religious Experience*, 249, citing Dwight, *Life of Edwards*, New York, 1830, 61.

155. Hilton, *The Scale of Perfection*, 27.

156. *The Cloud of Unknowing*, 18.

157. Ibid., 61, 227, 229.

Chapter 4. Process Theology and Classical Theism

1. Nikolai Berdyaev, *The Destiny of Man* (New York: Charles Schribner's Sons, 1937), 37–40.

2. Allan Watts, *Behold the Spirit* (New York: Pantheon Books 1947), 168–69.

3. H. F. Woodhouse, "Pneumatology and Process Theology," *Scottish Journal of Theology* 41 (1972):389.

4. Charles Hartshorne and William Reese, *Philosophers Speak of God*, (Chicago: University of Chicago Press, 1955), 34.

5. Watts, *Behold the Spirit*, 331.

6. Schubert Ogden, *The Reality of God*, (New York: Harper and Row, 1966), 51.

7. Thomas Aquinas, *Summa Theologia* (New York: Benzinger Bros., 1947), Pt. 1, Q. 13, Art. 7, p.66.

8. St. Anselm, *Prosologium*, (La Salle, Illinois: Open Court Publishing, 1903, 1945), 13–14.

9. Hartshorne and Reese, *Philosophers Speak of God*, 104.

10. Jean Calvin, L'Institution Cretienne, 4 vols. (Geneva: Labor et Fides, 1955), 2:2, 4.

11. Aurelius Augustine, *De Fide et Symbolo*, (Paris: Desclee de Brouwer, 1947), 57.

12. Thomas Rees, *The Holy Spirit*, (London: Duckworth, 1915), 119.

13. Henry Swete, *The Holy Spirit in the Ancient Church*, (London: Macmillan, 1912), 360.

14. Ibid., 32.

15. Lindsay Dewar, *The Holy Spirit and Modern Thought*, (London: A. R. Mowbray, 1954), 85.

16. Dewer, *Spirit and Modern Thought*, 85.

17. Swete, *Spirit in the Church*, 360.

18. Ibid., 119.

19. Rees, *The Holy Spirit*, 159.

20. Dewar, *Spirit and Modern Thought*, 101.

21. Irenaeus, *The Demonstrations of the Apostolic Preaching*, (New York: Macmillan, 1920), 231.

22. Emile Mersch, *The Whole Christ*, (London: Denis Dobson, 1938), 30.

23. Irenaus, *Treatise Against Heresies*, 4:38, 4, cited in Reinhold Niebuhr, *The Nature and Destiny of Man*, 2 vols. (New York: Charles Schribner's Sons, 1964), 1:173.

24. Edmund Fortman, *The Triune God*, (Philadelphia: Westminster Press, 1972), 57.

25. Ibid., 57.

26. Origen, *Selections from the Commentaries and Homilies*, (New York: Macmillan, 1929), 15–16.

27. Hartshorne and Reese, *Philosophers Speak of God*, 104.

28. Watts, *Behold the Spirit*, 165–67.

29. Plotinus, *The Enneads*, 2 vols. (London: George Bell, 1917–1924), 2:9.

30. Eusebius, *History of the Church*, trans. A. C. McGiffert (New York: Longmans, Green, and Co., 1890) 79, cited in Arthur C. McGriffert, *A History of Christian Thought* (London: Charles Schribner's Sons, 1932–33) 263.

31. Heinrich Optiz, ed., *Athanius: Werke* 3 vols. (Berlin: Walter de Gruyter, 1935), 1:35; Robert Gregg and Dennis Groh, *Early Arianism: A View of Salvation* (Philadelphia: Fortress Press, 1981), 2.

32. Opitz, *Athanasus: Werke*, 1:21–22; Gregg and Groh, *Early Arianism*, 37.

33. Athanasius in Philip Schaff and Henry Wace, eds., *A Select Library of the Nicene and Post-Nicene Fathers of the Christian Church* 27 vols. (Grand Rapids: Eerdmans Co., 1956), 4:531.

34. William Bright, ed., *The Orations of St. Athanasius Against the Arians According to the Benedictine Text* (Oxford: Clarendon Press, 1973), 181.

35. Arius, *Epistle to Eusebius*, 1:14–15, cited in Gregg and Groh, *Early Arianism*, 82.

36. John Pollard, "The Origins of Arianism," *Journal of Theological Studies* 9 (1958):106.

37. Opitz, *Athanasius*, 1:242, cited in Gregg and Grogh, 82.

38. Fortman, *The Triune God*, 205.

39. Robert Seeberg, *Textbook of the History of Doctrines* (Grand Rapids, Mich.: Baker Book House, 1966), 226.

40. George Hendry, *The Holy Spirit in Christian Theology* (Philadelphia: Westminster Press, 1956), 13.

41. Fortman, *The Triune God*, 85.

42. Arthur McGiffert, *A History of Christian Thought*, (London: Charles Schribner's Sons, 1932–1933), 226.

43. Reinhold Niebuhr, *The Nature and Destiny of Man*, (New York: Charles Schribner's Sons, 1964), 1:230.

44. Basil, *Traite du Sainte-Esprit* (Paris: Editions du Cerf, 1946), 147.

45. Philip Schaff and Henry Wace, eds., *A Select Library of the Nicene and Post-Nicene Fathers of the Christian Church* (Grand Rapids, Mich.: Eerdmans Co., 1956).

46. Ibid., Gregory of Nyssa, *On the Making of Man* 18, 5:442.

47. Rees, *The Holy Spirit*, 172.

48. Charles Shapland, ed., *The Letters of St. Athanasius Concerning the Holy Spirit* (New York: The Philosophical Library, 1951), 114.

49. John Cobb, *Christ in a Pluralistic Age* (Philadelphia: Westminster Press, 1975), 152.

50. Swete, *Spirit in the Church*, 249.

51. Shapland, *Letters of St. Athanasius*, 129.

52. Hartshorne and Reese, *Philosophers Speak of God*, 85.

53. Plotinus, *Complete Works*, 7 vols. (London: George Bell, 1918), 5:1115.

54. Hartshorne and Reese, *Philosophers Speak of God*, 223.

55. Ibid., 295.

56. Jarsolav Pelikman, *The Light of the World* (New York: Harper and Row, 1962), 44.

57. Gregg and Groh, *Early Arianism*, 178.

58. Bright, *Orations of St. Athanasius*, 53.

59. Hartshorne and Reese, *Philosophers Speak of God*, 187.

60. Aurelius Augustine, *Genesis in the Literal Sense* (unpublished translation by F. L. Battles and B. Reynolds, 1977), 23.

61. Aurelius Augustine, *The Confessions of St. Augustine* (New York: E. P. Dutton, 1907), 271–72, 275–77.

62. Calvin, *L'Institution Cretiénne*, 4 vols., 3:442.

63. Aurelius Augustine, *De Trinitate*, (Paris: Descleé de Brouwer, 1955), 453.

64. Augustine, *De Trinitate*, 31.

65. Ibid., 36.

66. Aurelius Augustine, *Johannis Evangelium* (Paris: Desclee de Brouwer, 1977), 181.

67. Aurelius Augustine, *De Doctrina Christiana* (Paris: Desclee de Brouwer, 1949), 6.

68. Aurelius Augustine, *The City of God* (London: Oxford University Press, 1963), 24.

69. Augustine, *De Trinitate*, 207–09.

70. Augustine, *City*, 544–545.

71. Ibid., 153.

72. Ibid., 550.

73. Ibid., 3, 5, 6.

74. Hartshorne and Reese, *Philosophers Speak of God*, 81–82.

75. Augustine, *City*, 4:14, 13.

76. Hartshorne and Reese, *Philosophers Speak of God*, 161.

77. Ibid., 243.

78. Ibid., 161–62.

79. Ibid., 161–62.

80. Augustine, *Genesis in the Literal Sense*, 37.

81. Hartshorne and Reese, *Philosophers Speak of God*, 284.

82. Augustine, *Genesis in the Literal Sense*, 25.

83. Augustine, *Genesis in the Literal Sense*, 9.

84. Calvin, *L'Institution* 2. 15.

85. Augustine, *City*, 192–93.

86. Augustine, *Genesis in the Literal Sense*, 23.

87. Ibid., 31.

88. Augustine, *Genesis in the Literal Sense*, 30; *City*, 21.

89. 30.

90. 8.

91. Hartshorne and Reese, *Philosophers Speak of God*, 286.

92. Augustine, *Genesis in the Literal Sense*, 40.

93. Thomas Ogletree, "A Christological Assessment of Dipolar Theism," in *Process Philosophy and Christian Thought*, D. Brown, R. James and G. Reeves, eds. (New York: Merrill Co., 1971,) 331–46, 343.

94. Augustine, *City*, 193.

95. Ibid., 452.

96. Augustine, *Genesis in the Literal Sense*, 25.

97. John Smith and William Ross, eds., *The Works of Aristotle* (Oxford: Clarendon Press, 1912), 1154, 1244–45.

98. Schubert Ogden, *The Reality of God*, (New York: Harper and Row, 1966), 222.

99. Charles Hartshorne, *The Divine Relativity: A Social Conception of God*, (New Haven: Yale University Press, 1948), 58.

100. Hartshorne and Reese, *Philosophers Speak of God*, 84.

101. Augustine, *De Trinitate*, 463–67.

102. Augustine, *De Trinitate*, 463–67.

103. Augustine, *City*, 451–52.

104. Augustine, *Genesis in the Literal Sense*, 41.

105. Lewis Ford, "Divine Persuasion and the Triumph of the Good," in Brown, James, and Reeves, *Process Philosophy*, 287–304, 289.

106. Augustine, *City*, 437.

107. Hartshorne and Reese, *Philosophers Speak of God*, 36–37.

108. Edgar Brightman, *The Problem of God*, (New York: Abingdon Press, 1930), 102–03.

109. Hartshorne and Reese, *Philosophers Speak of God*, 118.

110. Berdyaev, *The Destiny of Man*, 287.

111. Augustine, *Confessions*, 270.

112. Ibid., 7–17.

113. Niebuhr, *Nature and Destiny of Man*, 1:156.

114. Augustine, *Confessions*, 264.

115. 264.

116. 277.

117. Augustine, *Genesis in the Literal Sense*, 25.

118. Hartshorne and Reese, *Philosophers Speak of God*, 84.
119. Walter Channing, *A Sermon Delivered at the Ordination of the Rev. Jared Sparks*, (Boston: Hews and Goss, 1819), 5.
120. Hartshorne and Reese, *Philosophers Speak of God*, 20.
121. Calvin, *Institution*, 1–4.
122. Hartshorne and Reese, *Philosophers Speak of God*, 152.
123. Hartshorne and Reese, *Philosophers Speak of God*, 152.
124. Berdyaev, *Destiny of Man*, 74.
125. Augustine, *De Trinitate*, 1.
126. Ibid., 1.
127. Ibid., 537.
128. Aurelius Augustine, *Enarrantiones in Psalmos*, (Paris: Desclée de Brouwer, 1951), 10.
129. Augustine, *De Trinitate*, 523.
130. Ibid., 419.
131. Ibid., 449–51.
132. Walter Stokes, "God for Today and Tomorrow," in Brown, James, and Reeves, *Process Philosophy*, 244–63, 257.
133. Leon Wencelius, *L'Esthetique de Calvin* (Paris: Societe D'Edition "Les Belles Lettres," 1935), 9, 30.
134. Calvin, *L'Institution*, 3 55–56.
135. Ibid., 3, 13.
136. Ibid., 3, 13.
137. Ibid., 1, 68–71.
138. Hartshorne and Reese, *Philosophers Speak of God*, 209–10.
139. Augustine, *De Trinitate*, 537–39.
140. Swete, *Spirit in the Church*, 250.
141. Augustine, *Genesis in the Literal Sense*, 11–12.
142. Augustine, *De Trinitate*, 12.
143. Ibid., 445.
144. Augustine, *Genesis in the Literal Sense*, 11–12.
145. Leonard Hodgson, *The Doctrine of the Trinity* (New York: Charles Schribner's sons, 1944), 109.
146. Alfred Whitehead, *Process and Reality* (New York: Free Press, 1957), 411–13.
147. Augustine, *Johannis Evangelium*, 10; *De Vera Religione*, (Paris: Desclée de Brouwer, 1950), 72:72.
148. William Hill, *The Three-Personed God* (Washington, D.C.: Catholic University of America, 1982), 210.
149. Ibid., 313.
150. Ibid., 216.
151. David Burrell, *Aquinas: God and Action*, (Notre Dame, Ind.: University of Notre Dame Press, 1979), 85.
152. Aquinas, *Summa Theologiae*, cited in Burrell, *Aquinas: God and Action*, 85.
153. Burrell, *Aquinas: God and Action*, 88.
154. Charles Hartshorne, *Reality as Social Process*, (Glencoe, Illinois: Free Press, 1953), 139–41.
155. W. Norris Clarke, *The Philosophical Approaches to God: A Neo-Thomist Perspective*, (Winston-Salem, North Cardina: Wake Forest University, 1979), 91.
156. Clarke, *Philosophical Approaches*, 91.
157. Ibid., 90.
158. Ibid., 104.

159. Ibid., 104.

160. Burrell, *Aquinas: God and Action*, 6.

161. Charles Hartshorne, *Man's Vision of God and the Logic of Theism* (Chicago: Willet, Clark and Co., 1941), 124.

162. Hartshorne and Reese, *Philosophers Speak of God*, 131–33.

163. Ibid., 171.

164. Aquinas, *Summa*, Pt. 1, Q. 13, Art. 8, p.66.

165. Ibid., Pt. 1, Q. 13, Art. 8, p.66.

166. Hartshorne and Reese, *Philosophers Speak of God*, 132.

167. Ibid., 89.

168. Ibid., 43.

169. Hartshorne, *Divine Relativity*, 16.

170. Burrell, *Aquinas: God and Action*, 81.

171. Hartshorne, *Divine Relativity*, 41.

172. Charles Hartshorne, "Martin Buber's Metaphysics" in *The Philosophy of Martin Buber*, Library of Living Philosophers Series, eds. P. A. Schlipp and M. Friedman (Evanston, Ill.: Northwestern University Press, 1967), 61.

173. Hill, *The Three-Personed God*, 76.

174. Aquinas, *Summa*, Pt. 1, Q. 4, Art. 2, 21–24.

175. Ibid., Pt. 1, Q. 3, Art. 8, 19–20.

176. Clarke, *Philosophical Approaches*, 80.

177. Ibid., 54–55.

178. Aquinas, *Summa*, Pt. 1, Q. 8, Art. 3, 36.

179. Ibid., Pt. 1, Q. 8, Art. 3, 36.

180. Ibid., Pt. 1, Q. 3, Art. 8, 19–20.

181. Charles Hartshorne, *Aquinas to Whitehead*, (Milwaukee, Wis.: Marquette University Press, 1977), 10–11.

182. Hartshorne, *Aquinas to Whitehead*, 11.

183. Clarke, *Philosophical Approaches*, 109.

184. Aquinas, *Summa*, Pt. 1, Q. 9, Art. 1, 38.

185. Ibid., Pt. 1, Q. 3, Art. 2, 15–16.

186. Clarke, *Philosophical Approaches*, 55.

187. Ibid., 71–72.

188. Ibid., 74.

189. Ibid., 86.

190. Charles Hartshorne, "Whitehead's Novel Intuition," in *Alfred North Whitehead: Essays on His Philosophy*, ed. George Kline (Englewood Cliffs, N.J.: Prentice Hall, 1963), 22.

191. Hartshorne, *Aquinas to Whitehead*, 17.

Chapter 5. Summary

1. In Calvin, the concept of immanence must be distinguished from that of omniscience. The high God of Calvin is omniscient but is not an item or factor in the universe. Calvin, like Aquinas and also Augustine, adheres to the Aristotelian dictum that "a substance is not present in a subject" (later traversed by Whitehead's principle of relativity). The fact that God creates *ex nihilo* denotes the ontological separation between God and creatures. God in creating is no more included in his work than the sun is included in the object it illuminates. Chapters 11 and 21 of his *L'Institution* are devoted to this topic.

2. Alfred Whitehead, *Adventures of Ideas* (New York: Free Press, 1967), 168.

3. Ibid., 167.

4. John Calvin, *L'Institution Crétienne* (Geneva: Labor et Fides, 1955), 1, 13, 18, 167.

5. Thomas Aquinas, *Theologia* (New York: Benziger Bros., 1947). Pt. 1, Q. 3, Art. 8, 19–20.

6. For a fuller discussion of the docetic elements in Christology, both ancient and modern, see D. M. Baillie, *God Was In Christ* (New York: Charles Schribner's Sons, 1948). Of *anhypostasia*, Baillie notes that "it was in the controversy with Nestorius in the fifth century that this idea was set forth by Cyril of Alexandria (though some writers maintain that it was actually anticipated by the heretical Apollinarius). Nestorius, who refused to call the Virgin Mary, 'theotokos,' 'Mother of God,' maintaining that she was not the Mother of the eternal Divine Son but of the human Jesus, was accused of dividing Christ into two persons," (85–86). Baillie is critical of the modern Kenotic Theory of the Incarnation because it also presupposes a sharp divorce between the human and the divine, such that "He who formally was God changed Himself temporarily into a man, or exchanged His divinity for humanity," (96).

7. Charles Lowry, *The Trinity and Christian Devotion* (New York: Harper and Bros., 1946), 95.

8. John Illingworth, *The Doctrine of the Trinity, Apologetically Considered* (London: Macmillan, 1907), 143.

9. Lowry, *The Trinity and Christian Devotion*, 101; Leonard Hodgson, *The Doctrine of the Trinity* (New York: Charles Schribner's Sons, 1944), 89.

10. Joseph Bracken, "Process Philosophy and Trinitarian Thought," *Process Studies* 8, 4 (1979):217–30, 226.

11. Bracken, "Process Philosophy and Trinitarian Thought-II," *Process Studies* 11, 2 (1982):83–96, 89.

12. Whitehead, *Process and Reality* (New York: Free Press, 1959), 106.

13. Whitehead, *Process and Reality*, 413.

14. Norman Pittenger "How Was God in Christ?" *Expository Times* 96, 10 (July 1985):300–04.

15. Norman Pittenger, *The Divine Triunity* (Philadelphia: United Church Press, 1977), 43–44.

16. Lewis Ford, *The Lure of God* (Philadelphia: Fortress Press, 1978), 94.

17. Bracken, "Spirit and Society: A Study of Two Concepts," *Process Studies* 15, 4 (1986):244–55.

18. F. Wallack, *The Epochal Nature of Process in Whitehead's Metaphysics* (Albany: State University of New York, 1980), 8.

19. Bracken, "Spirit and Society," 255.

20. Whitehead, *Process and Reality*, 33.

21. Braken, "Spirit and Society," 250–51.

22. Most specifically here I am alluding to Aquinas's argument that God cannot be complex because whatever is complex is subject to change, contingency, and decay. Aquinas, *Summa*, Pt. 1, Q. 3, 17–20.

23. Whitehead, *Process and Reality*, 408.

24. Ford, *Lure of God*, 100.

25. Fredrich Schelling, *The Ages of the World*, (New York: Columbia University Press, 1942), 95–96.

26. Whitehead, *Process and Reality*, 411.

27. Ibid.

28. Aquinas, *Summa*, Pt. 1, Q. p, Art. 1, p. 38.

29. Whitehead, *Process and Reality*, 372.

30. Ibid., 411.

31. Charles Hartshorne, *The Divine Relativity: A Social Conception of God* (New Haven: Yale University Press, 1948), 49–51.

32. Schubert Ogden, *The Reality of God* (New York: Harper and Row, 1966), 60.

33. Whitehead, *Adventures of Ideas*, 357.

34. Whitehead, *Process and Reality*, 36.

35. John Cobb and David Griffin, *Process Theology: An Introductory Exposition* (Philadelphia: Westminster Press, 1976), 62.

36. Ogden, *The Reality of God*, 178.

37. Charles Hartshorne and William Reese, *Philosophers Speak of God* (Chicago: University of Chicago Press, 1953), 361.

38. Whitehead, *Adventures of Ideas*, 356–57.

39. Alfred Whitehead, *Religion in the Making* (New York: World Publishing, 1973), 146.

40. Aquinas, *Summa*, Pt. 1, Q. 3, Art. 3, 15–16.

41. Anders Nygren, *Agape and Eros* (Philadelphia: Westminster Press, 1953), 157.

42. Cobb and Griffin, *Process Theology*, 44.

43. Frederick Ferre, *Shaping the Future* (New York: Harper and Row, 1976), 128.

44. Reinhold Niebuhr, *The Nature and Destiny of Man* 2 vols. (New York: Charles Schribner's Sons, 1964), 1:51.

45. The spirit-matter dualism of classical theism is central here. It was assumed that God is pure Spirit, whereas human beings are plunged deep into a material world. There is then an unbridgeable ontological disjunction between God and creatures. Thus, absolutely nothing in creation can represent God. How can something uncreated be represented by images of created things? How can God, who is pure spirituality, be manifested by something material? Since God has no similarity to anything that could be made to represent him, it would abase his sovereign majesty and glory to make any sort of image of him. (See, for example, Calvin, *L'Institution*, 1, 11, 2, 121).

46. Hartshorne and Reese, *Philosophers Speak of God*, 82.

47. Robert Scott, *The Relevance of the Prophets* (New York: Macmillan, 1968), 120.

48. H. W. Wolff in *O.T. Hermeneutics*, 1963, 338, cited in Scott, Relevance of Prophets, 120.

49. Hartshorne and Reese, *Philosophers Speak of God*, 37.

50. Gerhard von Rad, *Old Testament Theology*, 2 vols. (New York: Harper and Row, 1965), 2:76.

51. Rufus Jones, *Pathways to the Reality of God* (London: Camelot Press, 1941), 41.

52. Sigmund Molwinckel, "Fullfilment and Promise," *Journal of Biblical Literature* LIII (1943), cited in Scott, *Relevance of Prophets*, 94.

53. Cobb and Griffin, *Process Theology*, 47; Hartshorne and Reese, *Philosophers Speak of God*, 37.

54. Hartshorne and Reese, *Philosophers Speak of God*, 83.

55. Ibid., 11.

56. Aurelius Augustine, *The City of God* (London: Oxford University Press, 1963), 8, 4, viii.

57. Augustine, *De Trinitate* (Paris: Desclée de Brouwer, 1955), 15, 389.

58. Ibid., 249.

59. Ibid., 13, 333.

60. Regis Prenter, *Spiritus Creator* (Philadelphia: Mulenberg Press, 1953), 100.

61. Calvin *L'Institution,* 3, 23, 2.

62. Ibid., 2, 3, 5.

63. Ibid., 1, 13, 18.
64. Ibid., 3, 22, 4.
65. Ibid., 3, 23, 2.
66. Ibid., 3, 23, 7.
67. Ibid., 3, 12, 11.
68. Ibid., 3, 23, 2.
69. Ibid., 3, 22, 11.
70. Ibid., 3, 22, 3.
71. Ibid., 3, 23, 8.
72. Ibid., 1, 16, 3.
73. Ibid., 1, 10, 2.
74. Ibid., 1, 1, 1–4.
75. Ibid., 3, 23, 7.
76. Ibid., 1, 16, 9, 234.
77. Ibid., 1, 17, 5, 242.
78. Ibid., 3, 2, 35.
79. Ibid., 3, 22, 11, 431.
80. Whitehead, *Adventures of Ideas*, 66.
81. Cobb and Griffin, *Process Theology*, 10.
82. Whitehead, *Religion in the Making*, 65–66.
83. Ferre, *Shaping the Future*, 91–92.
84. Whitehead, *Religion in the Making*, 56–57.
85. Ibid., 105.
86. Jurgen Moltmann, *Man* (Philadelphia: Fortress Press, 1964), 58.
87. Moltmann, *Man*, 20.
88. Whitehead, *Process and Reality*, 408.
89. Whitehead, *Religion in the Making*, 115.
90. Ibid., 96.
91. Gordon Jackson, "In Search of Adventure: The Aesthetic Project," (Draft for chapter 5 of a forthcoming book, 1981), 106.
92. Charles Hartshorne, *Man's Vision of God and the Logic of Theism* (Chicago: Willet, Clark, and Co., 1941), 244.
93. Charles Hartshorne, *Reality as Social Process* (Glencoe, Illinois: Free Press, 1953), 39.
94. Whitehead, *Process and Reality*, 410.
95. Whitehead, *Religion in the Making*, 60.
96. Cobb and Griffin, *Process Theology*, 69.
97. Ibid., 69.
98. Whitehead, *Adventures of Ideas*, 355.
99. Cobb and Griffin, *Process Theology*, 72.
100. Ibid., 70.
101. Ibid., 75.
102. Hartshorne and Reese, *Philosophers Speak of God*, 23.
103. Ibid., 110–11.
104. Lewis Ford, "Divine Persuasion and the Triumph of Good," 289, cited in *Process Philosophy and Christian Thought*, ed. D. Brown, R. James and G. Reeves (New York: Bobbs-Merrill, 1971), 282–304.
105. Hartshorne and Reese, *Philosophers Speak of God*, 23.
106. Whitehead, *Adventures of Ideas*, 189.
107. Cobb and Griffin, *Process Theology*, 121.
108. Whitehead, *Process and Reality*, 403.

109. Ibid., 408.

110. Ibid., 408.

111. William James, *The Varieties of the Religious Experience* (New York: Longmans, Green, and Co., 1917), 420.

112. *The Cloud of Unknowing* (London: J. M. Watkins, 1950), 77.

113. Robert Blakney, *Meister Eckhart* (New York: Harper and Row, 1941), 317.

114. Evelyn Underhill, *Mysticism* (New York: E. P. Dutton, 1961), 21.

115. John Cobb, *Christ in a Pluralistic Age* (Philadelphia: Westminster Press, 1975), 80.

116. Whitehead, *Adventures of Ideas*, 231.

117. Whitehead, *Process and Reality*, 164.

118. Ibid., 54–55.

119. Ibid., 408.

120. Ibid., 226.

121. Cobb, *Christ in a Pluralistic Age*, 79; Whitehead, *Adventures of Ideas*, 226.

122. Whitehead, *Adventures of Ideas*, 246.

123. Cobb, *Christ in a Pluralistic Age*, 79.

124. Ibid., 79.

125. Whitehead, *Adventures of Ideas*, 280.

126. Ibid., 383.

127. Ibid., 350.

128. Ibid., 350.

129. The mathematical equivalent of this concept is to be found in Whitehead's *Process and Reality*, part 4, "The Theory of Extension." An analogous concept of ulteriority is to be found in Edwyn Bevan's *Symbolism and Belief* (Boston: Beacon Press Paperback, 1957). Bevan writes:

> It seems that the artist can sometimes secure that the object has that halo of association which constitutes beauty by making it remind us of something more or less definite other than itself. If we do not attend to that other thing, or that other world of things, which the object suggests, still the fact in itself that the object does suggest something other than itself may give us the sense that we are apprehending other than our ordinary everyday world. (277).

130. John of the Cross, *The Ascent of Mount Carmel* (London: Thomas Baker, 1906), 259.

131. Whitehead, *Process and Reality*, 189.

132. David Prall, *Aesthetic Analysis* (New York: Thomas Y. Crowell Co., 1964), 149.

133. Prall, *Aesthetic Analysis*, 147–48.

134. Whitehead, *Science and the Modern World* (New York: Free Press, 1967), 54.

135. Whitehead, *Adventures of Ideas*, 250–51, 280.

136. One should bear in mind that, as emphasized in chapters 2 and especially 3, the *sine qua non* of mystical ecstasy is the fusion of subject and object. According to James, *The Varieties of the Religious Experience*: "This overcoming of all the usual barriers between the individual and the Absolute is the great mystical achievement. In mystic states we both become one with the Absolute and we become aware of our oneness. This is the everlasting and triumphant mystical tradition, hardly altered by differences of clime or creed. (410):".

137. Bernard Meland, *The Realities of Faith* (New York: Oxford University Press, 1962), 231–32.

138. James, *Varieties of the Religious Experience*, 212.

139. William Law, "Christian Regeneration," 158–60, cited in Underhill, *Mysticism*, 397.

140. Underhill, *Mysticism*, 396.

141. Whitehead, *Adventures of Ideas*, 214.

142. Whitehead, *Process and Reality*, 37.

143. Whitehead, *Adventures of Ideas*, 324.

144. Ibid., 325.

145. Whitehead, *Process and Reality*, 325.

146. Donald Sherburne, *A Whiteheadian Aesthetic: Some Implications of Whitehead's Metaphysical Speculations*, (New Haven: Yale University Press, 1961), 124–26.

147. Jackson, "In Search of Adventure," 114–15.

148. Whitehead, *The Function of Reason*, 6.

149. Ibid., 7.

150. Ibid., 8.

151. Ibid., 8, 33, 34.

152. Cobb, *Christ in a Pluralistic Age*, 85.

153. Ibid., 77, 94.

154. Whitehead, *Religion in the Making*, 156.

155. I find this concept of discovery to be in accord with many empirical observations of creativity, where beauty is intuitively grasped through a state of passive receptivity. New insights are grasped full-formed, "in a flash" in which the completed solution is grasped in its entirety. The novelist really hears the conversations of his or her characters. The painter sees the unpainted picture. The musician hears music that "pipes to the spirit ditties of no tone" (Underhill, *Mysticism*, 272). For example, Wagner reportedly heard music spontaneously. Brahms confessed that he heard fragments of his symphonies as a "inner harmony" (Charles Tart, ed., *Altered States of Consciousness* [New York: Doubleday and Co., 1970], 277–78). The German chemist, Kekule, after months of fruitless work, conjured up the image of the benzene ring when inspired by the drunken dream of a snake holding its tail in its mouth. Russell once remarked that in the development of the theory of relativity, Einstein began with a poetical or mystical discovery of the truth that took the form of visualizing the totality of the law in all its ramifications (Tart, *Altered States of Consciousness*, 470.)

156. Sherburne, *A Whiteheadian Aesthetic*, 180–81.

157. David Hume, *An Abstract of a Treatise of Human Nature* (New York: Liberal Arts Press, 1955), 185.

158. Whitehead, *Process and Reality*, 382.

159. Abraham Maslow, *Motivation and Personality* (New York: Harper and Row, 1954), 136.

160. Cobb, *Christ in a Pluralistic Age*, 76.

161. Jackson, "In Search of Adventure," 104.

162. Sherburne, *A Whiteheadian Aesthetic*, 191.

163. Whitehead, *Adventures of Ideas*, 343.

164. Ibid., 263–64.

165. Whitehead, *Process and Reality*, 373–74.

166. Ibid., (1929 ed.), 427.

167. Hartshorne, *Man's Vision of God*, 229.

Bibliography

Anselm, St. *Proslogium; Monlogium; An Appendix in Behalf of the Fool by Gaunilon; and Cur Deus Home*. Translated by S. N. Deane. La Salle, Ill. Open Court Publishing Company, 1903, 1945.

Aquinas, Thomas. *Summa Theologica*. New York: Benziger Brothers, 1947.

Arbman, Ernst. *Ecstasy or Religious Trance*. Vols. 1 and 2 Stockholm: Scandinavian University Press, 1963.

Augustine, Aurelius. *The City of God*. Translated by J. W. C. Wand. London: Oxford University Press, 1963.

Augustine, Aurelius. *The Confessions of St. Augustine*. Translated by E. Pusey. New York: E. P. Dutton, 1907.

Augustine, Aurelius. *De Fide et Symbolo*. Paris: Desclée de Brouwer, 1947.

Augustine, Aurelius. *De Doctrina Christiana*. Paris: Desclée de Brouwer, 1949.

Augustine, Aurelius. *De Trinitate*. Paris: Desclée de Brouwer, 1955.

Augustine, Aurelius. *Johnannis Evangelium*. Paris: Desclée de Brouwer, 1959.

Augustine, Aurelius. *De Vera Religione*. Paris: Desclée de Brouwer, 1959.

Augustine, Aurelius. *Genesis in the Literal Sense*. Translated by Ford Lewis Battles and Blair Reynolds. 1977.

Baillie, Donald. *God Was In Christ*. New York: Charles Scribner's Sons, 1948.

Baker, Augustine. *Holy Widsom; or Directions for the Prayer of Contemplation*. Edited by Abbot Sweeny. O.S.B. London, 1907.

Basil, St. *Traite du Saint-Esprit*. Translated by B. Pruche. Paris: Editions du Cerf, 1946.

Benz, Ernst. *Les Sources Mystiques de la Philosophia Allemande*. Paris: J. Vrin, 1968.

Berdyaev, Nikolai. *The Destiny of Man*. Translated by N. Duddington. New York: Charles Scribner's Sons, 1937.

_____. *Spirit and Reality*. Translated by G. Reavy. New York: Charles Scribner's Sons, 1939.

Berkhof, Hendrikus. *The Doctrine of the Holy Spirit*. Richmond: J. Knox, 1964.

Blakney, Robert. *Meister Eckhart* (trans.). New York: Harper and Row, 1941.

Blosius, Louis. *A Book of Spiritual Instruction*. Translated by B. A. Wilberforce. London: Burns and Oates, 1955.

Boehme, Jacob. *Samtliche Schriften*. Stuttgart: Fr. Frommans Verlag, 1957.

Bracken, Joseph. "Process Philosophy and Trinitarian Thought." *Process Studies* 8, 4 (1979): 217–30.

_____. "Process Philosophy and Trinitarian Thought—II." *Process Studies II* 11, 2 (1982): 83–96.

_____. "Spirit and Society: A Study of Two Concepts." *Process Studies* 15, 4 (1986): 244–55.

_____. *The Triune Symbol: Persons, Process and Comment*. Lanham, Maryland: University Press of America, 1985.

Bright, William, ed. *The Orations of St. Athanasium Against the Arians According to the Benedictine Text*. Oxford: The Clarendon Press, 1973.

Brightman, Edgar S. *The Problem of God*. New York: Abingdon Press, 1930.

Brown, Delwin; James, Ralph; Reeves, Gene, eds. *Process Philosophy and Christian Thought*. New York: Bobbs-Merrill, 1971.

Brown, Norman O. *Life Against Death: The Psychoanalytic Meaning of History*. London: Chaucer Press, 1970.

Burrell, David. *Aquinas: God and Action*. Notre Dame, Ind.: University of Notre Dame Press, 1979.

Butler, David. *Western Mysticism*. London: Everyman's Library, 1919.

Calvin, Jean. *L'Institution Crétienne*. Geneva: Labor et Fides, 1955.

Cargas, Harry, Lee, Bernard, eds. *Religious Experience and Process Theology*. New York: Paulist Press, 1967.

Catherine of Siena. *The Divine Dialogue of Catherine of Siena*. Translated by A. Thorold. London: Everyman's Library, 1906.

Channing, Walter E. *A Sermon Delivered at the Oration of the Rev. Jared Sparks*. Boston: Hews and Goss, 1819.

Christian, William A. *An Interpretation of Whitehead's Metaphysics*. New Haven: Yale University Press, 1959.

Clark, John M. *Meister Eckhart*. Edinburgh: Nelson and Sons, 1957.

Clarke, W. Norris. *The Philosophical Approach to God: A Neo-Thomist Perspective*. Winston-Salem, North Carolina: Wake Forest University, 1979.

The Cloud of Unknowing. London: J. M. Watkins, 1950.

Cobb, John B. *A Christian Natural Theology*. Philadelphia: Westminster Press, 1965.

_____. *Christ in a Pluralistic Age*. Philadelphia: Westminster Press, 1975.

_____., and Griffin, David R. *Process Theology: An Introductory Exposition*. Philadelphia: The Westminster Press, 1976.

Coe, George A. *The Psychology of Religion*. Chicago: University of Chicago Press, 1916.

Come, Arnold. *Human Spirit and Holy Spirit*. Philadelphia: Westminster University Press, 1959.

Dean, William. *Love Before the Fall*. Philadelphia: Westminster Press, 1976.

Deikman Arthur J. "Deautomatization and the Mystic Experience." In Charles Tart ed. *Altered States of Consciousness*. New York: Doubleday, 1970, pp. 25-46.

Deikman, Arthur J. "Experimental Mediation." In Charles Tart ed. *Altered States of Consciousness*. New York: Doubleday, 1970, pp. 203-23.

Delacroix, Henri. *Essai sur le Mysticism Speculatif en Allemangne*. Pairs: Alcan, 1900.

_____. *Les Grandes Mystiques Cretiens*. Paris: Alcan, 1938.

Dewar, Lindsay. *The Holy Spirit and Modern Thought*. London: A. R. Mowbray, 1954.

Emmet, Dorothy. *Whitehead's Philosophy of Organism*. New York: Macmillan, 1966.

Ferre, Frederick. *Shaping the Future*. New York: Harper and Row, 1976.

Ford, Lewis. "Divine Persuasion and the Triumph of Good." In Delwin Brown, Ralph James, and Gene Reeves, eds., *Process Philosophy and Christian Thought*. New York: Bobbs-Merrill, 1971, pp. 287-304.

Ford, Lewis. *The Lure of God*. Philadelphia: Fortress Press, 1978.

Fortman, Edmund. *The Triune God*. Philadelphia: Westminster Press, 1972.

Fremantle, Ann, ed. *The Protestant Mystics*. New York: Little Brown, 1964.

Gandillae, Maurice. *Oeuvres Completes du Pseudo-Denys* (trans.). Paris: Editions Montaigne, 1943.

Gregg, Robert, and Groh, Dennis. *Early Arianism: A View of Salvation*. Philadelphia: Fortress Press, 1981.

Haldane, Elizabeth, and Ross, George R. T. *The Philosophical Works of Descartes*. Cambridge: Cambridge University Press, 1911.

Hartshorne, Charles. *Man's Vision of God and the Logic of Theism*. Chicago: Willet, Clark, and Co., 1941.

Hartshorne, Charles. *The Divine Relativity: A Social Conception of God*. New Haven: Yale University Press, 1948.

Hartshorne, Charles. *Reality as Social Process*. Glencoe, Ill.: Free Press, 1953.

Hartshorne, Charles. "Whitehead's Novel Institution" in *Alfred North Whitehead: Essays on His Philosophy*, George Kline, ed. Englewood Cliffs, N. J.: Prentice Hall, 1963.

Hartshorne, Charles. "Martin Buber's Metaphysics" in *The Philosophy of Martin Buber*. Library of Living Philosophers Series, edited by P. A. Schlipp and M. Freidman. Evanston, Ill.: Northwestern University Press, 1967.

Hartshorne, Charles. *Aquinas to Whitehead*. Milwaukee, Wis.: Marquette University Press, 1977.

Hartshorne, Charles, and Reese, W. L. *Philosophers Speak of God*. Chicago: University of Chicago Press, 1953.

Hendry, George S. *The Holy Spirit in Christian Theology*. Philadelphia: Westminster Press, 1956.

Hill, William. *The Three-Personed God*. Washington, D.C.: Catholic University of America Press, 1982.

Hilton, Walter. *The Scale of Perfection*. Translated by D. G. Sitwell. London: Burns and Oates, 1953.

Hodgson, Leonard. *The Doctrine of the Trinity*. New York: Charles Schribner's Sons, 1944.

Hügel, von Baron. *The Mystical Element of Religion, as Studied in St. Catherine Genoa and her Friends*. 2 vols. London: Burns and Oates, 1908.

Hume, David. *An Abstract of a Treatise of Human Nature*. New York: Liberal Arts Press, 1955.

Huxley, Aldous. *The Doors of Perception*. New York: Harper and Row, 1963.

Illingworth, John R. *The Doctrine of the Trinity, Apologetically Considered*. London: Macmillan, 1907.

Irenaeus. *The Demonstrations of the Apostolic Preaching*. Translated by J. A. Robinson. New York: Macmillan, 1920.

Jackson, Gordon. "In Search of Adventure: The Aesthetic Project." Unpublished manuscript. 1981.

Jaegher, Paul, ed. *An Anthology of Mysticism*. Translated by D. Attwater. Maryknoll, Maryland: Newman Press, 1950.

James, William. *The Varieties of the Religious Experience*. New York: Longmans, Green and Co., 1917.

John of the Cross. *The Ascent of Mount Carmel*. Translated by D. Lewis. London: Thomas Baker, 1906.

_____. *The Dark Night of the Soul*. Translated by G. C. Graham. London: J. M. Watkins, 1922.

———. *The Complete Works of Saint John of the Cross.* Translated by David Attwater. Maryknoll, Md.: Newman Press, 1953.

———. *Studies in Mystical Religion.* London: Macmillan, 1909.

———. *Some Exponents of Mystical Religion.* London: Camelot Press, 1930.

Jones, Rufus. *Pathways to the Reality of God.* London: Camelot Press, 1941.

Kelley, Charles F. *Meister Eckhart on Divine Knowledge.* New Haven: Yale University Press, 1977.

Kline, George, ed. *Alfred North Whitehead: Essays on His Philosophy.* Englewood Cliffs, N. J.: Prentice Hall, 1963.

Lawrence, Nathaniel. *Whitehead's Philosophical Development.* Berkeley and Los Angeles: University of California Press, 1956.

Leclerc, Ivor. *Whitehead's Metaphysics.* New York: Macmillan, 1958.

Leuba, Jean H. *The Psychology of Religious Mysticism.* New York: Harcourt, Brace and Col., 1925.

Loomer, Bernard M. "Christian Faith and Process Philosophy." In Delwin Brown, Ralph James, and Gene Reeves eds. *Process Philosophy and Christian Thought.* New York: Bobbs-Merrill, 1971, pp. 70–982.

Lowry, Charles W. *The Trinity and Christian Devotion.* New York: Harper and Bros., 1946.

Mallory, Margaret M. *Christian Mysticism: Transcending Techniques.* Netherlands: Van Goreum and Co., 1977.

Maslow, Abraham. *Motivation and Personality.* New York: Harper and Row, 1954.

Maslow, Abraham. *Towards a Psychology of Being.* New York: Van Nostrand, 1962.

Maslow, Abraham. *Religions, Values, and Peak Experiences.* New York: Viking Press, 1970.

Maslow, Abraham. *The Farther Reaches of Human Nature.* New York: The Viking Press, 1971.

Masters, R. E. L., and Houston, Jean. *The Varieties of Psychedelic Experience.* New York: Dell Publishing Co., 1966.

McGiffert, Arthur C. *A History of Christian Thought.* London: Charles Schribner's, 1932–33.

Meland, Bernard. *Faith and Culture.* New York: Oxford University Press, 1953.

———. *Seeds of Redemption.* New York: Macmillan Co., 1947.

Meland, Bernard. *Higher Education and the Human Spirit.* Chicago: University of Chicago Press, 1953.

———. *The Realities of Faith.* New York: Oxford University Press, 1962.

Mersch, Emile. *The Whole Christ.* London: Denis Dobson, 1938.

Moltmann, Jurgen. *Man.* Philadelphia: Fortress Press, 1964.

Niebuhr, Reinhold. *The Nature and Destiny of Man,* vol. 1. New York: Charles Schribner's Sons, 1964.

Nygren, Anders. *Agape and Eros.* Translated by P. S. Watson. Philadelphia: Westminster Press, 1953.

Ogden, Shubert. *The Reality of God.* New York: Harper and Row, 1966.

Origen. *Selections from the Commentaries and Homilies*. Translated by R. B. Tollinton. New York: Macmillan, 1929.

Pardington, George. *Spirit Incarnate*. Ph.D. diss. University of California at Berkeley, 1972.

Pelikan, Jarsolav. *The Light of the World*. New York: Harper and Row, 1962.

Pfeiffer, Franz. *Deutsche Mystiker: Meiser Eckhart*. Gottigen: Vandenhoeck, 1914.

Pittenger, Norman. *The Divine Triunity*. Philadelphia: United Church Press, 1977.

_____. "How was God in Christ?" *Expository Times*. 96, 10 (July 1985): 300–04.

Plotinus. *Complete Works*. Translated by K. S. Guthrie. London: George Bell, 1918.

Plotinus. *The Enneads*. Translated by S. Mackenna London: George Bell, 1917–24.

Pollard, John T. "The Origins of Arianism." *Journal of Theological Studies*. 9 (1958): 61–71.

Prall, David. W., *Aesthetic Analysis*. New York: Thomas Y. Crowell Co., 1964.

Preger, Wilhelm. *Geschichte der deutschen Mystick im Mittelalter*. Leipzig: H. Hofman Verlag, 1874–93.

Prenter, Regis. *Spiritus Creator*. Philadelphia: Mulenberg Press, 1953.

Rad, Gerhard von. *Old Testament Theology*, vol. 2. Translated by D. M. G. Stalker. New York: Harper and Row, 1965.

Rees, Thomas. *The Holy Spirit*. London: Duckworth, 1915.

Reuther, Rosemary. "Critic's Corner." *Theology Today*. 27, 3 October 1970: 331–37.

Schaff, Philip, Wace, Henry, eds. *A Select Library of the Nicene and Post-Nicene Fathers of the Christian Church*. Grand Rapids, Mich.: Eerdmans Co., 1956.

Schelling, Fredrick W. J. *The Ages of the World*. Translated by F. de Wolfe Bolman. New York: Columbia University Press, 1942.

Schilling, Harold K. *The New Consciousness in Science and Religion*. Philadelphia: United Church Press, 1973.

Schlipp, Paul and Friedman, Maurice, eds. *The Philosophy of Martin Buber*. Evanston, Ill.: Northwestern University Press, 1967.

Scott, Robert. *The Relevance of the Prophets*. New York: Macmillan Co., 1968.

Seebert, Reinhold. *Textbook of the History of Doctrines*. Translated by C. E. Hay. Grand Rapids: Baker Book House, 1966.

Shapland, Charles R., ed. *The Letters of St Athanasius Concerning the Holy Spirit*. New York: The Philosophical Library, 1951.

_____. *A Whiteheadian Aesthetic: Some Implications of the Whiteheadian Metaphysical Speculation*. New Haven: Yale University Press, 1961.

Sherburne, Donald W. *A Key to Whitehead's Process and Reality*. Bloomington: Indiana University Press, 1966.

Sherburne, Donald W. "Whitehead Without God." In Delwin Brown, Ralph James, and Gene Reeves eds. *Process Philosophy and Christian Thought*. New York: Bobbs-Merrill, 1971, pp. 305–30.

Sittler, Joseph. *Essay on Nature and Grace*. Philadelphia: Fortress Press, 1972.

Smith, John A., and Ross, William D., eds. *The Works of Aristotle*. Oxford: The Clarendon Press, 1912.

Stokes, Walter E. "God for Today and Tomorrow." In Delwin Brown, Ralph James, and Gene Reeves, eds. *Process Philosophy and Christian Thought*. New York: Bobbs-Merrill, 1971, pp. 244–63.

Stroudt, John J. *Sunrise to Eternity*. Philadelphia: University of Pennsylvania Press, 1957.

Suchocki, Marjorie. "The Question of Immortality." *The Journal of Religion*. 57, 3 (July 1977): 288–306.

Suso, Henry. *Little Book of Eternal Wisdom, Little Book of Truth*. Translated by J. M. Clark. New York: Harper and Bros., 1949.

Swete, Henry B. *The Holy Spirit in the Ancient Church*. London: Macmillan and Co., 1912.

Tart, Charles, ed. *Altered States of Consciousness*. New York: Doubleday, 1970.

Teilhard de Chardin, Pierre. *Oeuvres*. Vols. 1–13. Paris: Editions du Seuil, 1955–76.

_____. *Le Phenomenene Humain*. Paris: Editions du Seuil, 1955–76.

Teresa of Avila, *The Life of St. Teresa of Jesus, Written by Herself*. Translated by D. Lewis. London: Macmillan, 1913.

Teresa of Avila. *Letters*. Translated by Benedictines of Stanbrook Abbey. London: Macmillan, 1919–24.

Teresa of Avila. *The Interior Castle*. Translated by E. A. Peers. New York: Image Books, 1961.

Theologica Germanica. Translated by S. Winkworth. New York: Pantheon Books, 1949.

Underhill, Evelyn. *The Essentials of Mysticism*. New York: E. P. Dutton, 1961.

_____. *Mysticism*. New York: E. P. Dutton, 1961.

Wallack, F. Bradford. *The Epochal Nature of Process in Whitehead's Metaphysics*. Albany: State University of New York, 1980.

Watts, Allan. *Behold the Spirit*. New York: Pantheon Books, 1947.

Webb, Charles J. *God and Personality*. New York: Macmillan, 1920.

Whitehead, Alfred. *Adventures of Ideas*. New York: Free Press, 1967.

Whitehead, Alfred. *The Principle of Relativity*. Cambridge: Cambridge University Press, 1922.

Whitehead, Alfred. *An Enquiry Concerning the Principles of Natural Knowledge*. Cambridge: Cambridge University Press, 1925.

Whitehead, Alfred. *The Concept of Nature*. Cambridge: Cambridge University Press, 1926.

Whitehead, Alfred. *Symbolism, Its Meaning and Effect*. New York: Macmillan, 1927.

Whitehead, Alfred. *Process and Reality*. New York: Macmillan, 1929.

Whitehead, Alfred. *Modes of Thought*. New York: Macmillan, 1938.

Whitehead, Alfred. *The Aims of Education and other Essays*. New York: New American Library, 1949.

Whitehead, Alfred. *Process and Reality*. New York: Free Press, 1957.

Whitehead, Alfred. *The Function of Reason*. Boston: Beacon Press, 1958.

Whitehead, Alfred. *Science and the Modern World*. New York: Free Press, 1967.

Whitehead, Alfred. *Religion in the Making*. New York: World Publishing, 1973.

Whitehead, Alfred. "Uniformity and Contingency." *Proceedings of the Aristotelian Society* 23 (1922–23): 1–18.

Woodhouse, H. F. "Pneumatoloty and Process Theology." *Scottish Journal of Theology* 41 (1972): 383–91.

Index

Actualization, 30
Ambrosius, Bishop, 81
Anakephalaiosasthai, 126
Angela of Foligno, Saint, 82, 83
Anhypostasia, 150
Anselm, Saint, 22, 104, 105, 158; and God's compassion, 160–7; *Proslogium* 106–7
Arianism, 113–16
Aristides, 109
Aristotelian logic, 19–20, 176
Aristotle, 14, 176
Arius, 113–14
Ascent of Mount Carmel, The (John of the Cross), 80, 83, 89, 102
Athanasius, Saint, 58, 114, 116, 117, 118; on the immutability of God, 118
Augustine, Saint, 9, 84, 104; *The City of God,* 121; and the concept of *quies,* 129; and the concept of Spirit, 120–22, 156; *The Confessions of Saint Augustine,* 121; *Contra Arius,* 115; *De Fide et Symbolo,* 108; divine passivity in, 120–25; and the doctrine of the Trinity, 133–39, 149–50; and the nature of God, 119–31
Aurora (Boehme), 74

Baker, Augustine, 93
Basil the Great, Saint, 116
Beauty, 178, 181
Benedictus of Nursia, Saint, 101–2
Benz, Ernst, 55
Bernard of Clairvaux, Saint, 90, 91
Bifurcation, 18–20, 55, 73
Blosius, Louis, 81, 84, 91, 92, 97, 101, 102
Boehme, Jacob, 9, 14, 44, 56, 92–93, 100; *Aurora,* 74; concept of Creatio ex Deo in, 76; concept of Divine Nothing *(Ungrund)* in, 74–75, 76, 151, 157; on cosmological mysticism, 101; and the Mysterium Magnum, 75; on the process of creation, 76; *Sendbriefen,* 74

Bracken, Joseph: theory of the Trinity in, 151–53; *The Triune Symbol,* 151
Brahman, 99, 102
Brhadaranyaka Upanishad, 99–100

Calvin, Jean, 9, 104, 108; on his view of the Spirit, 135–36, 149; on the will of God, 162–64
Camus, Albert, 106
Cappadocians, 116–17; their view of the Trinity, 136–37
Cartesianism, 55
Cassianus, Johannes, 81
Catherine of Genoa, Saint, 84, 178
Catherine of Ricci, Saint, 92
Catherine of Siena, Saint, 82, 96
Causal efficacy, 12, 39
Causality, 38
Christ, Jesus. *See* Jesus Christ
Christian, William, 37, 38
City of God, The (Augustine), 121
Clarke, W. Norris, 140–48; and Thomism, 140–48
Classical theism, 22, 31, 50; definition of God in, 105; process theology and, 104–47
Cloud of Unknowing, The, 78, 79, 86, 102
Coe, George A.: *The Psychology of Religion,* 95
Conceptual valuation, 23
Conciousness, 41
Concretion, 23
Confessions Aminatis (More), 86
Confessions of Saint Augustine, The (Augustine), 121
Contemplation, 79
Contra Arius (Augustine), 115
Council of Constantinople, 115
Council of Nicea, 115
Creativity, 11, 28–35, 41–43; as a concept in Whitehead, 11, 28–35, 180, 181; and the ontological principle, 11, 28, 30, 35
Cyprian, Saint, 110

DATE DUE

HIGHSMITH   # -45220